TERM PAPER
RESOURCE GUIDE
TO TWENTIETH-CENTURY
UNITED STATES HISTORY

TERM PAPER RESOURCE GUIDE TO TWENTIETH-CENTURY UNITED STATES HISTORY

Robert Muccigrosso, Ron Blazek
and Teri Maggio

Greenwood Press
Westport, Connecticut • London

Library of Congress Cataloging-in-Publication Data

Muccigrosso, Robert.
    Term paper resource guide to twentieth-century United States
history / Robert Muccigrosso, Ron Blazek, and Teri Maggio.
        p. cm.
    Includes bibliographical references and index.
    ISBN 0–313–30096–8 (alk. paper)
    1. United States—History—20th century—Chronology. 2. United
States—History—20th century—Bibliography. 3. Report writing—
Handbooks, manuals, etc. I. Blazek, Ron. II. Maggio, Teri.
III. Title.
    E741.M83 1999
    016.9739—dc21   98–44592

British Library Cataloguing in Publication Data is available.

Library of Congress Catalog Card Number: 98–44592
ISBN: 0–313–30096–8

First published in 1999

Greenwood Press, 88 Post Road West, Westport, CT 06881
An imprint of Greenwood Publishing Group, Inc.
www.greenwood.com

Printed in the United States of America

∞™

The paper used in this book complies with the
Permanent Paper Standard issued by the National
Information Standards Organization (Z39.48-1984).

10 9 8 7 6 5 4 3 2 1

973.9
m942

Contents

Historian's Preface

Research in the field of twentieth-century American history has become an increasingly complex enterprise. On the most basic level, researchers must consider the full sweep of historical events and developments that by now encompass nearly an entire century. They must also confront an enormous and rapidly accelerating amount of material that is available in traditional forms, as well as in sophisticated resources that stem from the century's more recent dramatic technological breakthroughs. The prospect is a formidable one. The purpose of this book is to assist researchers in both the selection of appropriate research topics and in locating useful bibliographical sources.

The selection of one hundred important historical events and developments invariably invites invidious comparisons and charges of arbitrary choice. Why some entries were chosen and not others is a fair question. In choosing topics, I have first and foremost sought to include those that undeniably are central to the nation's twentieth-century experience: wars; major political, economic, and social events; cultural transformations. A second criterion in the selection process has been the desire to include topics that seemingly would interest as well as inform contemporary students, while omitting, sometimes with strong reluctance, important topics that would generate only limited curiosity, such as creation of the federal reserve system. Every generation has its own particular historical concerns, and this book has tried to take today's into as much account as seems appropriate.

The events listed in the book appear in temporal sequence, but a

few explanatory words seem in order. Although most entries are accompanied by a date or dates, a significant number lack such notation,
and for compelling reasons. There is no way, for example, to offer a
precise date for such broadly construed events as "The Golden Age
of Television." The same holds true for such a pivotal event as the
Vietnam War. Did it begin during the Eisenhower, Kennedy, or
Johnson administration? Did it terminate with the peace accords of
1973 or with the fall of Saigon two years later? In a different vein,
the first entry, the Spanish-American War, is a nineteenth-century
event, but its proximity to and importance for the nation's twentieth-
century history warrant its inclusion. At the other end of the chronological spectrum, the list of entries ends with an event that took
place in 1993. The decision not to include more recent developments
came after much soul searching and reflects the judgment that such
occurrences seemed either not sufficiently important or germane to
replace others or that they remained in a state of flux at the time this
book went to print.

The audience for *Term Paper Resource Guide* is a varied one; this
book can substantially assist both those who are writing a research
paper and those who are guiding them in their enterprise. By selecting
a suitable event, turning to the suggestions for term papers (each
entry contains five suggestions), and then availing oneself of the wide
array of pertinent, up-to-date, annotated resource materials, researchers at all levels can learn more about the American experience and
how to write meaningfully about that experience. The task is not an
easy one, but the challenge and stimulation should provide ample
rewards.

Finally, my co-authors and I wish to thank our publisher for having
helped us with our challenge. We especially would like to express our
gratitude to Dr. Barbara A. Rader, the Executive Editor of the Board
Reference Program, to David Palmer, our production editor, and to
Beverly A. Miller, our copy editor, for their kind assistance.

Robert Muccigrosso
Las Vegas, Nevada

Bibliographer's Preface

Although there have been various bibliographic guides to the academic study of history, few have been geared especially to the needs of high school and undergraduate students. In providing bibliographic coverage of the major topics, issues, and events in modern U.S. history beginning with the Spanish-American War, along with emphasis on suitable term paper topics, Greenwood Press continues to serve the needs of both students and instructors in providing a useful and needed resource tool. Librarians will be especially pleased with the earnest attempt to include the most recent titles easily available in local libraries or through interlibrary loan for those pursuing the task of learning in these areas of inquiry. Also included are landmark or important titles of the past when appropriate, making this work a useful buying guide for those interested in building good collections in the field. Some of these earlier works are primary sources on the events in question. Even so, many of the titles listed are relatively recent, with a good proportion published in 1998. Videos and web sites also have been selected carefully. All entries are annotated briefly with the focus on content or scope of coverage of each work.

COMPOSITION OF THE GUIDE

Each of the 100 entries contain from 15 to 35 items under seven possible categories. Not all categories are represented in each entry except for *Audiovisual Sources* and *World Wide Web*, each containing at least one item for every entry. The categories in order of sequence are enumerated below.

Reference Sources—Historical bibliographies, encyclopedias, dictionaries, atlases, and others that may be devoted to the entry topic or treat the topic along with others; biographical reference books are listed under Biographical Sources. This category has been alphabetized by title; items in the other categories are alphabetized by author or editor.

General Sources—General histories or trade books that treat the entry topic along with others.

Specialized Sources—Books devoted to or centered on the entry topic. In some cases, this category has been subdivided by different themes or issues treated.

Biographical Sources—Individual or collective works on personalities associated with the entry topic. Biographical reference titles appear here rather than in Reference Sources.

Periodical Articles—In a few of the entries, certain periodical articles are included because they provided good insight into the entry topic; this is the least-used category.

Audiovisual Sources—At least one video is provided for each entry topic; they were selected for their capacity both to engage and enlighten learners.

World Wide Web—At least one web site is provided for each entry topic, and all were validated at the time of publication. These sites were selected for their relevance and ability to help users comprehend the topic.

Works of this kind cannot be completed without the help of others. We are deeply grateful to the students at the Florida State University School of Information Studies who over the past year have participated in the identification of worthy titles and location of reviews. Some of them worked as volunteers; others received credit as part of class work for LIS 5604, Library Information Services. These students are listed alphabetically:

Diane D' Angelo   Yuka Minei
Marta Demopoulos   Beth Morey
Lori Driscoll-Eagan   Tom Mueller
Ron Jarnagin   David Murphy

Patrick Johnson
Abby Krystal
Dianna McKellar

Billie Oakes
Patrick Reakes
Scott Routsong

Ron Blazek / Teri Maggio
Tallahassee, Florida

1. Spanish-American War (1898)

After 1895 Americans were largely unsympathetic to Spain's attempt to subdue Cuban rebels. Relations between the two countries steadily worsened with the sinking of the U.S. battleship *Maine*, an insulting letter from the Spanish minister Dupuy de Lôme, and a warmongering American press. War finally broke out in April 1898. This "splendid little war," as Secretary of State John Hay termed it, ended within a few months after decisive American victories in Cuba and the Philippines, with fewer than four hundred Americans killed in battle. Military and naval heroes included Colonel Theodore Roosevelt and Admiral George Dewey, with their victories at San Juan Hill and Manila Bay, respectively. By the terms of the Treaty of Paris, ratified in 1899, Cuba became independent; the United States acquired Puerto Rico, Guam, and the Philippines for $20 million. However, the treaty's terms sparked heated debate among Americans over whether their nation should join the ranks of colonial powers.

Suggestions for Term Papers

1. Analyze the impact of the sinking of the *Maine* on American public opinion, or discuss modern historians' theories about the cause of the battleship's loss.
2. Discuss whether William Randolph Hearst's yellow journalism contributed to the United States's entry into the war, and why.
3. Discuss the long-range impact of the war on the American presence in the Caribbean.
4. Discuss the war's impact on the future of Cuba or Puerto Rico, or both.
5. Argue that the war was the first modern war of the twentieth century or the last old-fashioned war of the nineteenth century.

Suggested Sources: See entry 2 for related items.

REFERENCE SOURCES

Historical Dictionary of the Spanish-American War. Westport, CT: Greenwood, 1996. Donald H. Dyal. A one-volume encyclopedia with sketches of individuals involved in the war and brief essays on all aspects of the war. Bibliographical references follow each entry.

The Late 19th Century U.S. Army, 1865–1898: A Research Guide. Joseph G. Dawson III. Westport, CT: Greenwood, 1990. Excellent for military campaigns of the Spanish-American War.

The Spanish-American War: An Annotated Bibliography. Anne Cipriano Venzon. New York: Garland, 1990. A supplement to Dawson (above entry) for naval operations, post-1898 operations in Cuba and the Philippines, and diplomatic and political matters.

The War of 1898 and U.S. Interventions, 1898–1934. Benjamin R. Beede, ed. Hamden, CT: Garland, 1993. An excellent analysis of leaders in the debate over the U.S. peacetime role in the former Spanish colonies.

SPECIALIZED SOURCES

The War and Its Aftermath

Blow, Michael. *A Ship to Remember: The Maine and the Spanish-American War.* New York: Morrow, 1992. Lively study with useful bibliography.

Bradford, James C., ed. *Crucible of Empire: The Spanish-American War and Its Aftermath.* Annapolis, MD: Naval Institute Press, 1993. Nine essays supplementing topics covered in David Trask's *War with Spain* (see below).

Cashin, Herschel V. *Under Fire with the 10th Cavalry.* (1899). Reprint. Boulder: University Press of Colorado, 1993. Eyewitness account.

Cohen, Stan. *Images of the Spanish-American War, April–August, 1898.* Missoula, MT: Pictorial Histories, 1997. Hundreds of photographs, prints, and maps about the war and events leading up to it.

Feuer, A. B. *The Santiago Campaign of 1898: A Soldier's View of the Spanish-American War.* Westport, CT: Praeger, 1993. Collection of contemporary soldiers' reminiscences. Helpful footnotes.

Foner, Philip S. *The Spanish-Cuban-American War and the Birth of American Imperialism, 1895–1902.* 2 vols. New York: Monthly Review Press, 1972. Reprint. Books on Demand. The first volume ends in 1898; second volume provides excellent coverage of the U.S. occupation. A study of the war's "imperialist" issues by a respected left-wing historian.

Golay, Michael. *The Spanish-American War.* New York: Facts on File, 1995. Informative and interesting account of the war from the explosion of the *U.S.S. Maine* to the end. Includes photographs and maps.

Gould, Lewis A. *The Spanish-American War and President McKinley.*

Lawrence: University of Kansas Press, 1982. A brief, informative examination of McKinley's presidency during the war. Based on an earlier work.

Roosevelt, Theodore. *The Rough Riders.* (1899). Reprint. New York: Da Capo, 1990. Roosevelt's account of the Cuban campaign.

Smith, Robert Freeman. *The United States and the Latin American Sphere of Influence.* 2 vols. Malabar, FL: Krieger, 1981, 1983. An excellent overview in volume 1 for Cuba and Puerto Rico before, during, and after the war.

Trask, David F. *The War with Spain in 1898.* New York: Macmillan, 1981. Standard modern history of the war.

Journalism and the War

Crane, Stephen. *Reports of War.* Charlottesville: University of Virginia Press, 1971. (Vol. 9 of the university edition of *The Works of Stephen Crane.*) More than one hundred pages of Crane's dispatches from Cuba and Puerto Rico, 1898–1899. The author of *The Red Badge of Courage* was also a well-known journalist.

Milton, Joyce. *The Yellow Kids: Foreign Correspondents in the Heyday of Yellow Journalism.* New York: Harper & Row, 1989. Lively novelistic approach to the yellow journalists who helped bring about the war.

BIOGRAPHICAL SOURCES

Blum, John Morton. *The Republican Roosevelt.* 2d ed. Cambridge: Harvard University Press, 1977. Standard one-volume biography of Theodore Roosevelt.

Dewey, George. *Autobiography.* [1913]. Reprint. Annapolis: Naval Institute Press, 1987. These memoirs available in several reprints.

Grant, George. *Carry a Big Stick: The Uncommon Heroism of Theodore Roosevelt.* Nashville, TN; Cumberland House, 1996. An interesting picture of Theodore Roosevelt's character.

Morris, Edmund. *The Rise of Theodore Roosevelt.* New York: Coward, McCann, 1979. Splendid account of Roosevelt's prepresidential career, including the Cuban campaign.

Swanberg, W. A. *Citizen Hearst: A Biography of William Randolph Hearst.* (1961). Reprint. New York: Simon & Schuster, 1981. Remains the definitive story of a publisher who helped start a war.

AUDIOVISUAL SOURCES

The Spanish-American War/World War I. Nashville: Knowledge Products, 1995. 2 audiocassettes. 90-minute tapes narrated by George C. Scott; part of The United States at War series.

The Splendid Little War. Kearny, NJ: Belle Grove Publishing Co., 1992. Videocassette. 55-minute documentary including recently recovered film documenting the war as the first conflict captured in moving images.

WORLD WIDE WEB

Spanish-American War Centennial Website. http://www.powerscourt.com/war/index.htm Currently under construction. Offers a chronology of the war and eventually will include background material, action reports, profiles, and other material.

2. Philippine Insurrection (1899–1902)

The United States acquired the Philippine Islands as a result of the Spanish-American War, despite demands for independence by Filipino nationalists, who had fought against Spanish rule. Led by Emilio Aguinaldo, insurgent forces clashed with U.S. troops as soon as word reached the islands of the terms of the peace treaty. Even before that treaty was ratified by the U.S. Senate by a close vote, America found itself at war again. The war deeply divided Americans at home. The U.S. military captured Aguinaldo in 1901, but the insurrection lasted until mid-1902. More than 4,000 American troops and possibly as many as 20,000 insurgents died; the death toll among civilians, largely from disease, was much higher. William Howard Taft's patient and compassionate work as governor of the Philippines did much to pacify the situation, and American missionaries made a significant contribution to public health and education in the islands in the forty years of U.S. occupation. Still, the moral legacy of the war remained vexatious. Not until the 1930s, however, was any plan put into effect to give Filipinos self-government; the Philippine Republic was granted independence in 1946. This occasion closed a troubled chapter in American foreign policy.

Suggestions for Term Papers

1. Compare contemporary arguments for and against the annexation of the Philippines.

2. Analyze the reasons for eventual U.S. military success against the Filipinos, as well as the methods Aguinaldo's guerrillas used to keep the Westerners at bay so long.

3. Discuss the long-range results of American rule in the Philippines on the native population, or compare America's occupation of the Philippines with the briefer military occupation of Cuba.

4. Why did it take the United States nearly half a century to grant independence to the Philippines?

5. Compare the opposition at home to America's war in the Philippines with later opposition to the war in Vietnam.

Suggested Sources: See entry 1 for related items, especially Bradford's *Crucible of Empire.*

REFERENCE SOURCES

The War of 1898 and U.S. Interventions 1898–1934: An Encyclopedia. Benjamin R. Beede, ed. Hamden, CT: Garland, 1994. Contains lengthy articles by nearly 100 scholars, as well as maps; treats all phases of intervention during that time period, including the Philippine War.

William Howard Taft: A Bibliography. Paolo E. Coletta. Westport, CT: Meckler, 1989. Guide to work about the man whose personality shaped early American occupation policy in the islands.

GENERAL SOURCES

Clymer, Kenton J. *Protestant Missionaries in the Philippines, 1898–1916: An Inquiry into the American Colonial Mentality.* Urbana: University of Illinois Press, 1986. Interesting study of America's most influential nonmilitary representatives in the Philippines.

Collin, Richard H. *Theodore Roosevelt, Culture, Diplomacy, and Expansion: A New View of American Imperialism.* Baton Rouge: Louisiana State University Press, 1985. Survey of Roosevelt's policies.

Damiani, Brian P. *Advocates of Empire: William McKinley, the Senate, and American Expansion, 1898–1899.* New York: Garland, 1987. Treats foreign relations and territorial expansion, including the Philippines and Spanish-American War.

Perry, John Curtis. *Sentimental Imperialists: The American Experience in East Asia.* New York: Harper & Row, 1981. American attempts to justify policy in the Philippines and other parts of Asia through religious and social arguments.

Pomeroy, William J. *American Neo-Colonialism: Its Emergence in the Philippines and Asia.* New York: International Publishers, 1970. Reprint. Books on Demand. Leftist analysis of the American presence in the Far East.

SPECIALIZED SOURCES

Bain, David H. *Sitting in Darkness: Americans in the Philippines.* Boston: Houghton Mifflin, 1984. Interesting and informative account of the capture of Aguinaldo by Major General Frederick Funston.

Brands, H. W. *Bound to Empire: The United States and the Philippines.* New York: Oxford University Press, 1992. Good, up-to-date survey and analysis beginning with the period prior to U.S. annexation to independence in 1946.

Hahn, Emily. *The Islands: America's Imperial Adventure in the Philippines.* New York: Coward, McCann, & Geoghegan, 1981. Focuses on early decades of American occupation.

Karnow, Stanley. *In Our Image: America's Empire in the Philippines.* New York: Random House, 1989. U.S. attempts to "educate" Filipinos for Western-style democracy.

Linn, Brian McAllister. *The United States and Counterinsurgency in the Philippine War: 1899–1902.* Chapel Hill: University of North Carolina Press, 1989. Operations on the island of Luzon; generally favorable conclusion regarding U.S. Army performance.

May, Glenn Anthony. *Battle for Batangas: A Philippine Province at War.* New Haven, CT: Yale University Press, 1991. Good description of life of both soldiers and civilians.

Miller, Stuart Creighton. *"Benevolent Assimilation": The American Conquest of the Philippines, 1899–1903.* (1982). Reprint. New Haven, CT: Yale University Press, 1984. Well-balanced coverage of the topic—an interesting contrast with the Sexton study listed next.

Sexton, William T. *Soldiers in the Sun: An Adventure in Imperialism.* (1939). Reprint. Freeport, NY: Books for Libraries Press, 1971. A history of U.S. forces in the Philippines at the turn of the century by a U.S. Army officer who served in the islands thirty years later and offers a soldier's view of the conflict.

BIOGRAPHICAL SOURCES

Burton, David H. *William Howard Taft in the Public Service.* Malabar, FL: Krieger, 1986. 2 vols. Focuses on Taft's public life.

Pringle, Henry F. *The Life and Times of William Howard Taft.* New York:

Farrar & Rinehart, 1939. The best overall life of Taft, although somewhat dated.

Steinbach, Robert H. *A Long March: The Lives of Frank and Alice Baldwin.* Austin: University of Texas Press, 1990. Concise, interesting, and informative account of the lives of a forty-four-year career officer and his wife; Baldwin was cited by President Roosevelt for his success in the Philippines.

Young, Kenneth R. *The General's General: The Life and Times of Arthur MacArthur.* Boulder, CO: Westview, 1994. Excellent biography of Douglas MacArthur's father, whose career spanned nearly fifty years in the military; his success in the Philippine war led to his appointment as military governor.

AUDIOVISUAL SOURCES

The U.S. and the Philippines: In Our Image. Alexandria, VA: PBS Home Video, 1989. Videocassette. 3-hour video dealing with America's first uneasy experiment with colonialism in Asia.

WORLD WIDE WEB

Zwick, Jim. "A Collaborative Exploration of the Cultural and Political Impacts of the Philippine Revolution and the Philippine-American War." *Sentenaryo/Centennial: The Philippine Revolution and the Philippine-American War.* June 1998. Updated continuously. http://home.ican.net/~zwick/centennial/ Numerous links to useful sites and contributed materials relevant to historical perspective such as Philippine-American War and Philippine history prior to the revolution.

3. Boxer Rebellion (1900)

After its defeat in the Sino-Japanese War (1894–1895), China was increasingly unable to resist the demands of European powers and Japan for increased economic rights and privileges in their respective spheres of influence. Angered and humiliated by the intrusion of these foreigners, the Boxers, a secret society (so-called because its symbol was a fist), attacked missionaries and then besieged the foreign legations in Peking. The various imperialist powers, including the United States, sent troops, who successfully defeated the Boxers and lifted the siege. The Chinese government subsequently was forced to pay large indemnities, although the United States remitted most of its share.

Suggestions for Term Papers

1. What accounts for America's growing interest in China during the 1890s?

2. What were the reasons for Secretary of State John Hay's Open Door policy? How did European powers react to this U.S. position?

3. Compare the importance of commerce and religion in the U.S. involvement with China during the 1890s.

4. What was the role of the U.S. military in suppressing the Boxer Rebellion?

5. What effect did the Boxer Rebellion have on America's future relations with China?

Suggested Sources: See entry 2 for related items.

REFERENCE SOURCES

The Encyclopedia of Propaganda. Armonk, NY: Sharpe Reference, 1998. 3 vols. Examines in detail the various aspects of propaganda. The Boxer Rebellion is one of over 500 topics treated.

GENERAL SOURCES

Barnett, Suzanne Wilson, and John King Fairbank, eds. *Christianity in China: Early Protestant Missionary Writings*. Cambridge, MA: Harvard University Press, 1985. This anthology of documents runs only through 1890, but the introductions for each section are worthwhile background reading.

Cohen, Warren I. *America's Response to China: A History of Sino-American Relations*. 3d ed. New York: Columbia University Press, 1990. Standard survey of U.S.-Chinese relations.

Gilbert, Martin. *A History of the Twentieth Century: Vol. 1: 1900–1933*. New York: William Morrow, 1997. The first volume of a planned three-volume set covering the entire century, year by year, place by place, and event by event. Contains extensive narrative detail on the Boxer Rebellion.

Hunt, Michael H. *The Making of a Special Relationship: The United States and China to 1914.* New York: Columbia University Press, 1983. An able discussion of the evolution of the relationship between the two nations up to World War I, emphasizing the changes wrought by the Boxer Rebellion.

SPECIALIZED SOURCES

The Boxers

Brandt, Nat. *Massacre in Shansi.* Syracuse, NY: Syracuse University Press, 1994. Lively account of a notorious incident of the rebellion.

Esherick, Joseph W. *The Origins of the Boxer Uprising.* Berkeley: University of California Press, 1987. Good survey of the Boxer movement and its history.

Keown-Boyd, Henry. *The Boxer Rebellion.* (1991). Reprint. New York: Dorset, 1995. Good recent account of the rebellion.

Martin, Christopher. *The Boxer Rebellion.* London: Abelard-Schuman, 1968. Concise and readable narrative of the rebellion; contains illustrations, maps, and portraits.

O'Connor, Richard. *The Boxer Rebellion.* London: Hale, 1974. Detailed history of the event. Published initially in 1973 under the title, *The Spirit Soldiers: A Historical Narrative of the Boxer Rebellion.*

Americans in China

Chong, Key Ray. *Americans and Chinese Reform and Revolution, 1898–1922: The Role of Private Citizens in Diplomacy.* Lanham, MD: University Press of America, 1984. The role of Americans in Chinese domestic affairs, examined by an Asian-born scholar.

Hunter, Jane. *The Gospel of Gentility: American Women Missionaries in Turn-of-the-Century China.* New Haven, CT: Yale University Press, 1984. An excellent source for the history of American women in Asia.

Neils, Patricia, ed. *United States Attitudes and Policies toward China: The Impact of American Missionaries.* Armonk, NY: Sharpe, 1990. A collection of essays on missionaries' role in shaping Americans' views of China.

Price, Eva Jane. *China Journal, 1889–1900: An American Missionary Family during the Boxer Rebellion.* New York: Scribner's, 1989. Collection of letters, journals, and illustrations that provide insight into the nature of the rebellion, as well as the missionary and his family, who were murdered by the Boxers.

PERIODICAL ARTICLES

Buck, David D. "Recent Studies of the Boxer Movement: Editor's Introduction." *Chinese Studies in History* 20:3–23 (1987). This journal publishes only English translations of studies originally published in Chinese. Buck's introduction to this special issue on the Boxer movement is well worth reading.

Deakin, T. J. "Relief Repeatedly Halted." *Military History* 7:38–44 (1990). Brief survey of the rebellion's suppression.

Garrity, John. "Which of These Men Is the Real Herbert Hoover?" *Smithsonian* 16:146–148 (May 1985). Entertaining account of a future president of the United States as a civilian hero of the Boxer Rebellion.

Miller, Michael. "Marines in the Boxer Rebellion." *American History Illustrated* 22:38–47 (1988). Narratives and illustrations from a museum exhibition on U.S. Marine Corps participation.

Skelly, Anne. "The Eagle and the Dragon." *American History Illustrated* 22:34–37 (1988). Overview of the U.S. military role in the rebellion.

Walsh, Tom. "Herbert Hoover and the Boxer Rebellion." *Prologue* 19:34–40 (1987). An account of Hoover's adventures in China.

BIOGRAPHICAL SOURCES

Nash, George H. *The Life of Herbert Hoover: The Engineer, 1874–1914.* New York: Norton, 1983. Interesting portrait of Hoover as a resourceful and business-minded engineer. Treats his mining ventures in China and Australia during that critical period.

AUDIOVISUAL SOURCES

Agonies of Nationalism, 1800–1927. Los Angeles: Metromedia Producers, 1972. 23-minute videocassette. Comprehensive treatment of modern Chinese history, including the Boxer Rebellion.

WORLD WIDE WEB

Buschini, J. "The Boxer Rebellion." Small Planet Communications. (1996). http://www.smplanet.com/imperialism/fists.html Informative illustrated essay on the rebellion with excellent links to maps, text of John Hay's first Open Door Note, and useful background histories of China and the Ch'ing dynasty.

4. Panama Canal

A long-standing desire for an interoceanic canal accelerated when the United States expanded its territories and interests in the Pacific at the end of the nineteenth century. Two treaties with Great Britain gave the United States the exclusive right to build and fortify such a canal, and Panama, a province of Colombia, was selected over Nicaragua as the site. Colombia refused to ratify the necessary treaty, but Panamanians, with the approval and connivance of President Theodore Roosevelt, successfully rebelled in late 1903 and negotiated the treaty that the United States had sought. An extraordinary feat of engineering, the Panama Canal opened to commercial traffic in 1914.

Suggestions for Term Papers

1. Why was the United States interested in an interoceanic canal, and why did it choose Panama as its site?
2. Analyze President Roosevelt's role in the acquisition of the canal.
3. Discuss the difficulties facing the builders of the canal.
4. Explain the long-range consequences of American acquisition and ownership of the canal on Panama.
5. Discuss the effects the canal had on U.S. military and strategic policies.

Suggested Sources: See entry 90 for related items.

GENERAL SOURCES

Collin, Richard H. *Theodore Roosevelt's Caribbean: The Panama Canal, the Monroe Doctrine, and the Latin American Context.* Baton Rouge: Louisiana State University Press, 1990. Thought-provoking examination of Roosevelt's Latin American policies.

Lael, Richard L. *Arrogant Diplomacy: U.S. Policy toward Colombia, 1903–1922.* Wilmington, DE: Scholarly Resources, 1987. U.S. policy toward Colombia during and after the Panamanian crisis.

SPECIALIZED SOURCES

Building the Canal

McCullough, David G. *The Path between the Seas: The Creation of the Panama Canal, 1870–1914.* New York: Simon & Schuster, 1977. A thorough, readable account of early attempts to launch an isthmian canal and of construction in Panama, 1904–1914.

The Canal in American History

Hogan, J. Michael. *The Panama Canal in American Politics: Domestic Advocacy and the Evolution of Policy.* Carbondale: Southern Illinois University Press, 1986. The canal's role as an issue in U.S. politics over the decades.

Major, John. *Prize Possession: The United States and the Panama Canal, 1903–1979.* New York: Cambridge University Press, 1993. An English author's perspective on the United States in the Canal Zone.

Richard, Alfred Charles. *The Panama Canal in American National Consciousness, 1870–1990.* New York: Garland, 1990. A survey of Americans' fascination with the possibilities—and the reality—of a canal tying the Atlantic and the Pacific.

BIOGRAPHICAL SOURCES

Anguizola, Gustave. *Philippe Bunau-Varilla: The Man behind the Panama Canal.* Chicago: Nelson-Hall, 1980. The Panamanian diplomat who signed the treaty ceding the Canal Zone to the United States.

Gibson, John M. *Physician to the World: The Life of General William C. Gorgas.* (1955). Reprint ed. Tuscaloosa: University of Alabama Press, 1989. Life of the army physician who eradicated yellow fever in the Canal Zone, thus making possible the canal's completion.

Gould, Lewis L. *The Presidency of Theodore Roosevelt.* Lawrence, KS: University of Kansas Press, 1991. A useful guide to the literature and issues of Roosevelt's years in the White House. Part of the American Presidency series.

Latham, Jean L. *George W. Goethals: Panama Canal Engineer.* Broomall, PA: Chelsea House, 1991. Biography of the army engineer who saw the canal through to completion and served as the Canal Zone's first civil governor.

PERIODICAL ARTICLES

Spellman, Robert L. "Misconceptions and Criminal Prosecutions: Theodore Roosevelt and the Panama Canal Libels." *American Journalism* 11: 39–60 (1994). The president's successful propaganda campaign to make the canal's story part of the legend of American ingenuity and determination.

AUDIOVISUAL SOURCES

A Man, a Plan, a Canal: Panama. Boston: WGBH Educational Foundation, 1987. Videocassette. 58-minute special on the construction of the canal.

Panama Canal. New York: A&E Home Video, 1995. Videocassette. 58-minute documentary that uses nineteenth-and early twentieth-century photographs and archival films.

TR and His Times. Santa Monica, CA: PBS Home Video, 1988. Videocassette. 58-minute discussion of Roosevelt and the era he shaped by Bill Moyers and biographer David McCullough.

WORLD WIDE WEB

Buschini, J. "The Panama Canal." *Small Planet*. 1996. http://www.smplanet.com/imperialism/joining.html Brief description of the construction of the canal as part of Roosevelt's plans to revitalize the navy. Array of interesting and relevant links, such as a movie of President McKinley and the Roosevelt Papers in the Library of Congress. Good pictures of canal construction.

5. Assassination of President McKinley (1901)

Less than six months into his second administration President William McKinley traveled to Buffalo to attend the Pan-American Exposition. On September 6, 1901, after delivering a speech to a crowd estimated at 50,000, he hosted a public reception, where he was shot by Leon Czolgosz, an anarchist. Despite his serious wound, the president asked that his assailant not be harmed. Physicians never found the bullet that lodged in McKinley's stomach, but his condition seemed improved. Nonetheless, he died on September 14 as a result of infection that stemmed from questionable medical treatment. Czolgosz was tried, convicted, and executed for the assassination.

Suggestions for Term Papers

1. Discuss why President McKinley attended the exposition.
2. Discuss why anarchists like Leon Czolgosz believed it was necessary to assassinate leaders like McKinley.
3. Did poor medical treatment lead to McKinley's death?
4. Did Czolgosz receive a fair trial, and was his execution justifiable?
5. What effect did McKinley's assassination have on American history?

REFERENCE SOURCES

William McKinley: A Bibliography. Lewis L. Gould. Westport, CT: Meckler, 1988. Serviceable guide to McKinley literature.

William McKinley, 1843–1901: Chronology, Documents, Bibliographical Aids. Harry J. Sievers, ed. Dobbs Ferry, NY: Oceana, 1970. Small collection of documents and source material; contains a chronology and bibliographical references.

William Thomas McKinley: A Bio-bibliography. Jeffrey S. Sposato. Westport, CT: Greenwood, 1995. Detailed bibliography providing references to McKinley's life and career.

GENERAL SOURCES

Dobson, John M. *Reticent Expansionism: The Foreign Policy of William McKinley.* Pittsburgh: Duquesne University Press, 1988. Brief overview of foreign relations and territorial expansion during the McKinley period up to the time of the President's assassination.

Ford, Franklin L. *Political Murder: From Tyrannicide to Terrorism.* Cambridge: Harvard University Press, 1985. Evolution of assassination as a political tool.

McElroy, Richard L. *William McKinley and Our America: A Pictorial History.* Canton, OH: Stark County Historical Society, 1996. Fine illustrated history of the McKinley years.

McKinley, James. *Assassination in America.* New York: Harper & Row,

1977. General account of assassination on politics and the American conscience.

BIOGRAPHICAL SOURCES

Collins, David R. *William McKinley, 25th President of the United States.* Ada, OK: Garret Educational, 1990. Brief and easy-to-read narrative describing McKinley's life beginning with his childhood.

Gould, Lewis L. *The Presidency of William McKinley.* Lawrence: University of Kansas Press, 1980. Good study of McKinley's life and political career. Part of the publisher's American Presidency Series.

Higgins, Eva. *William McKinley: An Inspiring Biography.* Canton, OH: Daring, 1989. Brief biography including McKinley's politics, philosophy, and events of his term.

Johns, A. Wesley. *The Man Who Shot McKinley.* South Brunswick, NJ: A. S. Barnes, 1970. The only book-length study of McKinley's assassin.

Morgan, H. Wayne. *William McKinley and His America.* Syracuse, NY: Syracuse University Press, 1963. Still the best book-length biography of McKinley.

Olcott, Charles S. *William McKinley.* (1916). Reprint. New York: AMS, 1972. 2 vols. Extensive and detailed biography of McKinley's life and presidency. First published under the title *The Life of William McKinley.*

PERIODICAL ARTICLES

Smith, T. Burton. "Assassination Medicine." *American Heritage* 43:116–119 (September 1992). Speculation on ways that modern medicine might have helped save McKinley and other nineteenth-century assassination victims.

Sneed, Don. "Newspapers Call for Swift Justice: A Study of the McKinley Assassination." *Journalism Quarterly* 65:360–375 (Summer 1988). How a biased press may have denied Czolgosz a fair trial.

AUDIOVISUAL SOURCES

From the Courthouse to the White House: The Life and Times of William McKinley. Canton, OH: Canton Preservation Society, 1990. Videocassette. 35-minute program prepared by the historical society of McKinley's home town.

William McKinley, 1843–1901, 25th President of the United States of America. Chatsworth, CA: Timeless Video, 1992. Videocassette. 18-minute video of footage from the Library of Congress showing

McKinley in office, at the Buffalo Exposition; shots of the McKinley funeral procession and Czolgosz's execution. Also available through the Library of Congress American Memory web site.

WORLD WIDE WEB

"Speech That Prompted Murderous Assault on the President." *The Goldman Papers—Emma Goldman Online Exhibition*. August 1996. http://sunsite.berkeley.edu/Goldman/Exhibition/assassination.html Reprint of article from *Chicago Daily Tribune*, September 8, 1901, attributing responsibility for the assassination to Goldman's speech delivered in Cleveland on May 6.

6. Wright Brothers Flight at Kitty Hawk (1903)

Wilbur and Orville Wright repaired and manufactured bicycles in Dayton, Ohio, beginning in 1892. By decade's end, they had become intrigued with the possibility of human flight. They carefully studied gliding, particularly the work of the German Otto Lilenthal, and in 1901 set up a wind tunnel for their own experiments. They developed aileron control and designed a workable propeller and lightweight engine. On December 17, 1903, at Kitty Hawk, Orville piloted a heavier-than-air, power-driven plane for 120 feet and thereby inaugurated the age of airplanes.

Suggestions for Term Papers

1. Why was there renewed interest in building airplanes at the turn of the century?
2. Analyze how the Wright Brothers experimented and built their plane.
3. Discuss the contributions of the astrophysicist and aeronautics experimenter Samuel P. Langley to aviation.
4. What were the immediate effects of the Kitty Hawk flight on aviation?

5. What further contributions to aeronautics did the Wright Brothers make after Kitty Hawk?

REFERENCE SOURCES

Kitty Hawk to Concorde: Jane's 100 Significant Aircraft. H. F. King, comp., and John W. R. Taylor, ed. London: Jane's Yearbooks, 1970. An excellent descriptive analysis and illustrations of 100 important airplanes starting with the Wright Brothers' invention. From the publisher's popular series.

GENERAL SOURCES

Bilstein, Roger E. *Flight in America, 1900–1983: From the Wrights to the Astronauts.* Baltimore: Johns Hopkins University Press, 1984. Good survey for the twentieth century.

Geibert, Ronald R., and Patrick B. Nolan. *Kitty Hawk and Beyond: The Wright Brothers and the Early Years of Aviation, a Photographic History.* Dayton, OH: Wright State University Press, 1989. Fine pictorial work of early aircraft; brief narrative text.

Gibbs-Smith, Charles H. *The Wright Brothers: A Brief Account of Their Work, 1899–1911.* 2d ed. London: HMSO, 1987. A forty-eight-page descriptive account of the brothers' work prior to, during, and after the Kitty Hawk flight. From the Science Museum in London.

Gollin, Alfred. *No Longer an Island: Britain and the Wright Brothers, 1902–1909.* Stanford, CA: Stanford University Press, 1984. Detailed account of Britain's attempts to monitor, then steal, the Wrights' secrets.

Scott, Phil. *The Shoulders of Giants: A History of Human Flight to 1919.* Reading, MA: Addison-Wesley, 1995. Antecedents of the Wrights.

Spick, Mike. *Milestones of Manned Flight: The Ages of Flight from the Wright Brothers to Stealth Technology.* New York: Smithmark, 1994. Good pictorial survey of the history of flight.

SPECIALIZED SOURCES

Chapman, William, and Jill K. Hanson. *Wright Brothers National Memorial: Historic Resource Study.* Atlanta: Southeast Field Area, National Park Service, U.S. Department of the Interior, 1997. Concise history of the Wright Brothers, the flight, and the memorial.

Jakab, Peter L. *Visions of a Flying Machine: The Wright Brothers and the*

Process of Invention. Washington, D.C.: Smithsonian Institution, 1990. The brothers' place in the history of technology.

The Papers of Wilbur and Orville Wright. (1953). Reprint. New York: Arno, 1972. 2 vols. Standard tool; excellent collection of annotated source materials, including the Chanute-Wright letters, and an extensive bibliography.

Parramore, Thomas C. *Triumph at Kitty Hawk: The Wright Brothers and Powered Flight*. Raleigh: Division of Archives and History, North Carolina Department of Cultural Resources, 1993. Concise, good history of the flight with lengthy bibliography.

BIOGRAPHICAL SOURCES

Aaseng, Nathan. *Twentieth-Century Inventors*. New York: Facts on File, 1991. A useful biographical dictionary with an interesting perspective on the Wright Brothers.

Combs, Harry, and Martin Caidin. *Kill Devil Hill: Discovering the Secret of the Wright Brothers*. Boston: Houghton Mifflin, 1979. Thorough study of the Wright Brothers and their marvelous feat.

Crouch, Tom D. *The Bishop's Boys: A Life of Wilbur and Orville Wright*. New York: Norton, 1989. Best current biography of the brothers. Excellent bibliography.

Foulois, Benjamin D., and C. V. Glines. *From the Wright Brothers to the Astronauts*. (1968). Reprint. New York: Arno, 1980. Good collective biography of individuals who have contributed to the space program.

Howard, Fred. *Wilbur and Orville: A Biography of the Wright Brothers*. New York: Knopf, 1987. Thorough and detailed biography with illustrations and a useful bibliography.

Kelly, Fred C. *The Wright Brothers: A Biography*. (1943). Reprint. New York: Dover, 1989. Standard biography by an expert.

————. *The Wright Brothers: A Biography Authorized by Orville Wright*. New York: Bantam Books, 1983. Adaptation by Bantam Books of the standard biography by Kelly initially issued in 1943.

Kirk, Stephen. *First in Flight: The Wright Brothers in North Carolina*. Winston-Salem, NC: J. F. Blair, 1995. Recent account with a good biography and historical perspective.

Reynolds, Quentin J. *The Wright Brothers: Pioneers of American Aviation*. (1950). Reprint. New York: Random House, 1997. Brief, readable account of the Wright Brothers and their achievement. From the publisher's Landmarks in History series.

AUDIOVISUAL SOURCES

Wilbur & Orville: Dreams of Flying. New York: A&E Home Video, 1994. Videocassette. 58 minutes. Fine presentation of the brothers. From the A&E Biography series.

The Wright Stuff. New York: Shanachie Entertainment, 1996. Videocassette. 58-minute segment of The American Experience presenting the story of the Wright brothers.

WORLD WIDE WEB

"First Flight at Kitty Hawk." *The Pilot Pitstop.* October 1997; updated January 1998. http://anna716.home.mindspring.com/pilot.htm Aviation buff's home page, equipped with sound and excellent links to relevant sites. Most useful is the detailed description by Orville Wright of the brothers' efforts in making the first successful flight.

7. Muckraking

During the Progressive era, a number of writers articulated and promoted a wide variety of reform causes that stemmed from such serious problems as corrupt politics, economic monopolies, harmful foods and medicines, and endangered natural resources. A small number of journals, most notably *McClure's,* led the movement, but certain novels, especially Upton Sinclair's *The Jungle,* also contributed. Major muckraking journalists included Lincoln Steffens and Ida Tarbell. Both highly popular and profitable for roughly a decade, muckraking journalism declined in importance just prior to World War I.

Suggestions for Term Papers

1. Why did muckraking originate when it did?
2. How does one account for the popularity and subsequent decline of muckraking?
3. How important was muckraking for achieving Progressive era reforms?
4. Analyze the contributions to reform made by a noted muckraker.

5. Compare the muckraking of the Progressive era with today's investigative journalism.

Suggested Sources: See entries 8 and 13 for related items.

GENERAL SOURCES

Camhi, Jane J. *Women Against Women: American Anti-Suffragism, 1880–1920.* Brooklyn, NY: Carlson Publishing, 1994. Interesting and provocative account of antisuffragist influences; full chapter on Ida Tarbell's life and work.

Ward, Hiley H. *Mainstreams of American Media History.* Needham Heights, MA: Allyn & Bacon, 1997. An excellent text on media history from ancient times to the computer age. Chapter 10 treats muckraking in detail.

SPECIALIZED SOURCES

Brasch, Walter M. *Forerunners of Revolution: Muckrakers and the American Social Conscience.* Lanham, MD: University Press of America, 1990. Links muckraking and twentieth-century American political and social activism.

Chalmers, David M. *The Social and Political Ideas of the Muckrakers.* Freeport, NY: Books for Libraries, 1970. Standard work identifying various muckrakers and their ideologies (Ida Tarbell, Lincoln Steffens, Upton Sinclair, and others).

Filler, Louis. *Appointment at Armageddon: Muckraking and Progressivism in the American Tradition.* Westport, CT: Greenwood, 1976. Detailed account providing insight into politics and government, with an examination of the social conditions that spurred the efforts of the crusading journalists.

————. *The Muckrakers.* (1968). Reprint. Stanford, CA: Stanford University Press, 1996. Major effort by a leading social historian and expert on the Progressive era; detailed examination of social conditions of the time and the activity of social reformers.

Fitzpatrick, Ellen, ed. *Muckraking: Three Landmark Articles.* Boston: Bedford Books/St. Martin's, 1994. Fine resource containing three landmark articles taken from the January 1903 issue of *McClure's* magazine.

Miraldi, Robert. *Muckraking and Objectivity: Journalism's Colliding Traditions.* Westport, CT: Greenwood, 1990. Good discussion of muckrakers' influence on American journalism, with a fine bibliography.

Weinberg, Arthur, and Lila Weinberg, eds. *The Muckrakers: The Era in Journalism That Moved America to Reform: The Most Significant Magazine Articles of 1902–1912*. New York: Simon & Schuster, 1961. Revealing collection of landmark articles annotated by the editors; critical treatment of social conditions and political corruption.

Wilson, Harold S. *McClure's Magazine and the Muckrakers*. Princeton, NJ: Princeton University Press, 1970. Important work providing insight into the relationship between the magazine and muckraking journalism.

BIOGRAPHICAL SOURCES

Applegate, Edd. *Journalistic Advocates and Muckrakers: Three Centuries of Crusading Writers*. Jefferson, NC: McFarland, 1997. Comprehensive collective biography of literary social reformers, including the leading muckrakers.

Brady, Kathleen. *Ida Tarbell: Portrait of a Muckraker*. New York: Seaview Books, 1984. Good introduction to this author.

Cather, Willa, ed. *The Autobiography of S. S. McClure*. (1914). Reprint. Lincoln: University of Nebraska Press, 1997. Standard source, with excellent introduction by Robert Thacker.

Cook, Fred J. *The Muckrakers: Crusading Journalists Who Changed America*. Garden City, NY: Doubleday, 1972. Collective biography providing informative biographical sketches of the reform journalists.

Griffith, Sally F. *Home Town News: William Allen White and the Emporia Gazette*. New York: Oxford University Press, 1989. Useful biography of the crusading Progressive journalist and editor.

Kaplan, Justin. *Lincoln Steffens: A Biography*. (1974). Reprint. New York: Simon & Schuster, 1988. Definitive work on Steffens.

Kochersberger, Robert C., ed. *More Than a Muckraker: Ida Tarbell's Lifetime in Journalism*. Knoxville: University of Tennessee Press, 1996. A collection of essays.

Scott, Ivan. *Upton Sinclair, The Forgotten Socialist*. Lewiston, NY: Edwin Mellen, 1997. Best book-length study of this writer.

PERIODICAL ARTICLES

Scriabine, Christine. "Upton Sinclair and the Writing of *The Jungle*." *Chicago History* 10(1): 26–37 (1981). Evolution of this milestone in muckraking fiction.

AUDIOVISUAL SOURCES

Upton Sinclair. Tustin, CA: Citadel Video, 1989. Videocassette. 30-minute interview with Sinclair covering his life as a writer and reformer.

WORLD WIDE WEB

"Muckrakers." *Progressive Era.* May 1997. http//www.mcps.k12.md.us/ schools/rmhs/instruct/ap-us-history/prog1/page7.html Well-executed and informative web site developed as a classroom study guide. Contains terms and people, as well as an excerpt from *The Jungle.* Most helpful is the discussion question and its key.

8. Conservation Movement during the Progressive Era

Neglected during most of the nation's history, the conservation of natural resources became a significant issue during the Progressive era. Dedicated environmentalists like John Muir alerted Americans to the need to preserve areas of wilderness; others, like Gifford Pinchot, argued for the rational use of resources. President Theodore Roosevelt made conservation an important part of his administration's agenda. Bitter controversies, like the Ballinger-Pinchot affair during the Taft administration and the battle to dam California's Hetch Hetchy Valley for a reservoir, sometimes surrounded conservation efforts.

Suggestions for Term Papers

1. Why did conservation become a popular issue?
2. Compare John Muir's and Gifford Pinchot's views on conservation.
3. Would the conservation movement have succeeded without Roosevelt's efforts?
4. How endangered were America's natural resources in 1900?
5. Analyze the Ballinger-Pinchot controversy.

Suggested Sources: See entries 7 and 13 for related items.

GENERAL SOURCES

Nash, Roderick, comp. and ed. *The American Environment: Readings in the History of Conservation.* 2d ed. Reading, MA: Addison-Wesley, 1976. Useful collection of source material and writings identifying the issues and environmental influences of their times.

Petulla, Joseph M. *American Environmental History: The Exploitation and Conservation of Natural Resources.* San Francisco: Boyd & Fraser Publishing, 1977. Revealing historical account of environmental policy over the years.

Richardson, Elmo R. *The Politics of Conservation: Crusades and Controversies, 1897–1913.* (1962). Reprint. Milwood, NY: Kraus, 1980. Good study of the relationship between reform and partisan politics.

Stefoff, Rebecca. *The American Environmental Movement.* New York: Facts on File, 1995. Provides a good historical overview, along with a reading list and chronology. Part of the publisher's Social Reform Movements series.

Williams, Michael. *Americans and Their Forests: A Historical Geography.* New York: Cambridge University Press, 1989. Thorough and detailed history of American forests, forestry, and forest products industry.

Wunder, John R. *Working the Range: Essays on the History of Western Land Management and the Environment.* Westport, CT: Greenwood, 1985. Collection of writings on land use and environmental land management in the American West.

SPECIALIZED SOURCES

Dorsey, Kurkpatrick. *The Dawn of Conservation Diplomacy: U.S.-Canadian Wildlife Protection Treaties in the Progressive Era.* Seattle: University of Washington Press, 1998. Informative examination of agreements on the environment reached by the two countries during the age of progressivism.

Hays, Samuel P. *Conservation and the Gospel of Efficiency: The Progressive Conservation Movement, 1890–1920.* (1959). Reprint. Pittsburgh: University of Pittsburgh, 1999. Revealing and insightful historical survey of the underlying themes regarding the environmental policies and conservation movement of the Progressive era.

Penick, James L., Jr. *Progressive Politics and Conservation: The Ballinger-Pinchot Affair.* Chicago: University of Chicago Press, 1968. Brief but revealing account of the controversy between Ballinger, the secretary of the interior, and Pinchot, the head of the Forest Service who was removed by Taft.

BIOGRAPHICAL SOURCES

Cohen, Michael P. *The Pathless Way: John Muir and the American Wilderness.* Madison: University of Wisconsin Press, 1984. Useful scholarly biography.

Cutright, Paul R. *Theodore Roosevelt: The Making of a Conservationist.* Urbana: University of Illinois Press, 1985. Covers Roosevelt's background as a naturalist and outdoorsman, which prepared him for his efforts on behalf of the conservation movement.

Fox, Stephen. *John Muir and His Legacy: The American Conservation Movement.* Boston: Little, Brown, 1981. Equally good as a biography and a history of conservationism.

Lucas, Eileen. *Naturalists, Conservationists and Environmentalists.* New York: Facts on File, 1994. Profiles John Muir and John James Audubon, plus ten other Americans.

Pinkett, Harold T. *Gifford Pinchot: Private and Public Forester.* (1970). Reprint. Ann Arbor: UMI, 1992. A brief, useful biography with a good bibliography, originally published by the University of Illinois.

Sterling, Keir B. *Biographical Dictionary of American and Canadian Naturalists and Environmentalists.* Westport, CT: Greenwood, 1997. Covers nearly 450 Canadian and American naturalists and conservationists. Entries average about two pages each.

Strong, Douglas Hillman. *Dreamers and Defenders: American Conservationists.* Rev. ed. Lincoln: University of Nebraska Press, 1988. Standard survey and collective biography of the American conservation effort.

PERIODICAL ARTICLES

Ponder, Stephen. " 'Nonpublicity' and the Unmaking of a President: William Howard Taft and the Ballinger-Pinchot Controversy of 1909–1910." *Journalism History* 19:111–120 (1994). Details this crucial battle.

Watkins, T. H. "Father of the Forests." *American Heritage* 42: 86–98 (February 1991). Pinchot's role in U.S. Forest Service.

AUDIOVISUAL SOURCES

The Wilderness Idea: Battle for Wilderness. Santa Monica, CA: PBS Home Video, 1989. Videocassette. Traces Pinchot's and Muir's careers and opposing views in 60-minute presentation from The American Experience series.

WORLD WIDE WEB

Library of Congress. "The Evolution of the Conservation Movement, 1850–1920." *American Memory.* April 1997. http://memory.loc. gov/ammem/amrvhtml/conshome.html Extraordinary source materials: photographs, hard-to-find printed works, and manuscripts. Exceptional year-by-year chronology.

9. Establishment of the National Association for the Advancement of Colored People (1909)

By the early 1900s African Americans in the South suffered from disenfranchisement, segregation, and widespread physical violence that included lynchings. Conditions in the North were not as appalling, yet usually brought second-class citizenship. On the centennial of Lincoln's birthday, February 12, 1909, a biracial group including W. E. B. Du Bois, John Dewey, Jane Addams, and Oswald Garrison Villard organized the NAACP to oppose segregation, promote equal educational opportunities, and fight for the enforcement of the Fourteenth and Fifteenth amendments. Du Bois was named an officer and editor of the organization's journal, *The Crisis.*

Suggestions for Term Papers

1. Why did racial segregation (Jim Crow laws) become the law in the South?
2. Compare the views of Booker T. Washington and W. E. B. Du Bois on how African Americans should deal with their problems.
3. Why was the NAACP established? What were its goals?
4. How does today's NAACP differ from the original organization?
5. Analyze Du Bois's changing views on racial problems in the United States.

Suggested Sources: See entries 71 and 73 for related items.

REFERENCE SOURCES

The African American Almanac. 7th ed. Detroit: Gale, 1997. Provides a range of current and historical information and description of topics, issues, events, and personalities.

The African-American Atlas: Black History and Culture—An Illustrated Reference. Molefi K. Asante and Mark T. Mattson. Old Tappan, NJ: Macmillan/Simon & Schuster, 1998. Provides both current and historical data regarding African American development. Good coverage of the rise of the NAACP.

Encyclopedia of African-American Culture and History. Old Tappan, NJ: Macmillan/Simon & Schuster, 1997. 5 vols. Well-developed treatment of the founding of the NAACP.

GENERAL SOURCES

Du Bois, W. E. B. *The Souls of Black Folk.* (1903). Reprint. New York: Penguin Books, 1996. A classic work by one of the NAACP's founders contains fourteen essays dealing with the difficulties of being a black American.

Villard, Oswald G. *Oswald Garrison Villard, the Dilemmas of the Absolute Pacifist in Two World Wars.* New York: Garland, 1983. Collection of articles, letters, and book excerpts by Villard that provide insight into his life's philosophy.

Wintz, Cary D., ed. *African American Political Thought, 1890–1930: Washington, Du Bois, Garvey, and Randolph.* Armonk, NY: M. E. Sharpe, 1996. Collection of essays by the foremost thinkers in setting the foundation for the modern black experience in the United States.

SPECIALIZED SOURCES

Finch, Minnie. *The NAACP: Its Fight for Justice.* Metuchen, NJ: Scarecrow Press, 1981. Introductory survey and good historical overview.

Harris, Jacqueline L. *History and Achievement of the NAACP.* New York: Franklin Watts, 1992. Concise and easy-to-read survey of the origin and history of the organization.

Kellogg, Charles Flint. *NAACP: A History of the National Association for the Advancement of Colored People.* Vol. 1. Baltimore: John Hopkins University Press, 1967. First of a projected two-volume history of the NAACP, covering the years 1909–1920. Available in reprint through University Microfilms.

Muse, Edward B. *Paying for Freedom: History of the NAACP and the Life Membership Program, 1909–1987*. Baltimore: National Association for the Advancement of Colored People, 1986. Interesting narrative of the program to finance the organization from the time of its inception.

Ovington, Mary White. *Black and White Sat Down Together: The Reminiscences of an NAACP Founder*. Ralph E. Luke, ed. New York: Feminist Press (CUNY), 1995. A fascinating and valuable memoir.

Zangrando, Robert L. *The NAACP Crusade against Lynching, 1909–1950*. Philadelphia: Temple University Press, 1980. Excellent history of this aspect of the association's work.

BIOGRAPHICAL SOURCES

Harlan, Louis. *Booker T. Washington*. (1972). Reprint. New York: Oxford University Press, 1983. 2 vols. Incomparable prize-winning study.

————, et al., eds. *The Booker T. Washington Papers*. Urbana: University of Illinois Press, 1972–1989. 14 vols. Extraordinary collection of sources for Washington and other African American leaders of his time.

Hovde, Jane. *Jane Addams*. New York: Facts on File, 1989. Concise biography of the influential social worker who helped create the NAACP.

Humes, Dollena J. *Oswald Garrison Villard, Liberal of the 1920s*. (1960). Reprint. Westport, CT: Greenwood, 1977. Biography of the journalist who helped found the NAACP.

Lewis, David Levering. *W. E. B. Du Bois: Biography of a Race, 1868–1919*. New York: H. Holt, 1993. First part of a projected two-volume effort. Detailed study with extensive bibliography.

Rockefeller, Steven C. *John Dewey: Religious Faith and Democratic Humanism*. New York: Columbia University Press, 1991. Detailed examination into Dewey's philosophy. Provides excellent insight into the life orientation of one of the NAACP founders.

Wedin, Carolyn. *Inheritors of the Spirit: Mary White Ovington and the Founding of the NAACP*. New York: Wiley, 1997. Recent study of Ovington's life and influence.

AUDIOVISUAL SOURCES

W. E. B. Du Bois: A Biography in Four Voices. San Francisco: California Newsreel, 1995. Four prominent African-Americans narrate a period in Du Bois's life.

WORLD WIDE WEB

National Association for the Advancement of Colored People. "What You Should Know About the NAACP." *NAACP Online.* September 1997. http://www.naacp.org/about/factsheet.html A fact sheet that provides an excellent overview of the NAACP and its development. Most interesting is the six-page history by Mary White Ovington as printed in 1914.

10. Triangle Shirtwaist Factory Fire (1911)

One major Progressive aim was to reform conditions for working women. On March 25, 1911, a fire broke out in the Triangle Shirtwaist Factory, a garment sweatshop in New York City. No fire escapes existed, and the doors of this upper-floor factory had been closed from the outside to keep employees from taking work breaks. As a result, 146 workers, most of them young immigrant women, perished from the fire itself or from jumping from windows. Following this tragedy, New York and other states enacted stricter codes for worker safety.

Suggestions for Term Papers

1. Were working conditions and wages in the Triangle Factory typical of other factories of the time?
2. Were labor unions responsive to the problems of working women at this time?
3. What employment opportunities did working women have in the early twentieth century?
4. Discuss public reaction to the fire.
5. To what extent did working conditions improve for women during the Progressive era?

Suggested Sources: See entries 7 and 13 for related items.

GENERAL SOURCES

Glenn, Susan A. *Daughters of the Shtetl: Life and Labor in the Immigrant Generation.* Ithaca, NY: Cornell University Press, 1990. Jewish immigrant women as workers in the United States.

Johnson, Gus. *The Fire Buff's Handbook of the New York Fire Department, 1900–1975.* New York: Fire Department of New York, 1977. A chronicle marking the seventy-fifth anniversary of the department, with material on the fire.

McCreesh, Carolyn Daniel. *Women in the Campaign to Organize Garment Workers, 1880–1917.* New York: Garland, 1985. Provocative investigation of the rise of women in organized labor.

Orleck, Annelise. *Common Sense and a Little Fire: Women and Working-Class Politics in the United States, 1900–1965.* Chapel Hill: University of North Carolina Press, 1995. Political activity of working women in America in the twentieth century.

Tyler, Gus. *Look for the Union Label: A History of the International Ladies' Garment Workers' Union.* Armonk, NY: Sharpe, 1995. A lively history of the union that reshaped the garment industry after the Triangle Fire.

Waldinger, Roger D. *Through the Eye of the Needle: Immigrants and Enterprise in New York's Garment Industry.* New York: New York University Press, 1986. Thorough discussion of newly arrived workers' role in the city's booming business.

SPECIALIZED SOURCES

Stein, Leon. *The Triangle Fire.* (1962). Reprint. New York: Carroll & Graf/ Quicksilver Books, 1985. Remains the best overall study of the subject.

BIOGRAPHICAL SOURCES

Malkiel, Theresa S. *The Diary of a Shirtwaist Striker.* (1910). Reprint. Ithaca, NY: ILR/Cornell University Press, 1990. Valuable first-person account of union organization of the needle trades.

PERIODICAL SOURCES

Crute, Sheree. "The Insurance Scandal behind the Triangle Shirtwaist Fire." *Ms* 11:81–83 (April 1983). A sidelight on the management of the Triangle Company.

Mitelman, Bonnie. "Rose Schneiderman and the Triangle Fire." *American*

History Illustrated 16(4): 38–47 (1981). Good brief account of one labor militant.

AUDIOVISUAL SOURCES

The Triangle Factory Fire Scandal. Van Nuys, CA: Live Entertainment, 1978. Videocassette. 100-minute tape of the 1978 television drama.

WORLD WIDE WEB

Kheel Center for Labor-Management Documentation and Archives. "The Triangle Shirtwaist Factory Fire—March 25, 1911." The Triangle Fire, Sweatshops, and Protective Legislation. (July 1998). http://www.ilr.cornell.edu/trianglefire/cover.html An excellent and authoritative site dealing with labor-management relations; treatment of the fire includes selections from the Stein book, *New York Times*, and *Chicago Tribune*, as well as photographs and political cartoons.

11. Presidential Election of 1912

Four familiar candidates competed for the presidency in 1912. Democrats chose Woodrow Wilson, reform governor of New Jersey; Republicans renominated President William Howard Taft. Convinced that the Taft forces had unfairly deprived him of the party nomination, former president Theodore Roosevelt ran as the third-party Progressive (or Bull Moose) candidate, while Eugene V. Debs was the Socialist party candidate. Both Wilson with his New Freedom program and Roosevelt with his New Nationalism program claimed to be the true reformer. Taft appealed to conservatives, Debs to radicals. The Roosevelt-Taft split cost the Republicans the presidency. Though obtaining only roughly 40 percent of the popular vote, Wilson won an overwhelming electoral victory. Debs received nearly 1 million votes.

Suggestions for Term Papers

1. Compare the New Nationalism and the New Freedom.
2. Was Roosevelt unfairly deprived of his party's nomination?

3. Why was Debs able to poll nearly 1 million votes?

4. Why was the Socialist party strong at this time?

5. What were the election's effects on American political and economic life?

Suggested Sources: See entries 2, 3, and 4 for related items, especially for material on Roosevelt and Taft.

GENERAL SOURCES

Burton, David H. *The Learned Presidency: Theodore Roosevelt, William Howard Taft, Woodrow Wilson.* Rutherford, NJ: Fairleigh Dickinson, 1988. Absorbing group portrait.

Cooper, John Milton. *The Warrior and the Priest: Woodrow Wilson and Theodore Roosevelt.* Cambridge, MA: Belknap Press of Harvard University Press, 1983. Essential for understanding the differing viewpoints of these two statesmen.

Debs, Eugene V. *Gentle Rebel: Letters of Eugene V. Debs.* Urbana: University of Illinois Press, 1995. Compilation of letters Debs sent to various political and societal figures; provides a comprehensive look at politics from the perspective of the leading American socialist of the time.

Roseboom, Eugene H., and Alfred E. Eckes, Jr. *A History of Presidential Elections, from George Washington to Jimmy Carter.* 4th ed. New York: Macmillan, 1979. Concise examination of the presidential elections, providing a quick overview.

SPECIALIZED SOURCES

Broderick, Francis L. *Progressivism at Risk: Electing a President in 1912.* Westport, CT: Greenwood, 1989. Solid examination of the topic.

Gable, John A. *The Bull Moose Years: Theodore Roosevelt and the Progressive Party.* Port Washington, NY: Kennikat, 1978. Detailed exposition of Roosevelt's involvement with and leadership of the Progressives.

BIOGRAPHICAL SOURCES

Clements, Kendrick A. *The Presidency of Woodrow Wilson.* Lawrence: University of Kansas Press, 1992. Brief, useful overview of Wilson's political life.

Fausold, Martin L. *Gifford Pinchot, Bull Moose Progressive.* (1961). Reprint. Westport, CT: Greenwood, 1973. Interesting and informative biography of the ardent conservationist-politician who supported Roosevelt in the election.

Ginger, Ray. *The Bending Cross: A Biography of Eugene Victor Debs.* (1949). Reprint. Kirksville, MO: Thomas Jefferson University Press, 1992. Thorough and detailed biography of Debs and his representation of the working class.

Link, Arthur, ed. *The Papers of Woodrow Wilson.* Princeton, NJ: Princeton University Press, 1966–1994. 69 vols. Incomparable annotated source materials for the study of Wilson's private and public life. Consult for topics 12–19 as well.

———. *Wilson.* Princeton, NJ: Princeton University Press, 1947–1965. 5 vols. to date. Monumental biography; although most volumes are out of print, it is well worth finding.

Salvatore, Nick. *Eugene V. Debs: Citizen and Socialist.* Urbana: University of Illinois Press, 1982. Pulitzer Prize–winning biography.

AUDIOVISUAL SOURCES

"The President's Collection II: TR & FDR." *The American Experience.* Santa Monica, CA: PBS Home Video, 1997. 4 videocassettes. 60-minute detailed treatment of all aspects of the administrations of both presidents. The events and considerations leading to the controversies between Roosevelt and Taft are examined in reporting the election of 1912.

WORLD WIDE WEB

"The Presidents—Theodore Roosevelt." *The American Experience.* September 1997. http:www.pbs.org/wgbh/pages/amex/presidents/nf/featured/tr/trdd.html This page from the PBS presentation focuses on the election of 1912. It has excellent links to presidential politics and days of decision among others.

12. Women's Suffrage

By 1896, only four states had granted women the vote; no other state would do so before 1910. Within the next decade, however, the suffrage movement greatly accelerated, culminating in the adoption of the Nineteenth Amendment in 1920. A change in tactics by the National American Woman Suffrage Association (NAWSA) helped achieve victory. Abandoning attempts to win the vote for women on a state-by-state basis, NAWSA pushed for a constitutional amendment, which Congress adopted in 1919. Significant leaders in the movement were Carrie Chapman Catt, Anna Howard Shaw, and the more radical feminist, Alice Paul.

Suggestions for Term Papers

1. Compare arguments for and against women's suffrage during the Progressive era.
2. Analyze the contributions of one important figure in the suffrage movement.
3. What were the long-range effects of women's suffrage on American politics?
4. What reforms other than suffrage did women in the movement seek during the Progressive era?
5. Did President Wilson support women's suffrage only because he wanted to win their votes in the 1920 election?

Suggested Sources: See entries 13 and 77 for related items.

REFERENCE SOURCES

The Encyclopedia of Women's History in America: Over 500 Years of Movements, Breakthroughs, Legislation, Court Cases and Notable Women. Kathryn Cullen-DuPont. New York: Facts on File, 1996. Comprehensive treatment of the women's movement.

Jewish Women in America: An Historical Encyclopedia. Paula Hyman and Deborah Dash Moore, eds. New York: Routledge, 1997. Covers personalities, activities, and organizations regarding Jewish women's participation in American life. A major essay examines their involvement with women's suffrage.

Protest, Power and Change: An Encyclopedia of Nonviolent Action from ACT-UP to Women's Suffrage. Roger S. Powers, ed. Hamden, CT: Garland, 1996. Comprehensive coverage of nonviolent resistance.

Reader's Guide to Women's Studies. Eleanor Amico, ed. Chicago: Fitzroy Dearborn, 1998. Essay and bibliography for 600 topics in women's studies; good treatment of suffrage.

Women in Modern American Politics: A Bibliography, 1900–1995. Elizabeth M. Cox. Washington, DC: Congressional Quarterly, 1997. Nearly

6,000 entries to writings on women in American political life from a wide variety of resources.

Women's Rights in the United States: A Documentary History. Winston E. Langley and Vivian C. Fox, eds. Westport, CT: Greenwood, 1994. Contains 125 documents organized into five chronological periods.

GENERAL SOURCES

Adickes, Sandra. *To Be Young Was Very Heaven: Women in New York before the First World War.* New York: St. Martin's, 1997. Well-conceived treatment of the high-energy period of Margaret Sanger and Mabel Dodge.

Frost-Knappman, Elizabeth, and Kathryn Cullen-DuPont. *Women's Rights on Trial: 101 Historic Trials from Anne Hutchinson to the Virginia Military Institute Cadets.* Detroit: Gale, 1997. Includes Susan B. Anthony's arrest for voting.

Giele, Janet Z. *Two Paths to Women's Equality: Temperance, Suffrage, and the Origins of Modern Feminism.* New York: Twayne, 1995. Examines social movements of the past to reveal the present; sees moderation as an effective policy.

Lunardini, Christine A. *Women's Rights.* Phoenix: Oryx, 1996. Comprehensive treatment of events and personalities integral to the women's rights movement. Part of the Social Issues in American History series.

Schneider, Dorothy, and Carl J. Schneider. *American Women in the Progressive Era, 1900–1920.* New York: Facts on File, 1993. Good historical survey of societal conditions regarding women during this period.

SPECIALIZED SOURCES

Frost, Elizabeth, and Kathryn Cullen-DuPont. *Women's Suffrage in America: An Eyewitness History.* New York: Facts on File, 1992. Variety of primary source materials (diaries, letters, speeches, etc.) provided for the period 1820 to 1920.

Gordon, Ann D., et al., eds. *African American Women and the Vote, 1837–1965.* Amherst: University of Massachusetts Press, 1996. Collection of essays by leading scholars.

Green, Elna C. *Southern Strategies: Southern Women and the Woman Suffrage Question.* Chapel Hill: University of North Carolina Press, 1997. Interesting exposition of a little-explored topic.

Joannou, Maraoula, and June Purvis, eds. *The Women's Suffrage Movement: New Feminist Perspectives.* New York: St. Martin's, 1998. Collection of essays of recent scholarship on the suffrage movement.

Law, Cheryl. *Suffrage and Power: The Women's Movement, 1918–1928.* New York: St. Martin's, 1997. Describes the transformation of the women's movement into a viable political force.

Marshall, Susan E. *Splintered Sisterhood: Gender and Class in the Campaign against Woman Suffrage.* Madison: University of Wisconsin Press, 1997. Up-to-date discussion.

Scott, Anne Firor, and Andrew Mackay. *One Half the People: The Fight for Woman Suffrage.* Urbana: University of Illinois Press, 1982. Brief history, with documents and useful bibliographic essay.

Terborg-Penn, Rosalyn. *African American Women in the Struggle for the Vote, 1850–1920.* Bloomington: Indiana University Press, 1998. Examination of the nature of the African American suffragist movement.

BIOGRAPHICAL SOURCES

Cullen-DuPont, Kathryn. *Elizabeth Cady Stanton and Women's Liberty.* New York: Facts on File, 1992. An excellent biographical description of Stanton's career. Part of the Makers of America series.

Goldsmith, Barbara. *Other Powers: The Age of Suffrage, Spiritualism, and the Scandalous Victoria Woodhull.* New York: Random House, 1998. Thorough and interesting biographical sketch of one of the most remarkable women in American history.

Helmer, Diana Star. *Women Suffragists.* New York: Facts on File, 1998. Profiles ten suffragists, including Alice Paul, Susan B. Anthony, and Victoria Woodhull. Part of the American Profiles series.

James, Edward T., and Janet W. James. *Notable American Women, 1607–1950: A Biographical Dictionary.* 3 vols. Cambridge, MA: Belknap Press, 1971. Basic source with good bibliographic notes.

Linkugel, Wil A. *Anna Howard Shaw: Suffrage Orator and Social Reformer.* Westport, CT: Greenwood, 1991. Brief, helpful study.

Lunardini, Christine A. *From Equal Suffrage to Equal Rights: Alice Paul and that National Woman's Party, 1910–1928.* New York: New York University Press, 1986. Stimulating life of this controversial feminist.

Sher, Lynn. *Failure Is Impossible: Susan B. Anthony in Her Own Words.* New York: Times Books, 1995. Biographical commentary along with excerpts from speeches, letters, diaries, and interviews.

Stuhler, Barbara. *Gentle Warriors: Clara Ueland and the Minnesota Struggle for Woman Suffrage.* St. Paul: Minnesota Historical Society, 1995. Interesting and readable account of an activist at the state level; excellent insight into the national suffrage movement.

Van Voris, Jacqueline. *Carrie Chapman Catt: A Public Life.* New York: Feminist Press (CUNY), 1987. Standard biography of Catt.

AUDIOVISUAL SOURCES

One Woman, One Vote. Santa Monica, CA: PBS Home Video, 1995. Videocassette. 60 minutes. From PBS's *The American Experience* series. There is a companion volume (with the same title), published by New Sage Press, 1995, providing an excellent collection of essays on various aspects of the movement for women's vote and women's rights.

WORLD WIDE WEB

Library of Congress. "Votes for Women—Selections from the National American Woman Suffrage Association Collection, 1848–1921." *American Memory*. July 1996. http://memory.loc.gov/ammem/naw/nawshome.html An extraordinary opportunity to use primary sources.

National Women's History Project. *Women Win the Vote*. August 1995. http://lcweb2.loc.gov/ammem/naw/nawshome.html Excellent site commemorating the seventy-fifth anniversary of woman suffrage. Links to collective biography of seventy-five suffragists, important dates, and brief history.

13. Progressive Reforms Enacted

Progressive era legislators enacted a host of political, economic, and social reforms at the city, state, and national levels of government. The agenda of reform politics included breaking the powers of political machines and extending the democratic process through women's suffrage, the direct election of senators, and the initiative, referendum, and recall. Economic reforms centered on regulating big business and banking practices. Protecting women and children workers was also an important issue for reformers. Perhaps no other social reform engendered as much controversy as did the battle to enact prohibition.

Suggestions for Term Papers

1. Who was the more important presidential reformer, Theodore Roosevelt or Woodrow Wilson?

2. Analyze the reform contributions of an important Progressive era governor or mayor.

3. How successful were efforts to destroy urban political machines?

4. Analyze Progressives' attitudes toward immigrants and minorities.

5. Did Progressive era reforms make the United States a substantially more democratic nation?

Suggested Sources: See entries 7, 8, and 13 for related items.

REFERENCE SOURCES

Progressive Reform: A Guide to Information Sources. John D. Buenker and Nicholas C. Burckel. Detroit: Gale Research, 1989. Comprehensive bibliography of progressivism in U.S. politics, beginning with the nineteenth century.

GENERAL SOURCES

Bruchey, Stuart W. *The Wealth of the Nation: An Economic History of the United States.* New York: Harper & Row, 1988. Brief, comprehensive economic history; treatment of the rise of big business and the Progressive movement is excellent.

Jensen, Joan M. *Army Surveillance in America.* New Haven, CT: Yale University Press, 1991. Lucid and readable historical examination of the use of army surveillance in the United States. Informative chapters on its use against organized labor during the early years of this century.

Ladd-Taylor, Molly. *Mother-Work: Women, Child Welfare, and the State, 1890–1930.* Urbana: University of Illinois Press, 1994. Informative study of motherhood and child raising over several decades, including the Progressive era.

Wiebe, Robert H. *The Search for Order, 1877–1920.* (1967). Reprint. Westport, CT: Greenwood, 1980. Important study by a leading historian challenging traditional reform claims for the Progressive era.

SPECIALIZED SOURCES

Berman, Jay S. *Police Administration and Progressive Reform: Theodore Roosevelt as Police Commissioner of New York.* Westport, CT: Greenwood, 1987. Brief survey of the Progressive movement and Roosevelt's early years as the police commissioner.

Chambers, John W. *The Tyranny of Change: America in the Progressive Era,*

1900–1917. 2d ed. New York: St. Martin's, 1992. Excellent coverage of all aspects of the era.

Colburn, David R., and George E. Pozzetta, eds. *Reform and Reformers in the Progressive Era.* Westport, CT: Greenwood, 1983. A collection of essays on various aspects of the Progressive era; looks at Al Smith, muckrakers, immigrants, John Reed, and others.

Diner, Steven J. *A Very Different Age: Americans of the Progressive Era.* New York: Hill & Wang, 1997. Good social history of working people during this time (industrial workers, farmers, immigrants, white-collar workers, etc.).

Frankel, Noralee, and Nancy Dye, eds. *Gender, Class, Race, and Reform in the Progressive Era.* Lexington: University of Kentucky Press, 1991. Stimulating series of essays presented at a conference held in 1988.

Link, William A. *The Paradox of Southern Progressivism, 1880–1930.* Chapel Hill: University of North Carolina Press, 1992. Good historical overview of the beginnings and development of the Progressive reform movement in the South.

Reese, William J. *Power and the Promise of School Reform: Grassroots Movements during the Progressive Era.* Boston: Routledge & Kegan Paul, 1986. Historical treatment of social reform in education during this period.

Sarasohn, David. *The Party of Reform: Democrats in the Progressive Era.* Jackson: University of Mississippi Press, 1989. Provocative study focusing on congressional Democrats as reformers.

Schneider, Dorothy, and Carl J. Schneider. *American Women in the Progressive Era, 1900–1920.* New York: Facts on File, 1993. Provides detailed and accurate treatment of both the domestic and working lives of American women.

Tiffin, Susan. *In Whose Best Interest? Child Welfare Reform in the Progressive Era.* Westport, CT: Greenwood, 1982. Examination of the child welfare movement.

Weisberger, Bernard A. *The La Follettes of Wisconsin: Love and Politics in Progressive America.* Madison, WI: University of Wisconsin Press, 1994. Story of America's most influential state Progressive leaders.

Weser, Robert F. *A Response to Progressivism: The Democratic Party and New York Politics, 1902–1918.* Chronological coverage of party politics in the Progressive era. Not limited to the Democratic party; also treats Republicans, Progressives, and Socialists in the peculiar makeup of New York City politics.

BIOGRAPHICAL SOURCES

Fitzpatrick, Ellen F. *Endless Crusade: Women Social Scientists and Progressive Reform.* New York: Oxford University Press, 1990. Collective biography of female social reformers and social scientists during the period.

AUDIOVISUAL SOURCES

The Progressive Movement. Wynewood, PA: Schlessinger/Library Video, 1996. Videocassette. 40-minute presentation on the roots of progressivism. Volume 14 of the 20-volume set, United States History Video Collection.

WORLD WIDE WEB

Schultz, Stanley K. *American History 102—Civil War to the Present.* (1998). http//hum.lss.wisc.edu/hist102/index.html University of Wisconsin course provides excellent narrative and relevant pictures. Click on "Student Web Notes" and see lectures 11 and 12 treating progressivism and morality of power with Roosevelt and Wilson.

14. Woodrow Wilson and the Mexican Crisis (1913–1917)

Events in revolutionary Mexico tested President Wilson's policy of "missionary diplomacy," which tried to infuse morality and idealism into foreign relations. When Mexican general Victoriano Huerta established a military dictatorship in 1913, Wilson refused to extend diplomatic recognition and supported the general's rival, Venustiano Carranza. In April 1914, Mexican authorities briefly arrested some American sailors in Tampico and shortly thereafter U.S. forces seized Veracruz. Perhaps only the mediation of the ABC Powers (Argentina, Brazil, and Chile) prevented war. The United States recognized the new Carranza government in 1915. The bandit Pancho Villa created grave concern by killing Americans in Mexico and in New Mexico. Wilson sent General John J. Pershing into Mexico in an unsuccessful attempt to capture Villa.

Suggestions for Term Papers

1. Compare Wilson's "missionary diplomacy" with Taft's "dollar diplomacy."

2. How significant was the ABC mediation?

3. Why did the Pershing expedition fail?

4. Did Wilson intervene in Mexico primarily to protect U.S. interests or to promote democracy?

5. Discuss the long-range consequences of the crisis on U.S.-Mexican relations.

Suggested Sources: See entries 11 and 14 for related items, especially Clements's *Presidency of Woodrow Wilson* and Link's edition of the *Woodrow Wilson Papers.*

GENERAL SOURCES

Calhoun, Frederick S. *Uses of Force and Wilsonian Foreign Policy.* Kent, Ohio: Kent State University Press, 1993. Places Mexican intervention in the broader context of Wilson's diplomacy.

Cumberland, Charles C. *Mexican Revolution: Genesis under Madero.* (1952). Reprint. Westport, CT: Greenwood, 1969. Informative survey of the beginning of the Mexican Revolution.

———. *Mexican Revolution: The Constitutionalist Years.* Austin: University of Texas Press, 1972. Detailed account of the Mexican Revolution through the Carranza period.

Haley, P. Edward. *Revolution and Intervention: The Diplomacy of Taft and Wilson with Mexico, 1910–1917.* Cambridge, MA: MIT Press, 1970. Thoughtful comparison of the two administrations.

Raat, W. Dirk. *Mexico and the United States: Ambivalent Vistas.* 2d ed. Athens: University of Georgia Press, 1996. Reliable survey with an excellent bibliography.

SPECIALIZED SOURCES

Clendenen, Clarence C. *The United States and Pancho Villa: A Study in Unconventional Diplomacy.* (1961). Reprint. Port Washington, NY: Kennikat, 1972. Informative examination of Mexican-American relations and the impact of Villa on the border region during this time.

Mason, Herbert M. *The Great Pursuit.* (1970). Reprint. New York: Smithmark, 1995. Fine study of Pershing's expedition.

Teitelbaum, Louis M. *Woodrow Wilson and the Mexican Revolution, 1913–1916: A History of United States–Mexican Relations from the Murder of Madero until Villa's Provocation across the Border.* New York: Exposition, 1967. Thorough coverage of the critical three-year period in which Carranza assumed control.

BIOGRAPHICAL SOURCES

Harris, Larry A. *Pancho Villa: Strong Man of the Revolution.* Silver City, NM: High Lonesome Books, 1989. Concise survey with good coverage of the Columbus Raid.

Katz, Friedrich. *The Life and Times of Pancho Villa.* Stanford, CA: Stanford University Press, 1998. The most recent examination of Villa and his influence on the revolutionary movement in Mexico.

Meyer, Harold J. *Hanging Sam: A Military Biography of General Samuel T. Williams from Pancho Villa to Vietnam.* Denton: University of North Texas Press, 1990. Interesting biography of an army officer's career that started with the Pershing expedition.

Smythe, Donald. *Pershing, General of the Armies.* Bloomington: Indiana University Press, 1986. Excellent biography of Pershing.

Tuck, Jim. *Pancho Villa and John Reed: Two Faces of Romantic Revolution.* Tucson: University of Arizona Press, 1984. Interesting pairing of the lives of Villa and Reed, the American socialist writer, as "romantic" revolutionaries.

Vandiver, Frank E. *Black Jack: The Life and Times of John J. Pershing.* College Station: Texas A&M University Press, 1977. Lengthy and detailed but readable and accurate. Considered a definitive biography.

AUDIOVISUAL SOURCES

Espinosa, Paul. "The Hunt for Pancho Villa." *The American Experience.* Santa Monica, CA: PBS Home Video, 1993. Videocassette. Television presentation; 56-minute documentary describing Pershing's unsuccessful pursuit of Villa.

"Pancho Villa, Mexican Revolutionary." *The Hispanic and Latin American Heritage Video Collection.* Bala Cynwyd, PA: Schlessinger Library Video, 1995. Videocassette. One of a series of 30-minute biographies providing an informative survey of the lives and achievements of notable individuals.

WORLD WIDE WEB

Dean, Paul. "Woodrow Wilson's Administration." *Presidents—Home Outlines, Essays, Texts, Biographies.* June 1997. wysiwyg://59/http://odur.let.rug.nl/~usa/P/ww28/about/wilsonxx.htm Excellent narrative overview of Wilson's political career with relevant links. Click on Part 2 "From New Freedom to World War I," which deals with the Mexican turmoil, among other things.

15. The Armory Show (1913)

Twentieth-century America responded to new movements in art. One group (known as "The Eight") focused on realistic, everyday scenes, earning the derisive nickname the "Ashcan School." And in February 1913, a larger group of U.S. artists staged a show at New York's National Guard Armory, which then toured Chicago, Philadelphia, and Boston. This huge exhibition of more than a thousand works by American and European artists was a watershed in the history of American art. Although many of the works were traditional, it was the avant-garde works of postimpressionism, cubism, fauvism, and expressionism, including ones by Pablo Picasso, Henri Matisse, Marcel Duchamps, and Wassily Kandinsky, that astonished and sometimes outraged audiences. The Armory Show represented the first truly major exhibit of modern art in the United States.

Suggestions for Term Papers

1. How did the Armory Show influence American cultural tastes?
2. Discuss the influence of the Ashcan painters on American art.
3. What was the general reaction of critics and the public to the Armory Show?
4. What was "modern" about modern art?
5. Discuss the career of a prominent American artist active at the time of the Armory Show.

GENERAL SOURCES

American Art: From the Limners to the Eight. Ashland, KY: Ashland Oil, 1976. Catalog of an exhibition held at Huntington Galleries (West Virginia) from February to May 1976.

Leeds, Valerie A. *The Independents: The Ashcan School and Their Circle from*

Florida Collections. Winter Park, FL: George D. and Harriet W. Cornell Fine Arts Museum, 1996. Catalog of paintings in Florida collections.

MacLeod, Glen G. *Wallace Stevens and Modern Art: From the Armory Show to Abstract Expressionism.* New Haven, CT: Yale University Press, 1993. Interesting perspective of the relationship of twentieth-century art and literature in the work of the Pulitzer Prize–winning poet.

Milroy, Elizabeth. *Painters of a New Century: The Eight and American Art.* Milwaukee: Milwaukee Art Museum, 1991. Catalog of an exhibition held at the museum from September to November 1991.

Perlman, Bennard B. *Painters of the Ashcan School: The Immortal Eight.* (1979). Reprint. New York: Dover, 1988. Evolution of U.S. art after the Civil War, with a focus on members of the Ash Can School; originally published as *The Immortal Eight.*

———, ed. *Revolutionaries of Realism: The Letters of John Sloan and Robert Henri.* Princeton, NJ: Princeton University Press, 1997. Interesting and revealing documentary record of the correspondence between two of the artists of the Ash Can School.

Prown, Jules David. *American Painting: From Its Beginnings to the Armory Show.* New York: Rizzoli, 1987. Well-illustrated historical survey.

Zurier, Rebecca, et al. *Metropolitan Lives: The Ashcan Artists and Their New York.* Washington, DC: National Museum of American Art/Norton, 1995. Catalog of an exhibition held at the museum from November 1995 to March 1996.

SPECIALIZED SOURCES

The Armory Show: International Exhibition of Modern Art, 1913. New York: Arno, 1972. 3 vols. Detailed catalog and collection of related documents providing insight into the nature of the show.

Brown, Milton W. *The Story of the Armory Show.* New York: Abbeville, 1988. Excellent description.

Green, Martin B. *The Armory Show and the Paterson Strike Pageant.* New York: Scribner, 1988. Informative history of the show within the political and social context of the times, including the strike of the Industrial Workers of the World in Paterson, New Jersey.

1913 Armory Show: 50th Anniversary Exhibition, 1963. Utica, NY: Munson-Williams-Proctor Institute, 1963. Reconstruction of the Armory Show held at the institute from February to March 1963.

Trapp, Frank A. *The 1913 Armory Show in Retrospect.* Amherst, MA: Amherst College, 1958. 34-page exhibition catalog for reconstructed exhibition held at Amherst College in 1958.

BIOGRAPHICAL SOURCES

Braider, Donald. *George Bellows and the Ashcan School of Painting.* Garden City, NY: Doubleday, 1971. Brief biography of one of the artists who presented harsh realities in his work.

Glackens, Ira. *William Glackens and the Eight: The Artists Who Freed American Art.* (1984). Reprint. New York: Writers and Readers, 1990. Valuable insight into modern art provided by the son of one of The Eight.

Green, Eleanor, et al. *Maurice Prendergast: Art of Impulse and Color.* College Park: University of Maryland Art Gallery, 1976. Good biography of Prendergast along with a chronology and catalog of an exhibition held at the university gallery from October to November 1976. The exhibition toured in 1977.

Perlman, Bennard B. *The Lives, Loves, and Art of Arthur B. Davies.* Albany: State University of New York Press, 1998. Recent biography of an artist who was part of the movement.

———. *Robert Henri: His Life and Art.* New York: Dover, 1991. Concise account of a member of the movement by the expert writer.

PERIODICAL ARTICLES

Dudar, Helen. "To John Marin, Art Became 'A Mad Wonder Dancing.' " *Smithsonian* 20:52–58 (Feb. 1990). Insight into the modernist painter who participated in the Armory Show.

AUDIOVISUAL SOURCES

A Wave from the Atlantic. Alexandria, VA: PBS Video, 1996. Videocassette. 58 minutes. Part of the American Visions series showing American history through its art.

Armory Show—1913–1963. Kent, CT: Creative Arts Television Archive, 1963. Videocassette. Tour of fiftieth anniversary re-creation of the Armory exhibition.

WORLD WIDE WEB

The Armory Show of 1913. December 1996. http://www.cwrl.utexas.edu/~slatin/20c_poetry/projects/relatproject/armory.html Brief description of the show and its impact; taken from Frank Trapp's *The Armory Show in Retrospect* (1958).

16. Sinking of the *Lusitania* (1915)

In early 1915, Germany announced that ships sailing in what it decreed the war zone around the British Isles would be sunk. On May 7, 1915, a German U-boat sank the British passenger liner *Lusitania*, which it claimed (correctly) was carrying arms, with the loss of 1,198 lives, 128 of them Americans. While declaring that "there is such a thing as a man being too proud to fight," President Woodrow Wilson promised to hold Germany to "strict accountability" and demanded an end to its unrestricted submarine warfare. Fearful that war might ensue, Secretary of State William Jennings Bryan resigned. Several months later, after a similar incident, Germany accepted the *Arabic* pledge, which provided for the safety of passengers on unarmed vessels.

Suggestions for Term Papers

1. Discuss the controversy concerning whether the *Lusitania* carried arms.

2. Compare American reaction to the sinking of the *Lusitania* with the sinking of the *Maine* before the Spanish-American War.

3. Should Americans have been allowed to travel on the *Lusitania*?

4. Should the United States have declared war on Germany after the sinking of the *Lusitania*?

5. Was the sinking of the *Lusitania* an important factor in the United States' eventual declaration of war against Germany?

Suggested Sources: See entries, 1, 11, 14, and 17 for related items.

REFERENCE SOURCES

Shipwrecks: An Encyclopedia of the World's Worst Disasters at Sea. David Ritchie. New York: Facts on File, 1996. Provides background on and descriptions of 400 significant shipwrecks; includes charts and illustrations. Includes the *Lusitania* and *Titanic*.

GENERAL SOURCES

Birnbaum, Karl E. *Peace Moves and U-Boat Warfare: A Study of Imperial Germany's Policy toward the United States, April 18, 1916–January 9, 1917.* Hamden, CT: Archon Books, 1970. Examines German policy developed one year after the *Lusitania* incident.

Gilbert, Martin. *The First World War: A Complete History.* New York: Holt, 1994. Nearly encyclopedic view of war.

Grant, Robert M. *U-Boat Intelligence, 1914–1918.* Hamden, CT: Archon Books, 1969. Brief account of intelligence gathering with respect to naval operations during the war.

Gray, Edwyn. *The Killing Time: The U-Boat War, 1914–1918.* New York: Scribner's, 1972. Revealing account of U-boat operations during the war; more detailed than the Grant effort above.

Rossler, Eberhard. *The U-Boat: The Evolution and Technical History of German Submarines.* Annapolis, MD: Naval Institute, 1981. Detailed, authoritative history of the development of U-boats. Translated from the German.

Terraine, John. *The U-Boat Wars, 1916–1945.* (1989). Reprint. New York: Holt, 1990. Detailed study of U-boat operations in World Wars I and II.

SPECIALIZED SOURCES

Bailey, Thomas A., and Paul B. Ryan. *The Lusitania Disaster: An Episode in Modern Warfare and Diplomacy.* New York: Free Press, 1975. Detailed and revealing study of the *Lusitania* and its implications for modern warfare.

Ballard, Robert D., and Spencer Dunmore. *Exploring the Lusitania: Probing the Mysteries of the Sinking That Changed History.* New York: Warner Books, 1995. Recent examination of the conditions attending the incident. Good bibliography.

Droste, Christian L., comp., and W. H. Tantum IV, ed. *The Lusitania Case.* (1915). Reprint. Riverside, CT: 7 C's Press, 1972. Originally published as volume 2 of *Documents on the War of the Nations from Neutral and Anti-German Sources,* shortly after the event. Good array of source material.

Hickey, Des, and Gus Smith. *Seven Days to Disaster: The Sinking of the Lusitania.* New York: Putnam, 1982. Indispensable basic study of the fateful voyage.

Hoehling, A. A., and Mary D. Hoehling. *The Last Voyage of the Lusitania.* (1956). Reprint. Lanham, MD: Madison Books, 1996. A standard popular history of the tragic voyage.

Simpson, Colin. *Lusitania*. (1972). Reprint. New York: Penguin Books, 1983. A standard history with a good bibliography.

BIOGRAPHICAL SOURCES

Ashby, LeRoy. *William Jennings Bryan: Champion of Democracy*. Boston: Twayne, 1987. Provides insight into Bryan's growing disenchantment with Wilson's anti-German policies and his resignation over the *Lusitania* notes. Helpful bibliography.
Link, Arthur S. *Woodrow Wilson and a Revolutionary World, 1913–1921*. Chapel Hill: University of North Carolina Press, 1982. Focuses on Wilson and European affairs.

AUDIOVISUAL SOURCES

The Lusitania. Orland Park, IL: MPI Home Video, 1989. Videocassette. 30 minutes. Part of the Secrets of the Unknown series. Host Edward Mulhare presents the intriguing story.

WORLD WIDE WEB

"Interviews—Winter: The Lusitania." *The Great War and the Shaping of the Twentieth Century*. September 1997. http://www3.pbs.org/ greatwar/ A multimedia project produced by PBS in association with the Imperial War Museum of London. Contains many pictures, a chronology, and interviews with historians. Click on the interview with Jay M. Winter, who briefly describes the conditions leading to the *Lusitania* incident.

17. The United States and World War I (1917–1918)

Citing Germany's repeated violations of America's rights as a neutral and vowing that the world "must be made safe for democracy," Woodrow Wilson asked Congress for a declaration of war on April 2, 1917. Congress, despite some opposition, assented. Nearly 5 million Americans enlisted or were drafted, and more than 50,000 died in battle before the fighting stopped. Mobilizing for war, the government created new regulatory agencies, and women and numerous

African Americans who had migrated northward toiled in factories as replacements for fighting men. The civil liberties of those opposed to the war were severely constrained.

Suggestions for Term Papers

1. Compare arguments made for and against U.S. entry into the war.
2. Analyze U.S. military contributions to the Allied victory.
3. Discuss the contributions of women and minorities to the war effort.
4. How effective was propaganda in winning domestic support for the war?
5. Analyze the effects of the war on domestic civil liberties.

Suggested Sources: See entries 16 and 18 for related items.

REFERENCE SOURCES

American Military History: A Guide to Reference and Information Resources. Daniel K. Blewett. Englewood, CO: Libraries Unlimited, 1995. Selectively annotated bibliography of reference sources treating all branches of the services and different wars. Separate chapter on World War I.

The Historical Atlas of World War I. Anthony Livesey. New York: Holt, 1994. Examines the war with over 100 color maps, along with photographs and illustrations.

The United States in the First World War: An Encyclopedia. Anne Cipriano Venzon, ed. Hamden, CT: Garland, 1995. Well-researched effort providing alphabetical arrangement of relevant topics and personalities regarding civil, political, and military aspects of the war.

The West Point Atlas of American Wars: The First World War. Brigadier General Vincent J. Esposito. New York: Holt, 1997. Large size with eighty-four full-color maps; up-to-date coverage from Bismarck's Prussia to the League of Nations.

GENERAL SOURCES

Snow, Donald M., and Dennis M. Drew. *From Lexington to Desert Storm: War and Politics in the American Experience.* Armonk, NY: Sharpe,

1992. Good coverage of both the military and political facets of all American wars, including World War I.

Tuchman, Barbara. *The Proud Tower: A Portrait of the World before the War, 1890–1914.* New York: Macmillan, 1966. Good background history of conditions prior to the war.

SPECIALIZED SOURCES

Background and Military Aspects

Bosco, Peter. *World War I.* New York: Facts on File, 1991. Complete account of U.S. participation with emphasis on the change from isolationism to intervention.

Brannen, Carl A., et al. *Over There: A Marine in the Great War.* College Station, TX: Texas A&M University Press, 1996. Based on Private Brannen's memoirs. A useful account of the life and routine of a foot soldier from training to combat.

Bristow, Nancy K. *Making Men Moral: Social Engineering during the Great War.* New York: New York University Press, 1996. Detailed description of Wilson's Commission on Training Camp Activities (1917), designed to prevent immoral and illegal behavior. From the publisher's American Social Experience series.

Dolan, Edward F. *America in World War I.* Brookfield, CT: Millbrook, 1996. Concise and easy-to-read history of the war from its causes and reasons for U.S. participation to its conclusion.

Esposito, David M. *The Legacy of Woodrow Wilson: American War Aims in World War I.* Westport, CT: Praeger, 1996. Fine account of Wilson's leadership during the war and his determination to create a lasting peace.

Halpern, Paul G. *A Naval History of World War I.* Annapolis, MD: Naval Institute, 1994. Up-to-date study.

Hansen, Arlen J. *Gentlemen Volunteers: The Story of the American Ambulance Drivers in the Great War, August 1914–September 1918.* New York: Arcade Publishing, 1996. Interesting and informative examination of the volunteer ambulance drivers who came from all walks of life and provided assistance even before the United States became involved in the war.

Harries, Meirion, and Susie Harries. *The Last Days of Innocence: America at War, 1917–1918.* New York: Random House, 1997. Focus on the last part of the war. Contains an extensive bibliography.

Hart, B. H. Liddell. *The Real War, 1914–1918.* (1930). Reprint. Boston: Little, Brown, 1964. Classic history by a leading military historian. Many consider this the best history of World War I.

Heyman, Neil M. *World War I.* Westport, CT: Greenwood, 1997. Good picture of the American role in the war and developments on the home front.

Jantzen, Steven L. *Hooray for Peace, Hurrah for War.* New York: Facts on File, 1990. A readable, informative work with illustrations that examines the American experience on the home front and the battlefield.

Kennett, Lee B. *The First Air War, 1914–1918.* New York: Free Press, 1991. Good overview of air participation.

Kirchberger, Joe H. *The First World War: An Eyewitness History.* New York: Facts on File, 1992. Firsthand accounts from speeches, letters, and newspapers. Includes chronologies and biographies.

O'Shea, Stephen. *Back to the Front: An Accidental Historian Walks the Trenches of World War I.* New York: Walker, 1997. Interesting account of a 500-mile walking tour of the trenches remaining from the war (Verdun, Somme, Vimy, etc.).

Trask, David. F. *The AEF and Coalition Warmaking, 1917–1918.* Lawrence: University of Kansas, 1993. Indispensable survey of the U.S. military contribution.

Tuchman, Barbara. *The Guns of August.* (1962). Reprint. New York: Macmillan, 1988. Pulitzer Prize–winning account of the heroism and valor in the war. Extensive bibliography.

Propaganda

Buitenhuis, Peter. *The Great War of Words: British, American and Canadian Propaganda and Fiction, 1914–1933.* Vancouver: University of British Columbia Press, 1987. Literature as propaganda.

Isenberg, Michael T. *War on Film: The American Cinema and World War I, 1914–1941.* Rutherford, NJ: Fairleigh Dickinson University Press, 1981. Excellent analysis of movies' effect on public morale.

Ross, Stewart Halsey. *Propaganda for War: How the United States Was Conditioned to Fight the Great War of 1914–1918.* Jefferson, NC: McFarland, 1996. Treats the packaging and promotion of the war as an exercise in mass persuasion.

Minorities

Cooper, Michael L. *Hell Fighters: African American Soldiers in World War I.* New York: Lodestar, 1997. Brief and readable story of a black regiment from New York.

Gavin, Lettie. *American Women in World War I: They Also Served.* Boulder, CO: University of Colorado Press, 1997. Comprehensive account of women's role in the war through treatment of service in the various branches, as physicians and nurses, and so forth.

Greenwald, Maurine W. *Women, War, and Work: The Impact of World War I on Women Workers.* Westport, CT: Greenwood, 1980. Examines the topic through case studies.

Patton, Gerald W. *War and Race: The Black Officer in the American Military, 1915–1941.* Westport, CT: Greenwood, 1981. Stories of pioneering African American military leaders.

Thom, Deborah. *Nice Girls and Rude Girls: Women Workers in World War I.* New York: St. Martin's, 1998. Uses official records, other primary sources, and oral history to examine the industrial role of women and its development during the war.

BIOGRAPHICAL SOURCES

Ferrell, Robert H. *Woodrow Wilson and World War I, 1917–1921.* New York: Harper & Row, 1985. Wilson as a wartime leader.

AUDIOVISUAL SOURCES

America over There: United States in World War I, 1917–1918. Venice, CA: TMW Media Group, 1996. Videocassette. 72-minute video originally produced as a motion picture in 1927; enhanced with voice track and music.

World War I. New York: CBS/Fox Video, 1994. Five videocassettes. Comprehensive eleven-episode documentary of the war from beginning to end.

WORLD WIDE WEB

Plotke, Jane, et al. *The World War I Document Archive.* February 1996; updated frequently. http://www.lib.byu.edu/~rdh/wwi/index.html Excellent collection of documents, images, articles, and biographies relevant to the study of the war.

18. Paris Peace Conference (1919)

During the course of World War I, President Wilson called for "peace without victory" and toward that end formulated his Fourteen Points as a statement of war aims. Germany, hoping for a lenient peace based on those proposals, acceded to an armistice on November 11, 1918. However, the subsequent peace conference, which began in January

1919, ended with the Allies forcing Germany to sign the punitive Treaty of Versailles in June. Wilson accepted the harsh measures largely to ensure that the Allies would heed his call for a League of Nations. At home, however, his refusal to compromise with Republican senators, notably Henry Cabot Lodge, who demanded treaty reservations, and with Senate "irreconcilables," who opposed the treaty in any form, doomed his handiwork. Wilson suffered an incapacitating stroke while campaigning for the treaty, which the Senate never ratified.

Suggestions for Term Papers

1. Discuss the origins of the League of Nations.
2. Was Wilson or Lodge more responsible for the Senate's refusal to ratify the treaty?
3. Could U.S. participation in the league have prevented World War II?
4. Discuss the effects of Wilson's stroke on foreign and domestic policy.
5. Compare the government crisis following Wilson's stroke with that which followed President Eisenhower's heart attack in September 1955.

Suggested Sources: See entries 11, 16, 17, and 67 for related items.

GENERAL SOURCES

Northedge, F. S. *The League of Nations: Its Life and Times, 1920–1946.* New York: Holmes & Meier, 1986. Standard history of the league.

SPECIALIZED SOURCES

Ambrosius, Lloyd E. *Woodrow Wilson and the American Diplomatic Tradition: The Treaty Fight in Perspective.* New York: Cambridge University Press, 1987. Contends that Wilson's efforts had a lasting influence even though he failed to get the country to join the League of Nations.

Boemke, Manfred F., et al., eds. *The Treaty of Versailles: 75 Years After.* New York: Cambridge University Press, 1998. Papers from the proceedings of an international conference examining the treaty and its results.

House, Edward M., ed. *What Really Happened at Paris: The Story of the Peace Conference, 1918–1919, by American Delegates.* (1921). Reprint. Westport, CT: Greenwood, 1976. Collection of papers written by U.S. representatives describing the conference in all its particulars.

Knock, Thomas J. *To End All Wars: Woodrow Wilson and the Quest for a New World Order.* New York: Oxford University Press, 1992. Highly regarded study of Wilson's vision.

Lentin, A. *Lloyd George, Woodrow Wilson and the Guilt of Germany: An Essay in the Pre-history of Appeasement.* Baton Rouge: Louisiana State University Press, 1985. Critical examination of the conduct of the Peace Conference.

Levin, Norman G., comp. *Woodrow Wilson and the Paris Peace Conference.* 2d ed. Lexington, MA: Heath, 1972. Standard account of Wilson's influence in Paris. Originally published in 1957 as *Wilson at Versailles.*

Lovin, Clifford R. *A School for Diplomats: The Paris Peace Conference of 1919.* Lanham, MD: University Press of America, 1997. Recent examination of the conference, with good insight into diplomacy.

Nielson, Jonathan M. *American Historians in War and Peace: Patriotism, Diplomacy, and the Paris Peace Conference, 1919.* Dubuque, IA: Kendall/Hunt, 1994. Interesting examination of the political activities of historians in securing the peace.

Rogers, James T. *Woodrow Wilson: Visionary for Peace.* New York: Facts on File, 1997. A carefully researched work focusing on Wilson's efforts in creating the League of Nations.

Walworth, Arthur. *Wilson and His Peacemakers: American Diplomacy at the Paris Peace Conference.* New York: Norton, 1986. Critical examination of the Wilson agenda at the conference.

BIOGRAPHICAL SOURCES

Lodge, Henry Cabot. *Early Memories.* (1913). Reprint. New York: Arno, 1975. Autobiography of Wilson's arch rival written six years before the conference. Provides insight into the life of the leisure class of the time.

Widenor, William C. *Henry Cabot Lodge and the Search for an American Foreign Policy.* Berkeley: University of California Press, 1980. Perceptive scholarly biography.

AUDIOVISUAL SOURCES

Woodrow Wilson: Fight for a League of Nations. Washington, DC: Capital Communications, 1972. 25-minute examination of Wilson's personal crusade for peace and a world government.

Woodrow Wilson: Peace and War and the Professor President. Chatsworth, CA: AIMS Multimedia, 1984. The career and achievements of the president, in a 23-minute narration by E. G. Marshall.

WORLD WIDE WEB

Schoenherr, Steve. *The Versailles Treaty—June 28, 1919.* November 1995; updated February 1997. http://ac.acusd.edu/History/text/versaillestreaty/vercontents.htm/ Contains complete treaty with access by sections; also provides cartoons, maps, and links to other relevant sites.

19. The Red Scare (1919–1920)

Fear of radicalism swept across the nation after World War I, largely as the result of the Bolshevik triumph in Russia and the threat of its spread. This fear heightened existing domestic tensions. In 1919, more than 4,000 labor strikes occurred, including a Seattle general strike and a Boston policemen's strike. Bombs were mailed to prominent figures, and an explosion killed thirty-eight persons on Wall Street. Attorney General A. Mitchell Palmer, whose front porch was bombed, moved to suppress radicalism, arresting 6,000 suspected radicals and ultimately having 556 deported. The Red Scare subsided in mid-1920 after a purported mass uprising of radicals failed to materialize.

Suggestions for Term Papers

1. How real was the threat of bolshevism to the United States?
2. Were the Boston police justified in striking?
3. Analyze the effect of the Red Scare on American civil liberties.
4. Discuss the long-range consequences of the Red Scare.
5. Should the radicals have been deported?

Suggested Sources: See entries 21 and 58 for related items.

REFERENCE SOURCES

Dictionary of 20th Century History. David M. Brownstone and Irene M. Franck. Paramus, NJ: Prentice-Hall, 1990. Brief historical overview of some 7,500 topics, several related to the Red Scare.

Great Events: The Twentieth Century. Pasadena, CA: Salem, 1992. 10 vols. Large-scale reference set with convenient coverage of nearly 475 important events, some related to the Red Scare. Contains background information, description, and outcomes or consequences.

GENERAL SOURCES

Baker, Nancy V. *Conflicting Loyalties: Law and Politics in the Attorney General's Office, 1789–1990.* Lawrence: University Press of Kansas, 1992. Examines the role of the attorney general in presidential politics. A. Mitchell Palmer is seen as an overly zealous advocate. Good narrative and exposition.

Buhle, Paul. *Marxism in the United States: Remapping the History of the American Left.* London: Verso/Methuen, 1987. Good general overview of the rise of working-class radicalism in the United States and the obstacles it faced.

Friedman, Lawrence M. *Crime and Punishment in American History.* New York: Basic Books, 1993. Comprehensive historical treatment of criminal law and justice in the United States, with a good description of the Red Scare.

Jensen, Joan M. *Army Surveillance in America, 1775–1980.* New Haven, CT: Yale University Press, 1991. Clearly written history of a little-covered topic. Excellent chapters on the use of the military against organized labor, including the period of the Red Scare.

Klehr, Harvey, and John E. Haynes. *The American Communist Movement: Storming Heaven Itself.* New York: Twayne, 1992. Concise and comprehensive coverage of the communist movement with a good analysis of its beginnings during the period of the Red Scare through its current state.

Morrison, Wilbur H. *Twentieth-Century Wars: Their Causes and Their Effects on American Life.* New York: Hippocrene, 1993. Narrative description of effects of wars on American life at home both during and after their conduct. Examines and analyzes World War I and the second Red Scare following World War II.

Murphy, Paul L. *World War I and the Origin of Civil Liberties in the United States.* New York: Norton, 1979. Excellent analysis of the role of wartime policies in developing the concept of civil liberties.

Parrish, Michael E. *Anxious Decades: America in Prosperity and Depression,*

1920–1941. New York: Norton, 1992. Interpretive overview from a liberal perspective, with brief treatments of personalities and events.

SPECIALIZED SOURCES

Kohn, Stephen M. *American Political Prisoners: Prosecutions under the Espionage and Sedition Acts.* Westport, CT: Praeger, 1994. Treatment of protesters and conscientious objectors, 1914–1918.

Murray, Robert K. *Red Scare: A Study in National Hysteria, 1919–1920.* (1955). Reprint. Westport, CT: Greenwood, 1980. A modern classic.

Polenberg, Richard. *Fighting Faiths: The Abrams Case, the Supreme Court, and Free Speech.* New York: Viking, 1987. Detailed and carefully crafted examination of this 1919 case involving five anarchist defendants and their denial of civil liberties during the Red Scare period.

BIOGRAPHICAL SOURCES

Carlson, Peter. *Roughneck: The Life and Times of Big Bill Haywood.* New York: Norton, 1983. Biography of America's most radical labor union leader of the day and one of Attorney General Palmer's prime targets.

Powers, Richard G. *Secrecy and Power: The Life of J. Edgar Hoover.* New York: Free Press, 1987. Complete story of Hoover's career, beginning with the period of the Red Scare.

Shipman, Charles. *It Had to Be Revolution: Memoirs of an American Radical.* Ithaca, NY: Cornell University Press, 1993. Good reading and provocative account of the progression of circumstances in the life and activity of an ex-communist.

PERIODICAL ARTICLES

Williams, David. "The Bureau of Investigation and Its Critics, 1919–1921: The Origins of Federal Political Surveillance." *Journal of American History* 68:560–579 (1981). Role of the newly created FBI.

AUDIOVISUAL SOURCES

The Great War. Wynewood, PA: Schlessinger Media/Library Video. Videocassette. 35-minute treatment of the Red Scare and Palmer raids following the war. Volume 16 of the publisher's twenty-volume set, United States History Video Collection.

WORLD WIDE WEB

MacLaury, Judson. "History of DOL, 1913–1988." 1988. U.S. Department of Labor. http://www.dol.gov/dol/asp/public/programs/history/hs75menu.htm Short recognition of the seventy-fifth anniversary of the department. The first chapter covers the first eight years and briefly treats the Red Scare as one of the major problems following the war.

20. Prohibition (1919–1933)

Ratification of the Eighteenth Amendment in January 1919 and the subsequent passage of the Volstead Act in October brought prohibition to the United States, polarizing "wets" and "drys," and proving enormously difficult to enforce. Despite the legendary efforts of dedicated agents such as Eliot Ness, illegal speakeasies flourished, as did organized crime, which reaped great profits. Al Capone was but one, if the most famous, of the many gangsters of the era. The Wickersham Report of 1931 noted the failures of prohibition but advocated its continuation, which President Herbert Hoover called an "experiment, noble in motive and far-reaching in purpose." Nonetheless, the Twenty-first Amendment, ratified in December 1933, repealed prohibition.

Suggestions for Term Papers

1. Why did the United States adopt prohibition?
2. Analyze why prohibition failed.
3. Discuss the career of a prominent prohibition era gangster.
4. What were the long-range consequences of prohibition?
5. Compare prohibition with today's attempts to ban addictive drugs.

Suggested Sources: See entry 32 for related items.

GENERAL SOURCES

Aaron, Paul, and David Musto. "Temperance and Prohibition in America: A Historical Overview." In Mark H. Moore and Dean R. Gerstein, eds., *Alcohol and Public Policy: Beyond the Shadow of Prohibition.* Washington, DC: National Academy Press, 1981. Good overview of and bibliography on temperance and prohibition. One of seven commissioned studies in this work.

Blocker, Jack S., Jr. *American Temperance Movements: Cycles of Reform.* Boston: Twayne, 1989. A comprehensive survey of the temperance and prohibition movements.

Friedman, Lawrence M. *Crime and Punishment in American History.* New York: Basic Books, 1993. Comprehensive and detailed history of crime and punishment in the United States, with a good treatment of the prohibition era. Lengthy bibliography.

Hamm, Richard F. *Shaping the Eighteenth Amendment: Temperance Reform, Legal Culture, and the Polity, 1880–1920.* Chapel Hill: University of North Carolina Press, 1995. An excellent study of the forces that created the prohibition period.

Woodiwiss, Michael. *Crime, Crusades, and Corruption: Prohibitions in the United States, 1900–1987.* Totowa, NJ: Barnes & Noble Books, 1988. Comprehensive general coverage of police corruption and development of organized crime and its link to crusades such as prohibition.

SPECIALIZED SOURCES

Behr, Edward. *Prohibition: Thirteen Years That Changed America.* New York: Arcade Publishing/Little, Brown, 1996. Interesting account of the legendary period, complete with gangsters, political corruption, and speakeasies.

Blocker, Jack S., Jr. *Retreat from Reform: The Prohibition Movement in the United States, 1890–1913.* Westport, CT: Greenwood, 1976. Examines the movement and how it distanced itself from all other social reforms to focus on the prohibition amendment.

Clark, Norman H. *Deliver Us from Evil: An Interpretation of American Prohibition.* New York: Norton, 1976. A useful survey of the prohibition period from 1918 to 1932.

Coffey, Thomas M. *The Long Thirst: Prohibition in America.* New York: Norton, 1975. Standard history of the period.

Englemann, Larry. *Intemperance, the Lost War against Liquor.* New York: Free Press, 1979. Examines the prohibition period in terms of the legal struggle against liquor. Treats the situation in Michigan.

Kerr, K. Austin. *Organized for Prohibition: A New History of the Anti-Saloon League*. New Haven, CT: Yale University Press, 1985. A fine history of the league, the leader in the movement to adopt prohibition.

Mason, Philip P. *Rumrunning and the Roaring Twenties: Prohibition on the Michigan-Ontario Waterway*. Detroit: Wayne State University Press, 1995. Covers the smuggling of liquor from Windsor, Canada, into Detroit.

Sinclair, Andrew. *Era of Excess: A Social History of the Prohibition Movement*. Boston: Little, Brown, 1962. Describes the movement and sees it as excessive and not worthy of being considered a progressive social reform.

BIOGRAPHICAL SOURCES

Cashman, Sean D. *America in the Twenties and Thirties: The Olympian Age of Franklin Delano Roosevelt*. New York: New York University Press, 1989. Good background of the period in which Roosevelt rode anti-prohibition sentiment to electoral victory.

Dorsett, Lyle W. "Sunday, Billy." In John A. Garraty, ed., *American National Biography*. New York: Oxford University Press/American Council of Learned Societies, 1998. 20 vols. A magnificent new set with thousands of detailed biographical sketches of and bibliographies on important Americans. The article by Dorsett traces Sunday's life and career as a ballplayer and preacher and his influence on the prohibition period.

Lender, Mark. *Dictionary of American Temperance Biography: From Temperance Reform to Alcohol Research, the 1600s to the 1980s*. Westport, CT: Greenwood, 1985. A collective biography of a variety of personalities over a broad spectrum of time.

Schoenburg, Robert J. *Mr. Capone*. New York: Morrow, 1992. Thorough and detailed biography of the man whose name was associated with organized crime; examines his many-sided personality as a thug, businessman, and charmer.

AUDIOVISUAL SOURCES

The Prohibition Era Collection. New York: A&E Home Video. 3 videocassettes: "The Dry Crusade," "The Roaring Twenties," and "The Road to Repeal." 50 minutes each. Narrated by Ed Asner.

WORLD WIDE WEB

Kerr, K. Austin. *Temperance and Prohibition*. 1997. http://www.cohums.ohio-state.edu/history/projects/prohibition   Informative and interesting web site maintained by the Ohio State University History Department. Table of contents is presented with the music from *Cheers* and leads to fine narratives and pictorials such as, "Why was there Prohibition in the United States?" and "American Prohibition in the 1920s."

21. Sacco–Vanzetti Trial (1921)

Nicola Sacco and Bartolomeo Vanzetti, Italian-born anarchists, were arrested in May 1920 on charges that they had committed robbery and murder in Braintree, Massachusetts. Their subsequent trial, set in the midst of the Red Scare, was marked by ambiguous evidence and prejudice on the part of the presiding judge, Webster Thayer. Found guilty, the defendants received death sentences. A special commission of three (Lowell Commission) reviewed and upheld the verdict. Sacco and Vanzetti were executed in August 1927 despite widespread international protest. Many believed that their radical politics and unpopular ethnicity had condemned the two. In 1968 the governor of Massachusetts issued a proclamation that acknowledged the trial's lack of fairness.

Suggestions for Term Papers

1. Discuss the differing views on whether Sacco and/or Vanzetti was guilty.
2. Analyze Judge Thayer's conduct during the trial.
3. How important were the defendants' ethnic background and political views in determining their fates?
4. Discuss the public protest against the verdict and the execution of Sacco and Vanzetti.
5. Compare the real case with a depiction, such as Upton Sinclair's novel *Boston* (1928), or the movie *Sacco and Vanzetti* (1971).

Suggested Sources: See entry 19 for related items.

REFERENCE SOURCES

Encyclopedia of the American Judicial System: Studies of the Principal Institutions and Processes of Law. Robert Janosik, ed. New York: Scribner,

1987. 3 vols. Thorough and comprehensive source of in-depth information on important court cases and judicial processes, including the Sacco and Vanzetti trial.

Encyclopedia of the American Left. Mari Jo Buhle, ed. Hamden, CT: Garland, 1990. Good, comprehensive coverage of personalities, events, organizations, and groups, including the Sacco and Vanzetti case.

Great American Trials. Edward W. Knappman, ed. Detroit: Gale, 1994. Informative summaries for 200 important trials, including Sacco and Vanzetti.

GENERAL SOURCES

Avrich, Paul. *Anarchist Voices: An Oral History of Anarchism in America.* Princeton, NJ: Princeton University Press, 1995. Based on interviews with anarchists and written by a leading authority on anarchist movements.

Fisher, David. *Hard Evidence: How Detectives inside the F.B.I.'s Sci-Crime Lab Have Helped Solve America's Toughest Cases.* New York: Simon & Schuster, 1995. Generally useful insight into the nature of forensic investigation, although the author accepts without question the judgments given by the lab technicians in controversial cases such as Sacco and Vanzetti.

SPECIALIZED SOURCES

Feuerlicht, Roberta S. *Justice Crucified: The Story of Sacco and Vanzetti.* New York: McGraw-Hill, 1977. Good introductory history of the time and the event in question based on interviews with participants. Points out certain injustices of the case.

Jackson, Brian. *The Black Flag: A Look at the Strange Case of Nicola Sacco and Bartolomeo Vanzetti.* Boston: Routledge and Kegan Paul, 1981. Brief, somewhat superficial history based on state police records. Contains some errors but does include Sacco's cross-examination at the trial, as well as the governor's proclamation issued in 1968 removing the stigma and disgrace suffered by Sacco and Venzetti.

Russell, Francis. *Sacco and Vanzetti: The Case Resolved.* New York: Harper & Row, 1986. By an author whose twenty years of research and reflection convinced him that Sacco, at least, was guilty as charged.

———. *Tragedy in Dedham: The Story of the Sacco-Vanzetti Case.* New York: McGraw-Hill, 1962. An investigation of what some have felt was an apparent miscarriage of justice.

Young, William, and David E. Kaiser. *Postmortem: New Evidence in the Case of Sacco and Vanzetti.* Amherst: University of Massachusetts Press,

1985. A recent investigation that concludes evidence was manipulated to frame the two men.

BIOGRAPHICAL SOURCES

Avrich, Paul. *Anarchist Portraits: An Oral History of Anarchism in America*. Princeton, NJ: Princeton University Press, 1988. Good collective biography and historical description of various personalities. Provides insight into the Italian anarchist world that produced Sacco and Vanzetti.

———. *Sacco and Vanzetti: The Anarchist Background*. Princeton, NJ: Princeton University Press, 1991. Well-designed and detailed examination of the two men in the context of European and American anarchism; nonjudgmental in tone.

Johnpoll, Bernard K., and Harvey Klehr, eds. *Biographical Dictionary of the American Left*. Westport, CT: Greenwood, 1986. Good collective biography providing informative sketches on personalities associated with radical movements.

AUDIOVISUAL SOURCES

The Trial of Sacco and Vanzetti. Washington, DC: American Bar Association, 1982. Two videocassettes. Historical reenactment of the trial based on the court record. Each video is 60 minutes.

WORLD WIDE WEB

Seventieth Anniversary of the Execution of Nicola Sacco and Bartolomeo Vanzetti. September 1997; updated January 1998. http://burn.ucsd.edu/~mai/sacco_venzetti.html Fine web site with pictures and relevant links to both primary and secondary source material. Of interest is the 1927 article by Felix Frankfurter, "The Case of Sacco and Vanzetti."

22. Ford Model T

Henry Ford introduced his Model T automobile in 1908. By 1913, he had developed the means to mass-produce his invention through a highly efficient assembly line. Determined that his workers and the average American should be able to afford an automobile, he used technology and labor efficiencies to hold down the cost of his product. During the 1920s, the automobile galvanized the economy. The number of registered automobiles soared, as did the automobile service industry. Under intense pressure from his chief rivals, General Motors and Chrysler, Ford built the last "Tin Lizzie" (Model T) in 1927 and introduced the Model A the following year.

Suggestions for Term Papers

1. Discuss the early years of automobile development in the United States.

2. Why did Henry Ford succeed while so many other automobile makers failed?

3. Analyze the challenge of General Motors and Chrysler to Ford during the 1920s.

4. How important was the automobile to the American economy during the 1920s?

5. How did the automobile change American life during the 1920s?

REFERENCE SOURCES

The ABC-CLIO Companion to Transportation in America. William L. Richter. Santa Barbara, CA: ABC-CLIO, 1995. Alphabetically arranged entries (persons, issues, themes) with comprehensive coverage of topic from prehistoric footpaths to space travel.

Encyclopedia of American Business History and Biography. New York: Facts on File, 1988–1990. 3 vols. Most important to this topic are the volumes edited by George S. May: *The Automobile Industry 1896–1920* (1990) and *The Automobile Industry 1920–1980* (1988), treating events, accomplishments, and personalities. The other volume, *Railroads of the 19th Century*, is edited by Robert L. Frey (1989).

GENERAL SOURCES

Dammann, George, and Jim Wrenn. *Packard*. Osceola, WI: Motorbooks International, 1996. Complete history of one of Ford's competitors from its beginning in 1899 to its demise in 1958.

SPECIALIZED SOURCES

Bryan, Ford R. *Henry's Lieutenants.* Detroit: Wayne State University Press, 1993. Good history of the company and its executives, as well as Ford.

Ford, Henry. *Ford on Management.* (1922, 1929). Reprint. New York: B. Blackwell, 1989. Ford's own story reprinted from two books, *My Life and Work* (1922) and *My Philosophy of Industry* (1929).

————, and Samuel Crowther. *Today and Tomorrow.* (1926). Reprint. Cambridge, MA: Productivity Press, 1988. Describes the management of the company.

Hooker, Clarence. *Life in the Shadows of the Crystal Palace, 1910–1927: Ford Workers in the Model T Era.* Bowling Green, OH: Bowling Green State University Popular Press, 1997. Examination of the lives led by the Ford industry workers in Highland Park, Michigan.

Sorensen, Lorin. *The American Ford.* (1975). Reprint. Osceola, WI: Motorbooks International, 1990. Brief, useful history of the company and the industry.

BIOGRAPHICAL SOURCES

Batchelor, Ray. *Henry Ford: Mass Production, Modernism, and Design.* New York: Manchester University Press/St. Martin's, 1994. Brief, informative biography of Ford, with an emphasis on his automobile design features and production.

Bryan, Ford R. *Beyond the Model T: The Other Ventures of Henry Ford.* Rev. ed. Detroit: Wayne State University Press, 1997. Treats the many sides of Ford in addition to his life as an automobile industrialist.

————. *The Fords of Dearborn.* Michigan Sesquicentennial, ed. Detroit: Harlo, 1987. A good treatment of the Ford family in covering the life of Henry Ford.

Gelderman, Carol W. *Henry Ford: The Wayward Capitalist.* New York: St. Martin's, 1989. An informative examination of the many faces and phases of Henry Ford.

Newton, James D. *Uncommon Friends: Life with Thomas Edison, Henry Ford, Harvey Firestone, Alexis Carrel and Charles Lindbergh.* San Diego: Harcourt Brace Jovanovich, 1987. The story of the author's friendship with some of the world's most celebrated personalities.

Olson, Sidney. *Young Henry Ford: A Picture History of the First Forty Years.* (1963). Reprint. Detroit: Wayne State University Press, 1997. A concise and interesting illustrated study of Ford and the industry.

Wik, Reynold M. *Henry Ford and Grass-Roots America.* (1972). Reprint. Norwalk, CT: 1989. The collector's edition of an earlier work published by the University of Michigan. Describes Ford's appeal in rural regions.

AUDIOVISUAL SOURCES

The Story of Henry Ford. Chicago: Questar Video, 1991. Videocassette. 55-minute presentation in black and white with original footage, along with commentary and interviews. Part of an eleven-volume series, *Famous Americans of the 20th Century.*

WORLD WIDE WEB

The Model T. 1997. http://www.fordlincmerc.com/vford932.html Provides a brief history from 1908 to 1927, as well as a picture of Ford with his auto. Useful examples of advertising and product literature, along with specifications and more photographs. Maintained by a Ford dealership in California.

23. Revival of the Ku Klux Klan

Influenced by D. W. Griffith's movie, *The Birth of a Nation*, William J. Simmons, a salesman and fraternal organizer, founded the twentieth-century KKK in 1915. Initially small, its membership reached 4.5 million by the mid-1920s. The chief reason for this popularity was its appeal to widespread anti-immigrant, anti-Catholic, anti-Jewish, anti–African American, and anti-wet sentiment. Its influence on political life was most significant at the state and local levels, but the Klan also was able to block the presidential nomination of Democrat Alfred E. Smith in 1924. A major scandal involving an Indiana Klan leader, David Stephenson, who was convicted of second-degree murder, and the efforts of anti-Klan groups led to the organization's decline by the end of the 1920s.

Suggestions for Term Papers

1. Compare the early twentieth-century KKK with the original Klan of the Reconstruction era.
2. Discuss why the Klan became powerful during the 1920s.
3. Discuss the opposition to the Klan.

4. Discuss the Stephenson scandal and its effect on the Klan.
5. Compare the Klan of the 1920s with the Klan of today.

Suggested Sources: See entry 9 for related items.

REFERENCE SOURCES

The Invisible Empire: A Bibliography of the Ku Klux Klan. William H. Fisher. Metuchen, NJ: Scarecrow, 1980. Comprehensive work that identifies writings on the Klan from its beginnings in the nineteenth century to its reemergence in 1915 and thereafter.

The Ku Klux Klan: A Bibliography. Lenwood Davis and Janet L. Sims-Wood, comps. Westport, CT: Greenwood, 1984. Comprehensive, thorough, and detailed listing of books and articles treating the entire history of the Klan.

The Ku Klux Klan: An Encyclopedia. Michael Newton and Judy Newton. New York: Garland Publishing, 1991. Alphabetical arrangement of entries covering issues, events, personalities, and so forth.

GENERAL SOURCES

Christensen, Terry. *Reel Politics: American Political Movies from Birth of a Nation to Platoon.* New York: Oxford University Press, 1987. Brief, interesting historical account of politics in motion pictures during the twentieth century, beginning with the Griffith classic.

Cook, Fred J. *The Ku Klux Klan: America's Recurring Nightmare.* Englewood Cliffs, NJ: J. Messner, 1989. Brief survey of the violence, bigotry, and intolerance associated with the entire history of the Klan. Easy to read and interesting.

Fleener-Marzec, Nickieann. *D. W. Griffith's The Birth of a Nation: Controversy, Suppression, and the First Amendment as It Applies to Filmic Expression, 1915–1973.* New York: Arno, 1980. Examines the controversy and censorship questions associated with the motion picture since it was released.

Jaffe, Steven H. *Who Were the Founding Fathers?* New York: H. Holt, 1996. Focuses on the Constitution and the Declaration of Independence, with an examination of interpretation by groups such as the Klan.

Lang, Robert, ed. *The Birth of a Nation: D. W. Griffith, Director.* New Brunswick, NJ: Rutgers University Press, 1994. Critical analysis and interpretation of Griffith and his work.

Lester, John C., and D. L. Wilson. *Ku Klux Klan: Its Origin, Growth, and Disbandment.* (1905). Reprint. New York: Da Capo, 1973. Concise and comprehensive general history of the Klan from its beginning to its decline in the late 1920s.

Platt, David, ed. *Celluloid Power: Social Film Criticism from the Birth of a Nation to Judgment at Nuremberg.* Metuchen, NJ: Scarecrow, 1992. More detailed study than the Christensen work above. Examines political aspects associated with motion pictures.

Ruiz, Jim. *The Black Hood of the Ku Klux Klan.* San Francisco: Austin & Winfield, 1997. Comprehensive recent history of the Klan beginning with its origin and treating its development.

SPECIALIZED SOURCES

Chalmers, David M. *Hooded Americanism: The History of the Ku Klux Klan.* 3d ed. (1981). Reprint. Durham, NC: Duke University Press, 1994. Detailed history of both the emergence of the Klan following the Civil War and its reemergence during World War I. Twenty-page bibliography.

Jackson, Kenneth T. *The Ku Klux Klan in the City, 1915–1930.* (1967). Reprint. Chicago: Ivan R. Dee, 1992. A revealing description of the Klan's urban development.

Katz, William L. *The Invisible Empire: The Ku Klux Klan Impact on History.* Upd. ed. Washington, DC: Open Hand Publishing, 1987. Concise and comprehensive in its treatment of the origin and subsequent rebirth of the Klan.

The Ku Klux Klan: A History of Racism and Violence. 5th ed. Montgomery: Klanwatch/Southern Poverty Law Center, 1997. Sixty-four-page report of the current situation, with a brief historical overview.

MacLean, Nancy. *Behind the Mask of Chivalry: The Making of the Second Ku Klux Klan.* New York: Oxford University Press, 1994. Provides excellent insight into the rebirth of the Klan in 1915.

Mecklin, John M. *The Ku Klux Klan: A Study of the American Mind.* New York: Russell & Russell, 1963. Standard study of the Klan's rebirth and the socioeconomic conditions behind its growth and resurgence.

Rice, Arnold S. *The Ku Klux Klan in American Politics.* (1962). Reprint. New York: Haskell House Publishers, 1972. Brief overview of the Klan's involvement with politics and government following its rebirth in the 1920s.

Stanton, Bill. *Klanwatch: Bringing the Ku Klux Klan to Justice.* New York: Weidenfeld, 1991. Examination of the role of Klanwatch, an anti-Klan group, in bringing the Klan to trial for its violations, with a survey of litigation efforts.

Tucker, Richard K. *The Dragon and the Cross: The Rise and Fall of the Ku Klux Klan in Middle America.* Hamden, CT: Archon Books, 1991. Account of the Klan in twentieth-century Indiana, with an emphasis on the Stephenson scandal.

Wade, Wyn C. *The Fiery Cross: The Ku Klux Klan in America.* (1987).

Reprint. New York: Oxford University Press, 1997. Well-researched description of the Klan in the twentieth century. Provides insight into the movement for white supremacy in the United States.

BIOGRAPHICAL SOURCES

Lutholtz, M. William. *Grand Dragon: D. C. Stephenson and the Ku Klux Klan in Indiana.* West Lafayette, IN: Purdue University Press, 1991. Examination of Stephenson's life and career as the ranking Klan official in Indiana; examines his violations, including murder.

McIlhany, William H. *Klandestine: The Untold Story of Delmar Dennis and His Role in the FBI's War against the Ku Klux Klan.* New Rochelle, NY: Arlington House, 1975. Interesting story of an agent's efforts to bring the Klan to justice.

Rowe, Gary T., Jr. *My Undercover Years with the Ku Klux Klan.* New York: Bantam Books, 1976. An interesting account of spy operations in Alabama.

Tarrants, Thomas A. *The Conversion of a Klansman: The Story of a Former Ku Klux Klan Terrorist.* Garden City, NY: Doubleday, 1979. Interesting biography of a former member who shifted his allegiance away from the Klan.

AUDIOVISUAL SOURCES

The Klan: A Legacy of Hate in America. Chicago: Films Inc. Video, 1982. Videocassette. 30-minute presentation of the current status of the Klan in the United States.

WORLD WIDE WEB

Cook, Carson C. *A Hundred Years of Terror.* 1996; updated March 1997. http://osprey.unf.edu/dept/equalop/oeop11.htm Detailed and thorough analytical report by the Southern Poverty Law Center of the origin, decline, and revival of the Klan.

24. First Radio Broadcasts

The first major radio broadcast took place in November 1920 when Westinghouse-owned station KDKA in Pittsburgh aired the presidential election results. Commercial programming began soon after and proved greatly popular. Both the National Broadcasting Company (NBC) and the Columbia Broadcasting Company (CBS) were established during the 1920s, as was the government's Federal Radio Commission, which became the Federal Communications Commission in 1934. By 1930 an estimated 40 percent of American households possessed radios, whose annual sales totaled more than $800 million. Popular radio figures of the era included singer Rudy Vallee and sports announcer Graham McNamee.

Suggestions for Term Papers

1. Identify the most popular radio programs of the 1920s and discuss why they were popular.
2. Compare radio's coverage of the 1920 presidential election with current media coverage of presidential elections.
3. What were the effects of radio on American life during the 1920s?
4. Discuss the early years of NBC or CBS.
5. Compare the early government regulation of radio broadcasting with today's government regulation of the media.

REFERENCE SOURCES

The ABC-CLIO Companion to the Media in America. Daniel W. Hollis. Santa Barbara, CA: ABC-CLIO, 1995. Alphabetically arranged entries treating people, events, and issues. A solid reference work that is part of the publisher's series.

The Big Broadcast, 1920–1950. Frank Buxton and Bill Owen. Blue Ridge Summit, PA: Scarecrow, 1996. Alphabetically arranged entries of important radio programs and topics. Includes narrative descriptions, cast lists, and theme music.

Handbook of Old-Time Radio: A Comprehensive Guide to Golden Age Radio Listening and Collecting. Jon D. Swartz and Robert C. Reinehr. Blue Ridge Summit, PA: Scarecrow, 1993. Treats more than 2,000 different programs with cast lists, network affiliation, announcers, length, story-lines, and availability.

Historical Dictionary of American Radio. Donald G. Godfrey and Frederic A. Leigh, eds. Westport, CT: Greenwood, 1998. Recent historical dictionary that covers issues, events, and personalities.

Radio and Television Pioneers: A Patent Bibliography. David W. Kraeuter. Blue Ridge Summit, PA: Scarecrow, 1992. Cites the patents of forty radio and television inventors in chronological order from the beginning of radio in the nineteenth century to 1976.

Radio Broadcasting from 1920 to 1990: An Annotated Bibliography. Diane F. Carothers. New York: Garland, 1991. Comprehensive bibliography covering the history of broadcasting from its beginnings to the present.

Radio Music Live: 1920–1950, a Pictorial Gamut. Morris N. Young and John C. Stoltzfus. Highland City, FL: Rainbow Books, 1998. Recent reference work providing a chronology of radio music along with numerous photographs.

GENERAL SOURCES

Aitken, Hugh G. J. *The Continuous Wave: Technology and American Radio, 1900–1932.* Princeton, NJ: Princeton University Press, 1985. Detailed history of American radio with an emphasis on technological considerations during the first three decades.

Barfield, Ray E. *Listening to Radio, 1920–1950.* Westport, CT: Greenwood, 1996. Recent, concise history of radio programs and programming beginning with the early years.

Campbell, Robert. *The Golden Years of Broadcasting: A Celebration of the First Fifty Years of Radio and TV on NBC.* New York: Scribner's 1976. Interesting and informative history of the network and its programming.

Chester, Edward W. *Radio, Television, and American Politics.* New York: Sheed and Ward, 1969. Revealing historical description of the media role in politics. The treatment of radio is more accurate than the treatment of television influences, which have changed considerably since the publication date.

MacDonald, J. Fred. *Don't Touch that Dial! Radio Programming in American Life, 1920–1960.* Chicago: Nelson-Hall, 1979. Interesting account of radio programming over a period of forty years, with insight into the nature of popular culture.

SPECIALIZED SOURCES

Douglas, George H. *The Early Days of Radio Broadcasting.* Jefferson, NC: McFarland, 1987. Concise and revealing history targeted to the early period.

Rosen, Philip T. *The Modern Stentors: Radio Broadcasters and the Federal Government, 1920–1934.* Westport, CT: Greenwood, 1980. Focused history on radio broadcasting and U.S. government policy during the early years.

Schmeckebier, Laurence F. *The Federal Radio Commission: Its History, Activities, and Organization.* (1932). Reprint. New York: AMS, 1974. Concise and informative account of the FRC. Originally issued as Number 65 of Service Monographs of the United States Government and developed by the Brookings Institution.

Smulyan, Susan. *Selling Radio: The Commercialization of American Broadcasting, 1920–1934.* Washington, DC: Smithsonian Institution, 1994. Brief examination of economic development through advertising and corporate sponsorship of radio broadcasting during the early years.

BIOGRAPHICAL SOURCES

DeLong, Thomas A. *Radio Stars: An Illustrated Biographical Dictionary of 953 Performers, 1920 through 1960.* Jefferson, NC: McFarland, 1996. Comprehensive work providing biographical sketches of radio personalities from the early years on.

Vallee, Eleanor, and Jill Amadio. *My Vagabond Lover: An Intimate Biography of Rudy Vallee.* Dallas: Taylor Publishing, 1996. Recent biography by the entertainer's widow.

Vallee, Rudy. *Let the Chips Fall.* Harrisburg, PA: Stackpole Books, 1975. Rudy Vallee's autobiography written when he was in his mid-seventies.

AUDIOVISUAL SOURCES

The Class of the 20th Century: 1901–1939. New York: A&E Home Video. 1992. Videocassette. The first of a six-part set extending to 1976–1990 that treats early radio in the context of parallel events. Narrated by Richard Dreyfuss. Each video is 96 minutes.

WORLD WIDE WEB

Messere, Fritz. "The Davis Amendment: Overview of the Controversy." *Documents of the Federal Radio Commission.* 1996. http://www.oswego.edu/~messere/FRCdavis.html Brief overview of the controversy surrounding this 1928 amendment to the Radio Act of 1927. Leads to other FRC documents.

25. Silent Movies

The 1920s represented a golden age for the movies. Enormously popular comedians such as Charlie Chaplin, Buster Keaton, Harold Lloyd, and Laurel and Hardy provided mirth for audiences. Sultry romances and sexual episodes also proved popular—and more controversial. Such Hollywood stars as Rudolph Valentino, Clara Bow, and Theda Bara brought sexuality to the silver screen. This sexuality, along with a scandal involving comedian Roscoe ("Fatty") Arbuckle, led to demands for reform and caused Hollywood to impose self-censorship under Postmaster General Will H. Hays, who resigned his cabinet position to devote himself to his new duties. Technological advancement brought the "talkies" to Hollywood in the later 1920s and doomed the "silents."

Suggestions for Term Papers

1. Why did Hollywood become the movie capital of the United States?
2. Discuss the career of a famous movie star during the 1920s.
3. Why did movies become so popular in the 1920s?
4. Compare movie censorship in the 1920s and today.
5. What happened to the "silent" stars when the "talkies" arrived?

Suggested Sources: See entry 23 for items relating to *Birth of a Nation*.

REFERENCE SOURCES

Charlie Chaplin, a Bio-bibliography. Wes D. Gehring. Westport, CT: Greenwood, 1983. Detailed bibliography of the life and career of one of the great comic geniuses of the silent era.

Roscoe "Fatty" Arbuckle: A Bio-bibliography. Robert Young, Jr. Westport, CT: Greenwood, 1994. Thorough bibliography of the life and career of a great comedian who rivaled Chaplin in popularity before a controversial scandal destroyed his career.

GENERAL SOURCES

Bakewell, William. *Hollywood Be Thy Name: Random Recollections of a Movie Veteran from Silents to Talkies to TV.* Blue Ridge Summit, PA: Scarecrow, 1991. Interesting and entertaining firsthand account of Hollywood.

Leff, Leonard J., and Jerold L. Simmons. *The Dame in the Kimono: Hollywood, Censorship, and the Production Code from the 1920s to the 1960s.* (1990). Reprint. New York: Anchor Books, 1991. Thorough account of censorship in Hollywood beginning with the silent era and running to the rebellious anti-Vietnam period.

Thomas, Tony. *The Best of Universal.* Lanham, MD: Vestal/National Book Network, 1990. Concise and interesting story of this important studio from its beginnings in 1912 to the present.

SPECIALIZED SOURCES

Bowers, Q. David. *Thanhouser Films, 1909–1917.* Lanham, MD: Vestal/National Book Network, 1998. An important history of this early company, which produced over a thousand quality films. An excellent resource on early film production.

Gardner, Gerald C. *The Censorship Papers: Movie Censorship Letters from the Hays Office, 1934–1968.* New York: Dodd, Mead, 1987. Interesting and informative collection of letters from Hays and Joe Breen, the official Hollywood censors, regarding the editing and censorship of movies.

Lloyd, Ann, and David Robinson, eds. *Movies of the Silent Years.* London: Orbis, 1984. Interesting history and criticism of films of the silent era.

Marks, Martin M. *Music and the Silent Film: Contexts and Case Studies, 1895–1924.* New York: Oxford University Press, 1997. A specialized source using examples that treat the inclusion of music with silent film offerings.

Sandburg, Carl. *Carl Sandburg at the Movies: A Poet in the Silent Era, 1920–1927.* Dale Featherling and Doug Featherling, eds. Metuchen, NJ: Scarecrow, 1985. Enlightening compilation of movie columns written by Sandburg for the *Chicago Daily News.*

Slide, Anthony. *Early American Cinema.* New and rev. ed. Blue Ridge Summit, PA: Scarecrow, 1994. A lucid and informative, concise history of the motion picture industry prior to 1920 by a leading film historian.

BIOGRAPHICAL SOURCES

Bellamy, Madge. *A Darling of the Twenties: The Autobiography of Madge Bellamy*. Lanham, MD: Vestal/National Book Network, 1989. An insider view of early Hollywood by one of the stars of the silent screen. Contains photographs and filmographies.

Doyle, Billy H. *The Ultimate Directory of Silent Screen Performers: A Necrology of Births and Deaths and Essays on 50 Lost Players*. Blue Ridge Summit, PA: Scarecrow, 1995. Entries for 7,500 deceased actors, directors, and writers, as well as politicians and sports figures who appeared in silent films.

Drew, William. *Speaking of Silents: First Ladies of the Screen*. Lanham, MD: Vestal/National Book Network, 1989. Interviews with ten glamorous stars of the early days that provide an important perspective on their careers and the early film industry.

Edmonds, Andy. *Frame-Up! The Untold Story of Roscoe "Fatty" Arbuckle*. New York: Morrow, 1991. Revealing account of how Arbuckle was falsely accused and maligned of a crime that did not occur.

Hays, Will H. *Come Home with Me Now—: The Untold Story of Movie Czar Will Hays by His Son*. Indianapolis: Guild Press of Indiana, 1993. Informative biography of the man who enforced the censorship codes, thus determining the moral limits of motion pictures for decades.

Lynn, Kenneth S. *Charlie Chaplin and His Times*. New York: Simon & Schuster, 1997. Recent, very detailed biography with numerous photographs.

Mackenzie, Norman A. *The Magic of Rudolph Valentino*. London: Research Publishing, 1974. Brief but informative account of the immensely popular dramatic actor.

Maltin, Leonard. *The Great Movie Comedians: Updated Edition from Charlie Chaplin to Woody Allen*. New York: Harmony Books, 1982. Paperback edition of popular earlier work providing biographical sketches of the great comedians from the silent era to our own time.

Slide, Anthony. *Silent Portraits: Stars of the Silent Screen in Historic Photographs*. Lanham, MD: Vestal/National Book Network, 1989. Brief biographies and photographs of over 500 personalities.

AUDIOVISUAL SOURCES

Movie Museum Series. Itasca, IL: Critics Choice Video, 1980. 5 videocassettes, each 2 hours. A thorough, detailed, and compelling history of the first twenty-five years of motion pictures.

WORLD WIDE WEB

Library of Congress. *Early Motion Pictures 1897–1916.* http://lcweb2. loc.gov/papr/mpixhome.html Great combination of graphics and narrative of historical interest not usually found in books; excellent links to little-known sites for film study.

Passi, Federico. "Cinema History: Silent Films." *The Cinema Connection.* 1995; updated continuously. http://www.socialchange.net.au/ TCC/Cinema_History/Silent_Films/index.html Many links to relevant sites and pages (Bow, Fields, Chaplin, Gish, Keaton, Lloyd, etc.).

26. Harlem Renaissance

World War I witnessed a significant migration of African Americans from the fields of the South to the factories of the North. Many settled in Harlem, which quickly became the mecca for African American writers and artists. Notable among the writers were Claude McKay, Countee Cullen, Jean Toomer, Zora Neale Hurston, Langston Hughes, and Alain Locke, who drew on their largely neglected African American heritage. Harlem also became home to a rich jazz culture during the 1920s. Denying that African Americans or their culture could ever find a home in the United States, Jamaican-born Marcus Garvey found popular support when he urged Harlemites to return to Africa.

Suggestions for Term Papers

1. Explain how Harlem became the center of African American cultural life.
2. Discuss the contributions to the Harlem Renaissance of a prominent African American writer, artist, or musician.
3. Why did jazz become widely popular during the 1920s?
4. Discuss the rise and fall of Marcus Garvey.
5. Compare the racial views of Marcus Garvey and the Ku Klux Klan.

Suggested Sources: See entries 9, 30, 72, and 73 for related items.

REFERENCE SOURCES

The Encyclopedia of African-American Heritage. Susan Altman and Joel Ke-
    melhor. New York: Facts on File, 1997. Good general encyclopedia
    with treatment of issues, topics, events, and personalities; informative
    entry on Harlem Renaissance.
The Harlem Renaissance: A Historical Dictionary for the Era. Bruce Kellner,
    ed. Westport, CT: Greenwood, 1984. Excellent reference source for
    brief information regarding personalities, titles, events, and so forth.
    Detailed bibliography as well as glossary.
The Harlem Renaissance: A Selected Bibliography. Robert A. Russ. New
    York: AMS, 1987. Extensive resource for identifying pertinent ma-
    terials on the topic.
*The Harlem Renaissance: An Annotated Reference Guide for Student Re-
    search.* Marie E. Rodgers. Englewood, CO: Libraries Unlimited,
    1998. Excellent historical overview of the years 1917–1933, with
    biographical sketches and annotated references.

GENERAL SOURCES

Hughes, Langston. *A Pictorial History of the Negro in America.* New York:
    Crown Publishers, 1983. Comprehensive illustrated history, with one
    chapter devoted to the Harlem Renaissance.
Katz, William L. *Black Legacy: A History of New York's African Americans.*
    New York: Atheneum Books, 1997. The Harlem Renaissance re-
    ceives emphasis in this general history of African Americans in New
    York. Well illustrated.
Schoener, Allon, ed. *Harlem on My Mind: Cultural Capital of Black Amer-
    ica.* New York: New Press/Norton, 1969. A good survey of the cre-
    ative energy coming out of Harlem. Originally issued as part of a
    museum exhibit.

SPECIALIZED SOURCES

Burkett, Randall K. *Garveyism as a Religious Movement: The Institutional-
    ization of a Black Civil Religion.* Blue Ridge Summit, PA: Scarecrow,
    1978. An informative examination of the religious dimensions asso-
    ciated with Garvey's mission. Still available from the publisher.
Chambers, Veronica. *The Harlem Renaissance.* Broomall, PA: Chelsea
    House Publishers, 1997. Concise and easy-to-read account of the
    personalities placed within the perspective of social and political in-
    fluences; art, literature, music, and other topics.
Harlem Renaissance: Art of Black America. New York: Studio Museum in

Harlem, 1987. Fine illustrated description of the visual arts as part of the Harlem Renaissance. Numerous examples.

Haskins, James. *The Harlem Renaissance*. Brookfield, CT: Millbrook, 1996. Easy-to-read, informative treatment of artists, musicians, writers, and others placed within the issues of the time and the ongoing debates regarding thematic material, social commentary, and other topics.

Hutchinson, George. *The Harlem Renaissance in Black and White*. Cambridge: Belknap Press of Harvard University Press, 1997. Detailed scholarly analysis of the impact and development of artistic expression in the movement. Examines the role of Alain Locke in promoting the arts.

Jacques, Geoffrey. *Free within Ourselves: The Harlem Renaissance*. New York: Franklin Watts, 1996. Brief, easy-to-read, informative introductory survey of the artistic productivity of the Renaissance; examines poetry, art, music, novels, theater, and other areas.

Lewis, David L. *When Harlem Was in Vogue*. New York: Knopf, 1981. Fine, readable history of this period of creativity. Informative and appealing.

Powell, Richard et al., eds. *Rhapsodies in Black: Art of the Harlem Renaissance*. Berkeley: University of California Press, 1997. Catalog of a traveling exhibition that opened in London. Excellent commentary on the work of artists, singers, photographers, actors, and others.

Roses, Lorraine E., and Ruth E. Randolph, eds. *Harlem's Glory: Black Women Writing, 1900–1950*. Cambridge: Harvard University Press, 1996. Interesting and informative compilation of writings on a wide range of topics from nearly sixty women, including Zora Neale Hurston and Jessie Fauset.

Spencer, Jon Michael. *The New Negroes and Their Music: The Success of the Harlem Renaissance*. Knoxville: University of Tennessee Press, 1997. Good study of the developments and obstacles faced by the black musicians and composers in New York at the time.

Wintz, Cary D. *Black Culture and the Harlem Renaissance*. Houston: Rice University Press, 1988. A useful examination of the history, geography, and ideas of the period. Emphasizes the emergence of cultural expression through writing, including publishing history.

———. *The Harlem Renaissance, 1920–1940: Interpretation of an African American Literary Movement*. New York: Garland, 1996. 7 vols. Primary sources, including lectures, essays, speeches, articles, and book reviews, in the first five volumes, and essays about the Harlem Renaissance by historians and others in the final two volumes.

BIOGRAPHICAL SOURCES

"Afro-American Writers from the Harlem Renaissance to 1940." *Dictionary of Literary Biography*. Detroit: Gale, 1987. Detailed and lengthy biographical descriptions of selected writers. Volume 51 continues the work of volume 50 treating writers before the Harlem Renaissance.

Coleman, Leon. *Carl Van Vechten and the Harlem Renaissance: A Critical Assessment*. Hamden, CT: Garland, 1998. Uses correspondence, manuscripts, memorabilia, and published material to evaluate Van Vechten's contribution to the Harlem Renaissance.

Roses, Lorraine E., and Ruth E. Randolph. *Harlem Renaissance and Beyond: Literary Biographies of 100 Black Women Writers*. Boston: G. K. Hall, 1990. Brief, cogent biographical sketches.

Rush, Theressa Gunnels, et al. *Black American Writers: Past and Present: A Biographical and Bibliographical Dictionary*. Blue Ridge Summit, PA: Scarecrow, 1975. A comprehensive tool providing biographical sketches of the Harlem Renaissance writers as well as others. Still in print and considered important.

Stein, Judith. *The World of Marcus Garvey: Race and Class in Modern Society*. Baton Rouge: Louisiana State University Press, 1986. Interesting and revealing biographical study and social history of black nationalism in its formative years.

Wall, Cheryl A. *Women of the Harlem Renaissance*. Bloomington: Indiana University Press, 1995. Treatment and critical commentary on literary black females Jessie Redmon Fauset, Zora Neale Hurston, and Nella Larsen; includes other writers and artists.

AUDIOVISUAL SOURCES

The Roaring Twenties. Wynnewood, PA: Schlessinger Media/Library Video. 1996. Videocassette. Seventeenth volume of a twenty-volume set (*United States History Video Collection*); covers Harlem Renaissance, Jazz Age, and other topics in the 40-minute tape.

Paul Robeson: One Man Show. Wilkes Barre, PA: Karol Video, 197?. A compelling performance by James Earl Jones in 118 minutes illustrates Robeson's character and motivation.

WORLD WIDE WEB

"Harlem Renaissance." *Geocities*. October 1997. http://www.geocities. com./Athens/Forum/4722/big.html Contains leads to "Poetry," "Politics," "Women," "Jazz," and "Theatre." Brief biographies and analyses; poetry section contains a selection of poems from different poets as well.

27. Scopes Trial (1925)

During the 1920s, the battle between religious fundamentalism and secularism focused most dramatically on Darwinism. In 1925 Tennessee outlawed the teaching of evolution in the state's public schools and colleges. John T. Scopes, a biology teacher in a Dayton high school, challenged the law. Clarence Darrow, the nation's most eminent defense lawyer, helped to defend Scopes, as did the American Civil Liberties Union. William Jennings Bryan, a leading fundamentalist, aided the prosecution. Found guilty, Scopes was fined $100, although a higher state court dismissed the case. Bryan died a few days after the original verdict was announced. The struggle between evolutionists and creationists continues to this day.

Suggestions for Term Papers

1. Why was religious fundamentalism strong in the 1920s?
2. Compare the roles played by Clarence Darrow and William Jennings Bryan in the trial.
3. Discuss the consequences of the Scopes trial.
4. Discuss the contemporary battle between evolutionists and creationists.
5. Compare the actual Scopes trial with a later depiction, such as the drama *Inherit the Wind* (1955), by Jerome Lawrence and Robert E. Lee, which was made into a film in 1960.

REFERENCE SOURCES

Clarence Darrow: A Bibliography. Willard D. Hunsberger. Metuchen, NJ: Scarecrow, 1981. An extensive bibliography on the important lawyer and the law.

GENERAL SOURCES

Hofstrop, Richard W. *The Scopes Trial; Dropping the Atomic Bomb on Japan; United States Versus Alger Hiss; Mississippi–Summer 1964*. Palm

Springs, CA: ETC Publications, 1990. Attempts to simulate these events in modern U.S. history, and provides a guide to using simulation in studying and teaching. From the publisher's United States History Simulations, 1925–1964 set.

SPECIALIZED SOURCES

Blake, Arthur. *The Scopes Trial: Defending the Right to Teach.* Brookfield, CT: Milbrook, 1994. An easy-to-read sixty-four-page tract on the trial. Emphasis on the teaching prerogatives. Contains an index and a brief bibliography.

Larson, Edward J. *Summer for the Gods: The Scopes Trial and America's Continuing Debate over Science and Religion.* New York: Basic Books, 1997. Up-to-date examination of the Scopes trial in terms of the lingering question of teaching evolution in public schools. Index and extensive bibliography.

The Monkey Trial and the Rise of Fundamentalism. Carol Stream, IL: Christianity Today, 1997. Issue 55 (volume 16, no. 3) of the periodical, *Christianity Today.* Forty-six-page treatment of the rise of fundamentalist-modernist controversy highlighting the role of the trial. Published as a separate monograph.

Nardo, Don. *The Scopes Trial.* San Diego: Lucent Books, 1997. An easy-to-read treatment of the Scopes trial, with a brief bibliography and an index.

Scopes, John Thomas, defendant. *The Scopes Trial. (World's most Famous Court Trial.* (1925). Reprint. Birmingham: Notable Trials Library, 1990. An important resource with a verbatim report of the trial with speeches, including Bryan's final speech, arguments, and testimony. Introduction by Alan Dershowitz.

Settle, Mary Lee. *The Scopes Trial: The State of Tennessee v. John Thomas Scopes.* New York: B. F. Watts, 1972. An easy-to-read history with brief bibliography.

BIOGRAPHICAL SOURCES

Ashby, LeRoy. *William Jennings Bryan: Champion of Democracy.* Boston: Twayne, 1987. Good study of Bryan with a useful bibliography. Part of the publisher's Twentieth-Century American Biography series.

Weinberg, Arthur, and Lila Weinberg. *Clarence Darrow, a Sentimental Rebel.* New York: Putnam, 1980. Sympathetic portrait of Darrow and his quest for justice.

AUDIOVISUAL SOURCES

The Monkey Trial. New York: History Channel/A&E Home Video, 1998. Videocassette. 50-minute presentation that examines the people and the agendas.

Rintels, David W. *Clarence Darrow.* Wilkes-Barre, PA: Karol Video, 1978. Videocassette. Much talent in this 81-minute production and acting (Henry Fonda) of the original 1974 NBC television play.

WORLD WIDE WEB

The Scopes Monkey Trial—July 10, 1925–July 25, 1925. 1997. http://xroads.virginia.edu/~UG97/inherit/1925home.html Overview of the conditions in which the play, *Inherit the Wind,* is cast. Provides an informative analysis of the background, conduct, and outcome of the trial.

28. Charles A. Lindbergh, Jr.'s Transatlantic Flight (1927)

Limited airmail service and the exhibitions of barnstorming pilots characterized aviation in postwar America. A $25,000 prize offered for the first nonstop crossing from the United States to Paris spurred interest. Several aviators had already failed or died in the attempt to cross the Atlantic, but Lindbergh, piloting his single-engine plane, *The Spirit of St. Louis,* succeeded. On May 21, 1927, with food and water but no parachute, he took off from Long Island and after a flight of some 3,500 miles that lasted more than thirty-three hours, he landed at Paris's Le Bourget airport. The flight made Lindbergh an international celebrity and stimulated the growth of the aviation industry.

Suggestions for Term Papers

1. Discuss the experiences of American aviators in World War I.
2. Why did Lindbergh's transatlantic flight succeed while others failed?

3. Analyze the consequences of Lindbergh's flight.

4. Discuss Lindbergh's later contributions to aviation.

5. Discuss the growth of the aviation industry during the 1920s.

REFERENCE SOURCES

Charles A. Lindbergh, a Bio-bibliography. Perry D. Luckett. Westport, CT: Greenwood, 1986. Brief biography with useful bibliography of materials relating to Lindbergh's life, career, and achievements.

World War I Aviation: A Bibliography of Books in English, French, German, and Italian, with a Price List Supplement. James P. Noffsinger. Rev. ed. Lanham, MD: Scarecrow, 1997. Comprehensive listing of writings with different views and perspectives. Recent revision of a bibliography originally issued in 1987.

GENERAL SOURCES

Beaty, David. *The Water Jump: The Story of Transatlantic Flight.* London: Secker & Warburg, 1976. Comprehensive coverage of flights over the Atlantic.

Cooke, David C. *Sky Battle, 1914–1918: The Story of Aviation in World War I.* New York: Norton, 1970. Informative historical survey of aerial operations during World War I.

Layman, R. D. *Naval Aviation in the First World War: Its Impact and Influence.* Annapolis, MD: Naval Institute, 1996. Up-to-date military history examining the naval aerial operations in World War I, including the role of seaplanes.

Pattillo, Donald M. *A History in the Making: 50 Turbulent Years in the American General Aviation Industry.* New York: McGraw-Hill, 1998. Recent examination of the history of the growth and development of the aviation industry in the United States.

SPECIALIZED SOURCES

Kent, Zachary. *Charles Lindbergh and the Spirit of St. Louis.* Parsippany, NJ: New Discovery Books, 1998. Concise and easy-to-read examination of the Lindbergh story, with emphasis given to the preparation for and conduct of the transatlantic flight.

Lindbergh, Charles A. *The Spirit of St. Louis.* (1953). Reprint. St. Paul: Minnesota Historical Society, 1993. Autobiographical account of

Lindbergh's career with detailed coverage of the airplane and its great flight.

Taylor, Richard L. *The First Solo Transatlantic Flight: The Story of Charles Lindbergh and His Airplane.* New York: Franklin Watts, 1995. Brief and easy-to-read biographical treatment, with emphasis given to the flight.

BIOGRAPHICAL SOURCES

Berg, A. Scott. *Lindbergh.* The first biography of the Lone Eagle based on unrestricted access to his papers. This is a major work.

Denenberg, Barry. *An American Hero: The True Story of Charles A. Lindbergh.* New York: Scholastic, 1996. Interesting and informative biography providing insight into Lindbergh's life and career.

Giblin, James. *Charles A. Lindbergh: A Human Hero.* New York: Clarion Books, 1997. Easy-to-read examination of Lindbergh's life, with all its tragedy, controversy, and achievement.

Gray, Susan M. *Charles A. Lindbergh and the American Dilemma: The Conflict of Technology and Human Values.* Bowling Green, OH: Bowling Green State University Popular Press, 1988. Interesting and informative examination of Lindbergh's views on technology, with treatment of societal aspects.

Hixson, Walter L. *Charles A. Lindbergh, Lone Eagle.* New York: HarperCollins, 1996. Brief biographical account examining Lindbergh's life and career, with a treatment of his personality.

Hunter, T. Willard. *The Spirit of Charles Lindbergh: Another Dimension.* Lanham, MD: Madison Books/National Book Network, 1993. Brief biographical treatment providing insight into Lindbergh's indomitable nature.

Lindbergh, Charles A. *Autobiography of Values.* (1978). Reprint. San Diego: Harcourt Brace Jovanovich, 1992. Lindbergh's own story setting forth his perspectives regarding the achievement of success.

Milton, Joyce. *Loss of Eden: A Biography of Charles and Anne Morrow Lindbergh.* New York: HarperCollins, 1993. Detailed narrative describing the lives and careers of both Lindbergh and his wife, the celebrated author.

Randolph, Blythe. *Charles Lindbergh.* New York: Franklin Watts, 1990. Brief and easy-to-read biographical overview of Lindbergh from his early years as a flier to his troubled later years.

Ross, Walter S. *The Last Hero, Charles A. Lindbergh.* Rev. ed. New York: Harper & Row, 1976. Detailed laudatory biography with slight changes to the earlier edition published in 1968.

Stoff, Joshua. *Charles A. Lindbergh: A Photographic Album.* New York: Dover, 1995. Brief biographical treatment, with photographs illustrating Lindbergh's career and achievements.

AUDIOVISUAL SOURCES

Famous American Speeches: A Multimedia History, 1850 to the Present. Phoenix: Oryx, 1996. CD-ROM. A comprehensive general source. The publisher uses Lindbergh as an example of a search to produce audio clips, video clips, photographs, subjects, additional references, and other materials.

Richardson, Cameron. *Are There Any Mechanics Here? Charles Lindbergh and the New York to Paris Flight.* New York: National Video Industries, 1995. Videocassette. Award-winning documentary of the transatlantic flight. Contains archival footage, newsreel material, and sound recordings in a 90-minute presentation.

WORLD WIDE WEB

"Ryan NYP 'Spirit of St. Louis': First Nonstop Solo Transatlantic Flight." *Milestones of Flight Gallery.* June 1996. http:www.nasm.edu/GALLERIES/GAL100/stlouis.html A brief descriptive commentary of the flight and its impact from the Smithsonian Institution (Gallery 100). Enumerates the design features of the airplane along with a small picture.

29. Opposition to Immigration in the 1920s

World War I stopped the flood of immigrants to the United States, but the influx of these newcomers, principally from southern and eastern Europe, then rebounded, reaching 800,000 in 1921. Writers such as Madison Grant fanned the flames of prejudice, as did Henry Ford, who published the fraudulent *Protocols of the Elders of Zion* in the early 1920s. The notoriety of Italian and Jewish gangsters also fueled prejudice. Congress enacted the Emergency Immigration Act of 1921, which restricted immigration, and the National Origins Act of 1924, which by 1929 was to set yearly immigration at 150,000 and discriminated against southern and eastern Europeans.

Suggestions for Term Papers

1. Why was anti-immigration legislation enacted during the 1920s?
2. How effective was Henry Ford in promoting anti-Semitism?
3. Compare the arguments for and against immigration restriction in the 1920s and today.
4. What was the reaction to Latino immigrants during the 1920s?
5. Compare the immigration restriction laws of the 1920s with current ones.

REFERENCE SOURCES

Atlas of American Migration. Stephen A. Flanders. New York: Facts on File, 1998. Important new resource tool that presents all aspects of immigration history and treats political developments, treaties, legislation, and court cases.

Dictionary of American Immigration History. Francesco Cordasco. Blue Ridge Summit, PA: Scarecrow, 1990. Well-conceived and easy-to-use informative compilation of facts regarding the history of immigration in the United States.

The Immigrant Experience: An Annotated Bibliography. Paul D. Mageli. Lanham, MD: Scarecrow, 1991. An introduction to and overview of the entire immigrant situation. Indexed with full annotations.

The Immigration History Research Center: A Guide to Collections. Suzanna Moody and Joe Wurl, comps., and eds. Westport, CT: Greenwood, 1991. An excellent listing of resources at this center at the University of Minnesota regarding immigrants and the immigration of southern, eastern, and central Europeans.

United States Immigration. E. Willard Miller and Ruby M. Miller. Santa Barbara, CA: ABC-CLIO, 1996. Primarily treats contemporary issues; the introductory essay, chronology, and treatment provide perspective of historical influences.

GENERAL SOURCES

Coan, Peter M. *Ellis Island Interviews: In Their Own Words.* New York: Facts on File, 1997. Oral histories of 130 people from all socioeconomic and ethnic backgrounds; descriptions of their dreams and their obstacles.

D'Innocenzo, Michael, and Josef P. Sirefman. *Immigration and Ethnicity:*

American Society—"Melting Pot" or "Salad Bowl"? Westport, CT: Greenwood, 1992. Treats assimilation and acculturation of different peoples (Greek-Americans, Italian-Americans, Jewish experience, etc.) with chapters by different authors. Prepared under the auspices of Hofstra University.

Parrish, Michael E. *Anxious Decades: America in Prosperity and Depression, 1920–1941.* New York: Norton, 1994. Detailed and comprehensive general history of the time period.

Purcell, L. E. *Immigration.* Phoenix: Oryx, 1995. Brief historical narrative of legal, societal, and cultural aspects of immigration to the United States from the seventeenth century to the present. Detailed bibliography and illustrations.

Siracusa, Joseph M. *Safe for Democracy: A History of America, 1914–1945.* Claremont, CA: Regina Books, 1993. Brief but comprehensive history of the thirty-year period treating briefly all societal issues.

Yans-McLaughlin, Virginia, and Marjorie Lightman. *Ellis Island: A Reader and Resource Guide.* New York: New Press, 1997. Interesting and informative collection of resources (interviews, oral histories, reports, photographs, excellent bibliography) from the eighteenth century to the present.

SPECIALIZED SOURCES

Barkai, Avraham. *Branching Out: German-Jewish Immigration to the United States, 1820–1914.* New York: Holmes & Meier, 1994. Describes the immigration and emigration of German Jews to the United States prior to the 1920s. Part of the publisher's Ellis Island series.

Cohn, Norman. *Warrant for Genocide: The Myth of the Jewish World Conspiracy and the Protocols of the Elders of Zion.* (1967). Reprint. London: Serif, 1996. Examines the myth promoted by Henry Ford and others regarding the Zionist determination to dominate the world.

Goldstein, Judith S. *The Politics of Ethnic Pressure: The American Jewish Committee Fight against Immigration Restriction, 1906–1917.* An examination of the politics involved in the struggle to allow Jewish immigration prior to the 1920s.

Grant, Madison. *The Conquest of a Continent.* (1933). Reprint. New York: Arno, 1977. One of the inflammatory and alarmist writings promoting the anti-immigration stance of the time.

Gurock, Jeffrey S., ed. *East European Jews in America, 1880–1920: Immigration and Adaptation.* New York: Routledge, 1997. Traces the pattern of immigration from the latter part of the nineteenth century that ultimately led to anti-immigration sentiment. Volume 3 of the eight-volume set, *American Jewish History.*

Simon, Rita James. *In the Golden Land: A Century of Russian and Soviet Jewish Immigration in America.* Westport, CT: Praeger, 1997. Brief examination of the historical conditions surrounding the immigration of Russian and Soviet Jewry to the United States.

Wieder, Alan. *Immigration, the Public School, and the 20th Century American Ethos: The Jewish Immigrant as a Case Study.* Lanham, MD: University Press of America, 1985. Brief and informative examination of the role of the school in the cultural assimilation of Jewish immigrants.

BIOGRAPHICAL SOURCES

Warren, Donald. *Radio Priest: Charles Coughlin, the Father of Hate Radio.* New York: Free Press, 1996. Detailed biography of Father Coughlin, the right-wing extremist who embarrassed the Catholic church with his anti-Jewish broadcasts during the 1920s and 1930s.

AUDIOVISUAL SOURCES

Immigration and Cultural Change. Wynewood, PA: Schlessinger Video/ Library Video Company, 1996. Videocassette. Number 12 of the twenty-volume set, United States History. Approximately 40 minutes. Informed treatment of immigration history with coverage of ethnic diversity and intolerance dating from the Chinese Exclusion Act of 1882.

WORLD WIDE WEB

Barnfield, Graham. "Addressing Estrangement: Federal Arts Patronage and National Identity Under the New Deal." *Communications Studies.* Updated September 1996. http://www.shu.ac.uk/schools/cs/ commstud/thirties/newdeal/intro.htm In setting the stage for the impact of New Deal legislation of the 1930s, part I examines the political fall-out of the National Origins Act and ethnic divisiveness of the 1920s.

30. Jazz Age Culture

The 1920s proved to be remarkably vibrant for both high and popular culture. Writers such as T. S. Eliot, Ernest Hemingway, F. Scott Fitzgerald, and Sinclair Lewis gained national and international fame.

Jazz, derived from African American roots, increasingly became popular, as did such upbeat dances as the Charleston. Many women, often collectively called "flappers," sought freer dress and lifestyles. Psychology, particularly of the Freudian and behavioral schools, gained new attention and respect. Sports—especially baseball (despite the Black Sox scandal of 1919), football, boxing, tennis, and golf—proved enormously popular, as did such sports figures as Babe Ruth and Jack Dempsey.

Suggestions for Term Papers

1. Discuss the career and influence of a prominent American writer of the 1920s.
2. Discuss the career and influence of a prominent American athlete of the 1920s.
3. Why did the popularity of sports increase during the 1920s?
4. Analyze the influence of Freudian psychology on American life and culture during the 1920s.
5. Why have the 1920s retained their popularity with later generations?

Suggested Sources: See entries 25 and 26 for related items.

REFERENCE SOURCES

Benny Goodman: Wrapping It Up. D. Russell O'Connor. Blue Ridge Summit, PA: Scarecrow, 1996. Excellent discography complementing O'Connor's earlier work, *Benny Goodman: Listen to his Legacy,* in providing the most complete guide to Goodman's career and recordings.

Duke Ellington: A Listener's Guide. Eddie Lambert. Blue Ridge Summit, PA: Scarecrow, 1998. A detailed and carefully executed discography with critical commentary from the leading expert on Ellington. Provides a good overview and exposition of Ellington's creative contributions.

Fashions of the Roaring '20s. Ellie Laubner. Atglen, PA: Schiffer Publishing, 1996. Illustrated guide to costume and fashion pieces with valuations of various apparel.

Historical Dictionary of the 1920s: From World War I to the New Deal. James

S. Olson. Westport, CT: Greenwood, 1988. Useful and convenient reference to quick information on all aspects of life in the 1920s.

GENERAL SOURCES

Jeansonne, Glen. *Transformation and Reaction: America, 1921–1945.* New York: HarperCollins, 1994. Brief, comprehensive history of the twenty-five-year period that witnessed broad changes in culture.

Piazza, Tom, ed. *Fifty Years of Great Jazz Liner Notes.* New York: Anchor Books, 1996. Recent history and criticism of jazz; liner notes provide insight into the nature of the music and the age.

Steele, Valerie. *Fashion and Eroticism: Ideals of Feminine Beauty from the Victorian Era to the Jazz Age.* New York: Oxford University Press, 1985. Comprehensive examination of fashion dictates and sex symbolism as represented in female dress.

SPECIALIZED SOURCES

Asinof, Eliot. *Eight Men Out.* New York: H. Holt, 1987. Interesting and informative account of the 1919 World Series and the Black Sox scandal; provided the basis for the recent motion picture.

Bruce, Kenneth R. *Yowsah! Yowsah! The Roaring Twenties.* Dubuque, IA: Kendall/Hunt, 1977. Brief and interesting overview of the people, events, social customs, and politics of the time.

Carter, Paul A. *The Twenties in America.* 2d ed. New York: Crowell, 1975. A brief but informative overview of the period embracing the Jazz Age. Part of the publisher's series on American history.

Cohen, Stanley. *Rebellion against Victorianism: The Impetus for Cultural Change in 1920s America.* New York: Oxford University Press, 1991. Informative account of the social conditions and cultural development of the Jazz Age.

Evensen, Bruce J. *When Dempsey Fought Tunney: Heroes, Hokum, and Storytelling in the Jazz Age.* Knoxville: University of Tennessee Press, 1996. Revealing examination of the athlete-heroes in boxing and the frenzy of their media buildup and popularity in this mad age.

Idema, Henry. *Freud, Religion, and the Roaring Twenties: A Psychoanalytic Theory of Secularization in Three Novelists: Anderson, Hemingway, and Fitzgerald.* Savage, MD: Rowman & Littlefield, 1990. Perceptive exposition of Freudian influences and secularism in the writing of three noted novelists of the period.

Olien, Roger M. *Easy Money: Oil Promoters and Investors in the Jazz Age.* Chapel Hill: University of North Carolina Press, 1990. Brief informative study of fraud, corruption, and speculation in the petroleum industry. See also the Tygiel work below.

The Roaring Twenties, 1920–1930. Alexandria, VA: Time-Life Books, 1991. Informative, illustrated survey of the social life and popular culture of the decade. Part of This Fabulous Century series.

Shaw, Arnold. *The Jazz Age: Popular Music in the 1920's.* New York: Oxford University Press, 1987. Critical history of popular music during the decade that featured jazz.

Studlar, Gaylyn. *This Mad Masquerade: Stardom and Masculinity in the Jazz Age.* New York: Columbia University Press, 1996. Examination of the sex role of men in motion pictures during this frivolous period.

Tygiel, Jules. *The Great Los Angeles Swindle: Oil, Stocks, and Scandal During the Roaring Twenties.* (1994). Reprint. Berkeley: University of California Press, 1996. An examination of corrupt practices in the petroleum industry. (See the Olien work above.) Focuses on the Julian Petroleum Corporation in Los Angeles.

BIOGRAPHICAL SOURCES

Anthony, Carl S. *Florence Harding: The First Lady, the Jazz Age, and the Death of America's Most Scandalous President.* New York: Morrow, 1998. Interesting biography of the wife of the president who served for two scandal-ridden years.

Cowley, Malcolm, and Robert Cowley. *Fitzgerald and the Jazz Age.* New York: Scribner's, 1966. Standard work on F. Scott Fitzgerald and his Jazz Age influences.

Eisenberg, Lisa. *The Story of Babe Ruth: Baseball's Greatest Legend.* Milwaukee, WI: Gareth Stevens Publishing, 1997. Brief, easy-to-read biography of one of the symbols of this fast-paced and frenetic time.

Grange, Red, and Ira Morton. *The Red Grange Story: An Autobiography.* (1953). Reprint. Urbana: University of Illinois Press, 1993. Well-written story of one of the sports idols of the Roaring Twenties.

Griffiths, David. *Hot Jazz: From Harlem to Storyville.* Blue Ridge Summit, PA: Scarecrow, 1998. Interview-based stories of over thirty musicians who served as the side-men in the big bands of the 1930s and 1940s.

Meyers, Jeffrey. *Hemingway, a Biography.* New York: Harper & Row, 1985. Detailed and thorough study of Hemingway's life and career.

Rimler, Walter. *Not Fade Away: A Comparison of Jazz Age with Rock Era Pop Song Composers.* Ann Arbor, MI: Pierian, 1984. Interesting collective biography and comparison of music personalities from two different eras.

Silverman, Kenneth. *Houdini: The Career of Erich Weiss.* New York: HarperPerennial, 1997. Thorough, detailed study of the world's greatest magician whose incredible feats amazed the nation during the Roaring Twenties.

Vache, Warren W. *Jazz Gentry: Aristocrats of the Music World.* Blue Ridge, PA: Scarecrow, 1998. Explores the years between the two world wars with the stories of musicians of the time. Based on interviews conducted over a twenty-year period.

Walsh, George. *Gentleman Jimmy Walker, Mayor of the Jazz Age.* New York: Praeger, 1974. Interesting biography of the dapper New York politician.

Yagoda, Ben. *Will Rogers: A Biography.* New York: Knopf, 1993. Detailed, interesting, and informative account of the life and career of one of the most influential political humorists of all time.

AUDIOVISUAL SOURCES

This Great Century: 1918–1939—The Years of Jazz/Great Illusions. New York: Central Park Media, 1996. Videocassette. 110 minutes. Treats the birth of jazz as well as Lindbergh's flight, Hindenburg tragedy, and other events. One of five videocassettes forming the This Great Century series.

WORLD WIDE WEB

Evans, Nick. *Culture in the Jazz Age.* 1996; updated July 1997. http:// cwrl.utexas.edu/~nick/e309k/jazzage.html A course taught at the University of Texas providing a well-constructed syllabus, listing of texts, and links to jazz sites. Most useful are the sophisticated analyses of important texts by F. Scott Fitzgerald and Langston Hughes, among others.

31. Stock Market Crash of 1929

Between 1927 and 1929, the stock market rose dramatically and, it turned out, dangerously. Prudent investment yielded to speculation as investors bet that they could reap huge profits. Stockbrokers compounded the risk by permitting investors to buy on margin, that is, by initially paying only a fraction of the stock's cost, with the balance to come from their profits. Fundamental weaknesses that included a slowing demand for goods and a diminished foreign trade resulting from the nation's own restrictive trade policies put an end to investor euphoria. In September and October 1929 the market weakened, and on October 29, "Black Tuesday," the worst day in market history, it plummeted. The great bull market had ended.

Suggestions for Term Papers

1. What weaknesses led to the stock market crash?
2. Could the market crash have been avoided?
3. How bad was Black Tuesday?
4. What were the long-range effects of the market crash?
5. Compare the crash of 1929 with the stock market plunge of October 1987.

Suggested Sources: See entry 32 for relevant items.

GENERAL SOURCES

Beaudreau, Bernard. *Mass Production, the Stock Market Crash, and the Great Depression: The Macroeconomics of Electrification.* Westport, CT: Greenwood, 1996. Brief history of industrialization and the stock market crash and Great Depression.

SPECIALIZED SOURCES

Axon, Gordon V. *The Stock Market Crash of 1929.* New York: Mason and Lipscomb, 1974. Brief examination of the economic conditions surrounding the crash.

Bierman, Harold. *The Causes of the 1929 Stock Market Crash: A Speculative Orgy or a New Era?* Westport, CT: Greenwood, 1998. The most recent analysis of the stock exchanges and the causes of the crash.

————. *The Great Myths of 1929 and the Lessons to Be Learned.* Westport, CT: Greenwood, 1991. Good description and analysis of the 1929 crash, with comparison and application to the decline in 1987.

Dillon, Gadis J. *The Role of Accounting in the Stock Market Crash of 1929.* Atlanta: Georgia State University Press, 1984. An examination of the stock market crash with special emphasis on accounting methods employed.

Feinberg, Barbara S. *Black Tuesday: The Stock Market Crash of 1929.* Brookfield, CT: Millbrook, 1995. An easy-to-read, brief description of the conditions leading to the crash, the onset of the Great Depression, and remedial steps taken.

Hiebert, Ray E. *The Stock Market Crash, 1929: Panic on Wall Street Ends the Jazz Age.* New York: Franklin Watts, 1970. An examination of nine of the most significant days leading to the crash. Similar to the Feinberg book above in being easy to read.

Millichap, Nancy. *The Stock Market Crash of 1929.* New York: New Discovery Books, 1994. An easy-to-read description from the publisher's American Events series.

AUDIOVISUAL SOURCES

"The Crash of 1929." *The American Experience.* Santa Monica, CA: PBS Home Video, 1991. Videocassette. 60-minute documentary of the stock market crash and its aftermath.

The Great Depression: 1929–1939. Mount Kisco, NY: Center for Humanities, 1968. Videocassette. 32-minute overview of the Great Depression; begins with Black Thursday and the panic on Wall Street.

WORLD WIDE WEB

Associated Press. "Stock Market Crash of 1929, Oct. 29, 1929." *Washington Post.* September 1997. http://washingtonpost.com/wp-srv/business/longterm/biztalk/grassol/102929.htm Reprint of October 30 article describing the stock market plunge the previous day.

32. The Great Depression

Many believed that the severe recession that followed the stock market crash of 1929 would be relatively brief. By mid-1931, however, it was clearly turning into a profound depression. Between 1929 and 1933, industrial and farm prices declined precipitously, and unemployment soared to 25 percent of the workforce. Although he feared the creation of a welfare state, President Hoover, unlike some orthodox economists, did not believe in letting the depression run its course. Yet the various measures his administration took failed to restore prosperity. By the end of his term as president, Hoover, who was internationally famous for earlier humanitarian efforts, had become widely reviled.

Suggestions for Term Papers

1. Was President Hoover unfairly blamed for having failed to end the depression?
2. Discuss why the Great Depression is considered the worst one in U.S. history.
3. What effect did the depression in the United States have on other nations?
4. Discuss how the depression affected your home town or your relatives.
5. Analyze the causes of the Great Depression.

Suggested Sources: See entries 30–31 and 33–39 for related items.

REFERENCE SOURCES

The Great Depression: A Historical Bibliography. Santa Barbara, CA: ABC-Clio Information Services, 1984. Identifies material relevant to study of the Great Depression (social conditions, economic conditions, government policy, etc.).

New Day/New Deal: A Bibliography of the Great American Depression, 1929–1941. David E. Kyvig and Mary-Ann Blasio, comps. Westport, CT: Greenwood, 1988. Good bibliography of writings on the Great Depression and the Roosevelt years up to World War II.

GENERAL SOURCES

Liebovich, Louis. *Bylines in Despair: Herbert Hoover, the Great Depression, and the U.S. News Media.* Westport, CT: Praeger, 1994. Examination of press coverage and the media influences surrounding Herbert Hoover during the Depression.

Nash, Gerald D. *The Crucial Era: The Great Depression and World War II, 1929–1945.* 2d ed. New York; St. Martin's, 1992. Concise, comprehensive historical overview of the period embracing the Depression years and World War II.

Rothermund, Dietmar. *The Global Impact of the Great Depression, 1929–1939.* New York: Routledge, 1996. Brief, handy, and useful survey of the Depression. Places the American scene within perspective of international consequences.

Soule, George H. *Prosperity Decade: From War to Depression, 1917–1929.* (1947). Reprint. Armonk, NY: M. E. Sharpe, 1989. Good firsthand account of the economic conditions in the decade prior to the Depression by an author who lived through it.

SPECIALIZED SOURCES

Bauman, John F., and Thomas H. Coode. *In the Eye of the Great Depression: New Deal Reporters and the Agony of the American People*. DeKalb, IL: Northern Illinois University Press, 1988. Good social history providing sketches of reporters like Lorena Hickok and Harry Hopkins and their work in reporting, illustrating, and exposing the conditions of the time.

Beito, David T. *Taxpayers in Revolt: Tax Resistance during the Great Depression*. Chapel Hill: University of North Carolina Press, 1989. Interesting and informative account of tax collection and taxpayer compliance during the Depression.

Bernstein, Michael A. *The Great Depression: Delayed Recovery and Economic Change in America, 1929–1939*. New York: Cambridge University Press, 1987. Concise description of the economic conditions surrounding the Depression and the early period of recovery.

Brinkley, Alan. *Voices of Protest: Huey Long, Father Coughlin, and the Great Depression*. New York: Knopf, 1982. Examination of two radically different dissenters and their ideas.

Burg, David. *The Great Depression*. New York: Facts on File, 1996. Examines the Depression from its onset to the 1940s through the eyes of its affected citizens. Includes documents, biographical sketches, maps, photographs, and bibliographic references. From the publisher's Eyewitness History series.

Dubofsky, Melvyn, and Stephen Burwood, eds. *Women and Minorities during the Great Depression*. New York: Garland, 1990. Treats social conditions surrounding women and minorities during the time. Part of the publisher's The Great Depression and the New Deal series.

Ellis, Edward R. *A Nation in Torment: The Great Depression, 1929–1939*. New York: Kodansha International, 1995. Thorough, vivid, anecdote-filled historical account of the events and personalities of the time.

Freemon, David K. *The Great Depression in American History*. Springfield, NJ: Enslow Publishers, 1997. Easy-to-read brief historical treatment of causes of the Depression and important figures. Part of the publisher's series.

Garraty, John A. *The Great Depression: An Inquiry into the Causes, Course, and Consequences of the Worldwide Depression of the Nineteen-Thirties, as Seen by Contemporaries and in the Light of History*. San

Diego: Harcourt Brace Jovanovich, 1986. Important work on the Depression by a leading historian.

Hill, Kim Q. *Democracies in Crisis: Public Policy Responses to the Great Depression.* Boulder, CO: Westview, 1988. Brief, handy examination of economic policies intended to counter the Depression.

McElvaine, Robert S. *The Great Depression: America, 1929–1941.* New York: Times Books, 1984. Well-received and thorough account of the Depression and its aftermath up to the time of U.S. entry into World War II.

Meltzer, Milton. *Brother, Can You Spare a Dime: The Great Depression of 1929–1933.* New York: Facts on File, 1990. Firsthand accounts of workers, farmers, businessmen, and others, with photographs, maps, and a bibliography. Part of the publisher's Library of American History series.

Rose, Nancy E. *Put to Work: Relief Programs in the Great Depression.* New York: Monthly Review, 1994. Brief description of government programs enacted to provide relief and create jobs.

Terkel, Studs. *Hard Times: An Oral History of the Great Depression.* (1970). Reprint. New York: Pantheon Books, 1986. Important work providing personal narratives of a variety of people who lived through the Depression.

Watkins, T. H. *The Great Depression: America in the 1930s.* Boston: Little, Brown, 1993. Informative survey history of the difficult decade and the programs designed to alleviate suffering.

Wenger, Beth S. *New York Jews and the Great Depression: Uncertain Promise.* New Haven, CT: Yale University Press, 1996. Analysis of the Depression and its impact on one segment of the population.

BIOGRAPHICAL SOURCES

Jeansonne, Glen. *Messiah of the Masses: Huey P. Long and the Great Depression.* New York: HarperCollins, 1993. Brief account of the life and career of the populist Louisiana governor who was developing a national following at the time of his death in 1935.

Smith, Richard Norton. *An Uncommon Man: The Triumph of Herbert Hoover.* New York: Simon and Schuster, 1984. A scholarly and sympathetic biography.

Warren, Harris G. *Herbert Hoover and the Great Depression.* (1959). Reprint. Westport, CT: Greenwood, 1980. Well-received biographical account of President Hoover and his administration during the Depression.

AUDIOVISUAL SOURCES

The Great Depression: New Deal/New York. Santa Monica, CA: PBS Home Video, 1993. Videocassette. Fine 60-minute documentary examining FDR's association with Mayor Fiorello La Guardia in expanding social reforms to combat the Depression in New York.

WORLD WIDE WEB

Kangas, Steve. "The Great Depression: Its Causes and Cure." *Liberalism Resurgent.* May 1997. http://www.scruz.net/~kangaroo/THE__ GREAT__DEPRESSION.htm Analysis of the Depression from the liberal perspective. Useful links to time line and summary.

33. The Bonus Army (1932)

In 1924, Congress legislated a bonus for World War I veterans, to be paid to them or their heirs in 1945. But the Great Depression led perhaps as many as twenty thousand unemployed veterans and their families to march to Washington in the spring of 1932 to demand immediate payment. Unsuccessful, most of the Bonus Army left their makeshift quarters at Anacostia Flats outside the Capitol and went home. In July, President Hoover reluctantly ordered the remaining occupied government buildings cleared. Ultimately, General Douglas MacArthur led hundreds of troops in dispersing the squatters. In the melee, scores of civilians were injured and a baby was accidentally killed. The incident diminished Hoover's popularity further.

Suggestions for Term Papers

1. Was the government justified in using force to evict the Bonus Army?

2. Discuss public reaction to the Bonus Army and its dispersal.

3. Compare the Bonus Army's march on Washington with that of Coxey's Army in 1894.

4. Compare the Bonus Army's march on Washington with that of the Poor People's Campaign in 1968.

5. Should the Bonus Army have received its bonus in 1932?

Suggested Sources: See entry 32 for related items.

REFERENCE SOURCES

General Douglas MacArthur, 1880–1964: Historiography and Annotated Bibliography. Eugene L. Rasor. Westport, CT: Greenwood, 1994. Good bibliography covering all aspects of the general's career.

GENERAL SOURCES

Allen, Frederick L. *Only Yesterday: An Informal History of the Nineteen-Twenties.* New York: Harper, 1931. Important and well-received firsthand account by the editor of *Harper's* magazine of the social and economic conditions that led to the Great Depression and the Bonus March.

————. *Since Yesterday: The Nineteen-Thirties in America, September 3, 1929-September 3, 1939.* New York: Harper, 1940. Allen's second important work treats the history of the next decade examining the Bonus March among other aspects of the Depression.

Bernstein, Michael A. *The Great Depression: Delayed Recovery and Economic Change in America, 1929–1939.* New York: Cambridge University Press, 1987. More recent coverage of the period treated by Allen in the work above.

Ellis, Edward R. *A Nation in Torment: The Great American Depression, 1929–1939.* (1970). Reprint. New York: Kodansha International, 1995. An examination of this difficult period and its momentous events such as the Bonus March.

McElvaine, Robert S. *The Great Depression: America 1929–1941.* New York: Times Books, 1984. Even-handed history of New Deal by a leftist historian. Good background for understanding the sociopolitical conditions surrounding the Bonus Army.

Mitchell, Broadus. *Depression Decade: From New Era through New Deal, 1929–1941.* (1947). Reprint. Armonk, NY: M. E. Sharpe, 1989. Detailed firsthand account of the Depression by a writer who lived through it and such events as the Bonus March.

Watkins, T. H. *The Great Depression: America in the 1930s.* Boston: Little, Brown, 1993. A recent history of the turbulent decade that provides good coverage of the Bonus March.

SPECIALIZED SOURCES

Lisio, Donald. *Hoover, MacArthur, and the Bonus Riot.* 2d ed. New York: Fordham University Press, 1994. Recent examination and interpretation of both MacArthur and Hoover in respect to the calamity at Anacostia Flats. Extensive bibliography.

Waters, Walter W. *B. E. F.: The Whole Story of the Bonus Army.* (1933). Reprint. New York: AMS, 1970. Firsthand account written just after it happened. The major source on the event.

BIOGRAPHICAL SOURCES

Payne, Darwin. *The Man of Only Yesterday: Frederick Lewis Allen, Former Editor of Harper's Magazine, Author, and Interpreter of His Times.* New York: Harper & Row, 1975. Detailed biography of the well-known author of the 1920s and 1930s.

Perret, Geoffrey. *Old Soldiers Never Die: The Life of Douglas MacArthur.* New York: Random House, 1996. The most recent biography of the general. New material sheds more light on the directives given MacArthur in the assault on the Bonus Army.

AUDIOVISUAL SOURCES

Fayer, Steve. "After the Crash." *The American Experience.* Santa Monica, CA: PBS Home Video, 1991. Videocassette. 60-minute television presentation examining the events that led to the creation of the Bonus Army, as well as the tragic riot that ensued.

WORLD WIDE WEB

"WWI Veterans' Bonus March 1932." *UMI: Great Events.* 1997. http://www.umi.com/hp/Support/K12/GreatEvents/WWIBonus.html Fine narrative describing the situation, along with a reading list and questions for comprehension. Accompanies microfiche as part of Resources for Schools package.

34. The Presidential Election of 1932

Republicans again nominated incumbent Herbert Hoover as their presidential candidate in 1932; Democrats, despite some strong opposition, chose New York governor Franklin D. Roosevelt. Roosevelt, breaking with tradition, accepted the nomination in person and promised "a new deal for the American people." Throughout the campaign, he and his advisers, notably three Columbia University professors known collectively as the brain trust, attacked Hoover's failure to end the Depression and outlined a general, and sometimes contradictory, course of government activism to be pursued. Voters elected Roosevelt by a landslide vote and gave him strong Democratic majorities in Congress.

Suggestions for Term Papers

1. Why did the Democrats select FDR as their presidential candidate?
2. Compare the campaigns and promises of Hoover and Roosevelt.
3. Discuss the contributions of the brain trust to Roosevelt's campaign and election.
4. Analyze the failure of the Socialist party to attract more votes.
5. What was "new" about the New Deal?

Suggested Sources: See entry 32 for related items.

REFERENCE SOURCES

America at the Polls: A Handbook of American Presidential Election Statistics. Alice V. McGillivray and Richard M. Scammon. Washington, DC: Congressional Quarterly, 1994. 2 vols. Volume 1 treats the elections from Harding to Eisenhower. Good presentation and analysis of election returns in summaries by state and county.

Congressional Quarterly's Guide to U.S. Elections. 3d ed. John L. Moore, ed. Washington, DC: Congressional Quarterly, 1994. Similar to the previous book but with a less detailed analysis of presidential elections. Also provides treatment of the House and Senate elections.

Encyclopedia of the American Presidency. Leonard W. Levy and Louis Fisher, eds. New York: Simon & Schuster, 1994. 4 vols. Excellent coverage with great detail. Over 1,000 entries from over 300 experts covering individuals, issues, cases, and other materials. Fine bibliographic references.

The Presidents Speak: The Inaugural Addresses of the American Presidents from Washington to Clinton. David N. Lott. New York: Holt, 1994. In addition to the inauguration speech, provides a biography, interpretation of events at the time, and analysis of the speeches. Informative and interesting.

Student's Atlas of American Presidential Elections, 1789–1996. Fred L. Israel. Washington, DC: Congressional Quarterly, 1997. Statewide voting shown with color-coded maps for each election along with charts. Includes data on minor parties. The display for the 1932 election clearly illustrates Roosevelt's victory.

The World Almanac of Presidential Campaigns. Eileen Shields-West. Mahwah, NJ: Pharos/World Almanac, 1992. Popular compilation of statistics, fascinating facts, anecdotes, and ephemera about each election. Describes the selection of the ticket, the candidates, slogans, songs, and other facets of the campaign.

The Young Oxford Companion to the Presidency of the United States. Richard M. Pious. New York: Oxford University Press, 1994. Brief alphabetically arranged articles on personalities, events, issues, concepts, and so forth. Even-handed, balanced treatment, with a good bibliography.

GENERAL SOURCES

Boller, Paul F. *Presidential Campaigns.* Rev. ed. Cleveland: World Almanac Education, 1996. Treatment of every presidential campaign in American history with a brief description and highlights.

Lichtman, Allan J., and Ken DeCell. *The Thirteen Keys to the Presidency.* Lanham, MD: Madison Books, 1990. Thirteen historical factors (the keys) that helped to determine the outcomes of presidential elections since 1860—four political keys, seven performance, and two personality.

Parrish, Michael. *Anxious Decades: America in Prosperity and Depression, 1920–1941.* New York: Norton, 1992. Liberal interpretation of these tension-filled years. Good understanding of the conditions on which the 1932 campaign was fought.

BIOGRAPHICAL SOURCES

Crompton, Samuel. *The Presidents of the United States.* New York: Smithmark, 1992. Brief narrative summary of personal, social, and political events for each term of office. With illustrations.

Havel, James T. *U.S. Presidential Candidates and the Elections: A Biographical and Historical Guide.* New York; Macmillan, 1996. 2 vols. Good compilation of statistics (vol. 2) biographical and historical narrative about some 3,500 persons (vol. 1).

Lyons, Eugene. *Herbert Hoover: A Biography.* (1964). Reprint. Norwalk, CT: Easton, 1989. Readable but somewhat dated biography of Hoover.

Miller, Nathan. *FDR: An Intimate History*. New York: Doubleday, 1983. Comprehensive treatment of FDR prior to and during the presidency. Popular and readable, and based on secondary sources.

AUDIOVISUAL SOURCES

Roosevelt and U.S. History (1930–1945). Columbus, OH: Coronet/MTI Film & Video, 1977. Videocassette. 32-minute documentary narrated by Michael Redgrave and Anthony Quayle. Begins with the Depression years under Hoover and traces Roosevelt's career.

WORLD WIDE WEB

Ripon College. "Franklin Delano Roosevelt." American Presidents. August 1997. http://www.ripon.edu/dept/pogo/presidency/Pres.List.HTML Provides outline and textual coverage of every American president from Washington to Clinton, including treatment of each election. Brief but informative description of the campaign and election of 1932, including voting statistics and enumeration of states carried.

35. Civilian Conservation Corps (CCC) (1933)

Established on March 31, 1933, the Civilian Conservation Corps (CCC) was an attempt to reduce the country's massive unemployment. Authorized initially to employ 250,000 young men between the ages of eighteen and twenty-five, the CCC ultimately employed more than 2 million before Congress abolished it in 1943. These youths, who had come from urban areas, wore uniforms and lived in camps run along military lines. They undertook such tasks as reforestation, soil conservation, and general improvements in the nation's parks and could also enroll in educational courses. Most of their small monthly wages was sent home to their families.

Suggestions for Term Papers

1. Discuss the origins of the CCC.
2. Discuss how various participants viewed their experience in the program.

3. Did the achievements of the CCC outweigh its shortcomings?

4. Should Congress have abolished the CCC?

5. Compare the CCC with similar contemporary programs.

Suggested Sources: See entry 32 for related items.

REFERENCE SOURCES

Encyclopedia of American History. 7th rev. ed. Richard B. Morris and Jeffery B. Morris, eds. New York: HarperCollins, 1996. Basic source of information with chronologies, biographies, and numerous tables. Good coverage of the CCC.

Historical Dictionary of the New Deal: From Inauguration to Preparation for War. James S. Olson, ed. Westport, CT: Greenwood, 1985. The most comprehensive reference work on the New Deal. Treats 700 personalities, political groups, agencies, legislation, and various topics in clear, concise fashion. Good coverage of the CCC.

The Presidents: A Reference History. 2d ed. New York: Macmillan Library Reference USA, 1997. Comprehensive history of the American presidency from Washington to Clinton. Good treatment of FDR and all his programs.

GENERAL SOURCES

Daynes, Byron W., et al., eds. *The New Deal and Public Policy.* New York: St. Martin's, 1998. Collection of papers from a recent conference covering various aspects of the New Deal. Contains an interesting description of CCC as an idea whose time had come.

Eden, Robert, ed. *The New Deal and Its Legacy: Critique and Reappraisal.* Westport, CT: Greenwood, 1989. Collection of essays—some brief, some probing, some angry about the impact of the New Deal. Written from a neoconservative point of view.

Leuchtenburg, William E. *The FDR Years: On Roosevelt and His Legacy.* New York: Columbia University Press, 1995. Excellent insight into Roosevelt and his tremendous impact. Compelling, informed analysis of the New Deal included.

Rosenbaum, Herbert D., and Elizabeth Bartelme, eds. *Franklin D. Roosevelt: The Man, the Myth, the Era, 1882–1945.* Westport, CT: Greenwood, 1987. Comprehensive coverage and assessment of many aspects of FDR's presidency in twenty-three papers from a professional conference. Treats several aspects of the New Deal.

Rozell, Mark J., and William Pederson, eds. *FDR and the Modern Presi-*

dency: Leadership and Legacy. Westport, CT: Praeger, 1997. Collection of new essays exploring the impact of FDR on the modern presidency. The New Deal is one of several topics examined.

SPECIALIZED SOURCES

Kiefer, E. Kay, and Paul E. Fellows. *Hobnail Boots and Khaki Suits: A Brief Look at the Great Depression and the Civilian Conservation Corps as Seen through the Eyes of Those Who Were There.* Chicago: Adams, 1983. Brief examination of the CCC with observations of its role in alleviating the suffering of the Depression.

Lacy, Leslie A. *The Soil Soldiers: The Civilian Conservation Corps in the Great Depression.* Radnor, PA: Chilton, 1976. Excellent history of the CCC. Examines the activities of recruits and provides background detail.

Lange, Howard E. *The CCC, a Humanitarian Endeavor During the Great Depression.* New York: Vantage, 1984. Brief history of the CCC with a positive interpretation of its noble intent.

Merrill, Perry H. *Roosevelt's Forest Army: A History of the Civilian Conservation Corps, 1933–1942.* Montpelier, VT: P. H. Merrill, 1981. Contains extensive quotations from CCC participants, with summaries of activity state by state. Privately published. Order through interlibrary loan.

Salmond, John A. *The Civilian Conservation Corps, 1932–1942: A New Deal Case Study.* Durham, NC: Duke University Press, 1967. Considered the best history on the origin, development, failure, and successes of the CCC. Written clearly with excellent documentation.

BIOGRAPHICAL SOURCES

Alsop, Joseph. *FDR, 1882–1945: A Centenary Remembrance.* (1982). Reprint. New York: Gramercy, 1998. Classic work by a noted author that examines FDR's personal and political lives, with some insight into the New Deal.

Maney, Patrick J. *The Roosevelt Presence: The Life and Legacy of FDR.* (1992). Reprint. Berkeley: University of California Press, 1998. Well-written, concise biographical work with balanced account of the New Deal as well as foreign policy. Somewhat critical assessment of FDR.

Morgan, Ted. *FDR: A Biography.* New York: Touchstone/Simon & Schuster, 1986. A well-researched examination of FDR in clear and readable terms. Sees FDR as an important agent of change.

AUDIOVISUAL SOURCES

The Great Depression: 1929–1939. Mount Kisco, NY: Center for Humanities, 1968. Videocassette. Brief (32 minutes) but comprehensive examination of the Great Depression that provides insight into New Deal legislation such as that establishing the CCC.

WORLD WIDE WEB

Civilian Conservation Corps Museum. (Nov. 1997). http//www.sos.state. mi.us/history/museum/museccc.html Overview of the museum dedicated to the Michigan participation in CCC. Link to "Roosevelt's Tree Army" provides a detailed historical narrative.

36. Tennessee Valley Authority (TVA) (1933)

The origins of TVA date back to the 1920s and the debate over public versus private development and ownership of the nation's power facilities. A radical New Deal measure, the creation of the TVA in May 1933 was intended to harness for public benefit the power of the Tennessee River, which cut through seven southern states. Multipurpose in goals, the TVA offered jobs, provided inexpensive fertilizers, improved and built dams, reforested depleted areas, and, most controversially, provided cheap public electricity to compete with more costly private power.

Suggestions for Term Papers

1. Analyze the Muscle Shoals (Alabama) project controversy of the 1920s.

2. Discuss the reaction of private utility companies to the establishment of the TVA.

3. Discuss the reaction to presidential candidate Barry Goldwater's suggestion in 1964 to privatize the TVA.

4. Compare the original TVA with today's TVA.

5. Discuss the long-range effects of the TVA.

Suggested Sources: See entry 32 for related items.

GENERAL SOURCES

Durant, Robert F. *When Government Regulates Itself: EPA, TVA, and Pollution Control in the 1970s.* Knoxville: University of Tennessee Press, 1985. Brief examination of the activity of both the Environmental Protection Agency and the TVA in combating pollution in line with government legislation.

SPECIALIZED SOURCES

Callahan, North. *TVA: Bridge over Troubled Waters.* South Brunswick, NJ: A. S. Barnes, 1980. Well-written history of the TVA describing its obstacles and its progressive growth and development.

Chandler, William U. *The Myth of TVA: Conservation and Development in the Tennessee Valley, 1933–1983.* Cambridge, MA: Ballinger, 1984. Well-written and popular, somewhat revisionist history of the TVA. The myth was its alleged design to assist the small farmer rather than the large farm organizations that actually benefited most.

Colignon, Richard A. *Power Plays: Critical Events in the Institutionalization of the Tennessee Valley Authority.* Albany: State University of New York Press, 1997. Historical treatment of events in the development of TVA as an electric utility and government corporation.

Grant, Nancy. *TVA and Black Americans: Planning for the Status Quo.* Philadelphia: Temple University Press, 1990. Interesting history of the employment and relocation of African Americans in accordance with the requirements of the TVA.

Hargrove, E. C. *Prisoners of Myth: The Leadership of the Tennessee Valley Authority, 1933–1990.* Princeton, NJ: Princeton University Press, 1994. Comprehensive history of the TVA from its beginnings to the present. Examines the effectiveness of its leaders over time.

———, and Paul K. Conkin, eds. *TVA, Fifty Years of Grass-roots Bureaucracy.* Urbana: University of Illinois Press, 1983. Contains papers drawn from a symposium held at Vanderbilt University covering history, management, activity, image, and public interest issues.

Hodge, Clarence L. *The Tennessee Valley Authority: A National Experiment in Regionalism.* (1938). Reprint. New York: Russell & Russell, 1968. Early examination of the TVA, written five years after its creation.

Hubbard, Preston J. *Origins of the TVA: The Muscle Shoals Controversy, 1920–1932.* Nashville, TN: Vanderbilt University Press, 1961. In-depth description of the Muscle Shoals situation leading to the creation of the TVA.

Lilienthal, David E. *TVA: Democracy on the March.* (1953). Reprint. Westport, CT: Greenwood, 1977. Noncritical treatment of the agency by one of its leaders. Reprint of a publication commemorating the TVA's twentieth anniversary.

McCraw, Thomas K. *TVA and the Power Fight, 1933–1939.* Philadelphia: Lippincott, 1971. Provides insight into the nature of the struggle for power within a critical six-year period. (See McCraw in "Biographical Sources" below.)

McDonald, Michael J., and John Muldowny. *TVA and the Dispossessed: The Resettlement of Population in the Norris Dam Area.* Knoxville: University of Tennessee Press, 1982. Detailed look at the relocation of poor people in the Norris Lake region as part of the TVA's program.

Neal, Harry E. *The People's Giant: The Story of TVA.* New York: J. Messer, 1970. Brief, easy-to-read, laudatory description of the history, accomplishments, and importance of the TVA.

Nurick, Aaron J. *Participation in Organizational Change: The TVA Experiment.* New York: Praeger, 1985. Description of certain aspects of progressive management attempted at the TVA, with case studies of employee participation and perceived benefits.

Owen, Marguerite. *The Tennessee Valley Authority.* New York: Praeger, 1973. Straightforward description of the TVA—its development and its activity.

BIOGRAPHICAL SOURCES

McCraw, Thomas K. *Morgan vs. Lilienthal: The Feud within the TVA.* Chicago: Loyola University Press, 1970. Treats the careers of the two leaders and their professional disagreement. (See McCraw in "Specialized Sources" above.)

Talbert, Roy. *FDR's Utopian: Arthur Morgan of the TVA.* Jackson: University of Mississippi Press, 1987. Informative biography of one of the TVA's leaders. Part of the Twentieth-century America series.

AUDIOVISUAL SOURCES

Tennessee Valley Authority. New York: A&E Home Video. 1997. Videocassette. Part of the twenty-three-volume Modern Marvels: Engineering Achievements of the 20th Century Series examining the stories of the construction of great engineering wonders. 50 minutes.

WORLD WIDE WEB

"From the New Deal to a New Century: A Short History of TVA." *TVA*.
    1997; updated 1998. http://www.tva.gov/whatis/history.htm In-
    formative historical sketch along with photographs.

37. Growth of Organized Labor during the 1930s

During the 1930s, organized labor grew significantly, its membership
trebling from 3.6 million in 1930 to more than 10 million in 1941.
New Deal legislation, particularly the National Labor Relations Act
(better known as the Wagner Act), aided this growth, as did the
efforts of New Dealers such as Secretary of Labor Frances Perkins.
So too did the unionization of unskilled workers that followed the
split within the ranks of the American Federation of Labor (AFL) and
the formation of the Congress of Industrial Organization (CIO) in
1938. The surge in CIO membership resulted largely from the successful unionization of the automobile and steel industries after bitter
strikes.

Suggestions for Term Papers

1. Discuss the impact of the New Deal on organized labor.
2. Discuss the split within the AFL and the formation of the CIO.
3. Discuss the unionization of the steel industry.
4. Discuss the unionization of the automobile industry.
5. Discuss the career of John L. Lewis as a labor leader.

Suggested Sources: See entries 32 and 34 for related items.

REFERENCE SOURCES

The ABC-CLIO Companion to the American Labor Movement. Paul F. Tay-
    lor. Santa Barbara, CA: ABC-CLIO, 1993. Alphabetically arranged
    entries of personalities, events, issues, and other areas. Good chro-
    nology. Part of the publisher's series.

Historical Dictionary of Organized Labor. James C. Docherty. Blue Ridge, PA: Scarecrow, 1996. Valuable for its comprehensive treatment of organized labor on an international scale. Places the American labor movement into perspective. Entries treat personalities, events, organizations, and other areas.

GENERAL SOURCES

Boyle, Kevin, ed. *Organized Labor and American Politics, 1894–1994: Essays on the Labor-Liberal Alliance.* Albany: State University of New York Press, 1998. Newly published collection of writings on liberalism and labor union political activity.

Clark, Gordon L. *Unions and Communities under Siege: American Communities and the Crisis of Organized Labor.* Cambridge, UK: Cambridge University Press, 1989. Study of industrial relations, with a focus on trade unions and community development, by a British scholar.

Draper, Alan. *Conflict of Interests: Organized Labor and the Civil Rights Movement in the South, 1954–1968.* Ithaca, NY: ILR, 1994. Good account of organized labor in the South and its relationship to race relations in the years following the emergence of labor as a political force. Published as part of Cornell Studies in Industrial and Labor Relations.

Foner, Philip S. *Organized Labor and the Black Worker, 1619–1981.* 2d ed. New York: International Publishers, 1982. Comprehensive general history of blacks and the labor struggle.

Goldfield, Michael. *The Decline of Organized Labor in the United States.* Chicago: University of Chicago Press, 1987. Examination of the setbacks organized labor has faced in the past few decades following its period of expansion.

Goode, Bill. *Infighting in the UAW: The 1946 Election and Ascendancy of Walter Reuther.* Westport, CT: Greenwood, 1994. Treats the struggle of Walter Reuther to become president of the United Auto Workers. Part of the publisher's Contributions in Labor Studies series.

Halpern, Rick, and Roger Horowitz. *Meatpackers: An Oral History of Black Packinghouse Workers and Their Struggle for Racial and Economic Equality.* New York: Twayne, 1996. A history of the union beginning in the 1930s to the 1960s. Based on interviews with members of the union.

Nelson, Daniel. *Shifting Fortunes: The Rise and Decline of American Labor, from the 1820s to the Present.* Chicago: Ivan R. Dee, 1997. Brief historical survey of the role of workers with attention to governmental policy as a factor.

Puette, William. *Through Jaundiced Eyes: How the Media View the Organized Labor*. Ithaca, NY: ILR, 1992. Interesting treatment of press coverage given to trade unions and to industrial relations.

Tomlins, Christopher L. *The State and the Unions: Labor Relations, Law and the Organized Labor Movement in America, 1880–1960*. New York: Cambridge University Press, 1985. General overview of labor legislation and its relationship to trade unions.

Zieger, Robert H., ed. *Organized Labor in the Twentieth-Century South*. Knoxville: University of Tennessee Press, 1991. Collection treating trade unions and race relations in the South.

SPECIALIZED SOURCES

Bernstein, Irving. *A Caring Society: The New Deal, the Worker, and the Great Depression, a History of the American Worker, 1933–1941*. Boston: Houghton Mifflin, 1985. Informative history of the working class from the Depression to the outbreak of World War II.

Horowitz, Ruth L. *Political Ideologies of Organized Labor: The New Deal Era*. New Brunswick, NJ: Transaction Books, 1978. Concise, informative examination of the period of the New Deal and the rise of the CIO.

Paulsen, George E. *A Living Wage for the Forgotten Man: The Quest for Fair Labor Standards, 1933–1941*. Selinsgrove, PA: Susquehanna University/Associated University Presses, 1996. First important study of the passage of the Fair Labor Standards Act in 1938 and its significance for labor history.

Roberts, John W. *Putting Foreign Policy to Work: The Role of Organized Labor in American Foreign Relations, 1932–1941*. New York: Garland, 1995. Detailed analysis of the considerations of organized labor in the development of foreign relations prior to World War II.

Simonds, Patricia. *The Founding of the AFL and the Rise of Organized Labor*. Englewood Cliffs, NJ: Silver Burdett, 1991. Easy-to-read sixty-four-page account of the AFL and other early unions in their struggle for better conditions. Good background material.

BIOGRAPHICAL SOURCES

Colman, Penny. *A Woman Unafraid: The Achievements of Frances Perkins*. New York: Atheneum, 1993. Easy-to-read brief biography of the first woman cabinet member and fighter for labor reform.

Dubofsky, Melvyn, and Warren Van Tyne. *John L. Lewis: A Biography*. Abr. ed. Urbana: University of Illinois Press, 1986. Well-focused and en-

lightening biography of the important labor leader. Admirably short-
ened to 387 pages from the initial 1977 effort of 619 pages.

Lichtenstein, Nelson. *Walter Reuther: The Most Dangerous Man in Detroit.*
(1995). Reprint. Urbana: University of Illinois Press, 1997. Detailed
and thorough biography of the life and career of one of the foremost
labor leaders.

O'Donnell, L. A. *Irish Voice and Organized Labor in America: A Biographical Study.* Westport, CT: Greenwood, 1997. Collective biography
of Irish American officials and leaders of the various trade unions.

AUDIOVISUAL SOURCES

The Great Depression and the New Deal. Wynnewood, PA: Schlessinger Me-
dia/Library Video. 1996. Videocassette. The eighteenth of twenty
titles in the United States History Video Collection, this 35-minute
presentation treats the Wagner Act and growth of unions, as well as
the Depression and growth of welfare.

Zwerin, Charlotte M. "Sit Down and Fight: Walter Reuther and the Rise
of the Auto Workers Union." *The American Experience.* Santa Monica, CA: PBS Home Video. 1993. Videocassette. 1-hour profile of
the life of Walter Reuther, with emphasis on the early development
of the union.

WORLD WIDE WEB

"Federal Labor Law." *History of U.S. Labor Law.* April 1995. http://gar-
net.berkeley.edu:3333/.labor/.files/.archive/.labor.law.html   Summary of important legislation, drawn from the *Congressional Digest*,
June–July 1993, beginning with the Clayton Act of 1914 and ending
with the Landrum-Griffin Act of 1959.

38. The Dust Bowl

Throughout the 1930s, severely arid conditions in parts of Arkansas,
Texas, and Oklahoma and on the Great Plains uprooted topsoil, turning these areas into huge dust bowls. In 1938, the worst year, an
estimated 850 million tons of soil were lost. Unable to produce or
to pay their mortgages, numerous farmers abandoned their home sites
and headed westward in search of work. Many of these "Arkies" and
"Okies" settled in California, whose population soared during the

1930s. Once there, many became underpaid, overworked migrant laborers, whose plight John Steinbeck vividly described in *The Grapes of Wrath* (1939).

Suggestions for Term Papers

1. Discuss the experiences of the Okies and other migrant farmers during the era of the Dust Bowl.
2. Why did California grow so rapidly during the 1930s?
3. Discuss the Great Depression novels of John Steinbeck.
4. Should the government have done more to combat the plight of farmers during the Depression?
5. What were the long-range consequences of the Dust Bowl?

Suggested Sources: See entry 32 for related items.

GENERAL SOURCES

Carter, Vernon G., and Tom Dale. *Topsoil and Civilization*. Rev. ed. Norman: University of Oklahoma Press, 1974. Agricultural history of the effects of topsoil on civilization and human ecology.

Mitchell, Don. *The Lie of the Land: Migrant Workers and the California Landscape*. Minneapolis: University of Minnesota Press, 1996. Historical overview of the plight of migrant agricultural workers in California during the twentieth century.

SPECIALIZED SOURCES

Andryszewski, Tricia. *The Dust Bowl: Disaster on the Plains*. Brookfield, CT: Milbrook, 1993. Easy-to-read and concise history of the severe dust storms that created the Dust Bowl during the Depression era.

Bonnifield, Mathew P. *The Dust Bowl: Men, Dirt, and Depression*. Albuquerque: University of New Mexico Press, 1979. Informative historical account of the depressed economic circumstances of the Great Plains caused by the dust storms.

Farris, John. *The Dust Bowl*. San Diego: Lucent Books, 1989. Easy-to-read, brief description of the severe drought in the Great Plains and the impact on the farmers.

Genzel, Bill. *Dust Bowl Descent*. Lincoln: University of Nebraska Press,

1984. Interesting pictorial work providing photographic records of the stark and dry landscape of the Great Plains during the time.

Gregory, James N. *American Exodus: The Dust Bowl Migration and Okie Culture in California.* New York: Oxford University Press, 1989. Informative social history of the western migration of rural families from the Great Plains and their relocation to California.

Hurt, R. Douglas. *The Dust Bowl: An Agricultural and Social History.* Chicago: Nelson-Hall, 1981. Brief historical overview of agricultural and social conditions of the Great Plains during the period of the dust storms.

Johnson, Vance. *Heaven's Tableland: The Dust Bowl Story.* (1947). Reprint. New York: Da Capo, 1974. Historical narrative of the New Deal and its impact on the depressed Great Plains states.

Shindo, Charles J. *Dust Bowl Migrants in the American Imagination.* Lawrence: University of Kansas Press, 1997. Collection of illustrations of migrant agricultural workers and their plight during the depressed period.

Stanley, Jerry. *Children of the Dust Bowl: The True Story of the School at Weedpatch Camp.* New York: Crown, 1992. Brief and easy-to-read account of the life led by families of migrant workers in a federal labor camp in California.

Stein, Walter J. *California and Dust Bowl Migration.* Westport, CT: Greenwood, 1973. Examination of conditions regarding the migration to California of people escaping from the Dust Bowl.

Worster, Donald. *Dust Bowl: The Southern Plains in the 1930s.* New York: Oxford University Press, 1979. Informative agricultural history of the regions affected by the dust storms during the Depression.

BIOGRAPHICAL SOURCES

Low, Ann M. *Dust Bowl Diary.* Lincoln: University of Nebraska Press, 1984. Case history based on the diary kept by a woman in North Dakota recording the depressed social and economic conditions of the time.

Rutland, Robert A. *A Boyhood in the Dust Bowl, 1926–1934.* Niwot: University Press of Colorado, 1995. Brief autobiography providing a social history of life and customs in a small town in Oklahoma during the Depression.

Svobida, Lawrence. *Farming the Dust Bowl: A First-hand Account from Kansas.* (1940, 1968). Reprint. Lawrence: University of Kansas Press, 1986. Provides insight into the struggle against droughts, dust storms, and soil erosion. Originally published as *An Empire of Dust* prior to World War II.

AUDIOVISUAL SOURCES

Steinbeck, John. *The Grapes of Wrath.* Los Angeles: FoxVideo, 1940. Videocassette. No better insight is provided into the plight of the Okies than was contained in this book made into a motion picture. Henry Fonda provides a stirring performance as a migrant worker in this 129-minute feature.

WORLD WIDE WEB

The Dust Bowl. January 1996. http://drylands.nasm.edu:1995/bowl.html Brief description along with four photographs illustrating the desolation of this natural catastrophe.

39. Establishment of Social Security (1935)

Despite the urgings of early twentieth-century reformers and the example of European nations, the United States lacked a national system of welfare assistance to its needy. Spurred on by the popular promises of the Townsend Plan and by the efforts of Secretary of Labor Frances Perkins, Congress in 1935 passed the Social Security Act. The measure focused on three major goals: (1) a pension plan for retirees age sixty-five and over, to be financed equally by employers and workers; (2) a more uniform state code of unemployment compensation; and (3) federal assistance to states for such welfare matters as aiding dependent children and disabled persons.

Suggestions for Term Papers

1. Analyze why European nations generally had a social security system before the United States did.
2. Was the Townsend Plan a realistic proposal?
3. Analyze the arguments both for and against social security during the New Deal era and today.
4. Discuss the origins of the Social Security Act.
5. Compare today's social security system in the United States with that of a European nation.

Suggested Sources: See entry 32 for related items.

REFERENCE SOURCES

Basic Readings in Social Security: 25th Anniversary of the Social Security Act, 1935–1960. U.S. Department of Health, Education and Welfare Library. (1960). Reprint. New York: Greenwood, 1968. Useful bibliography of publications treating social security and public welfare.

Social Security, Its Development from Roosevelt to Reagan. Alva W. Stewart. Monticello, IL: Vance Bibliographies, 1982. One of the Vance bibliographies done by and for librarians; thirteen-page listing of pertinent publications.

GENERAL SOURCES

Eliot, Thomas H. *Recollections of the New Deal: When the People Mattered.* Boston: Northeastern University Press, 1995. Excellent historical treatment by one of the chief designers of the Social Security Act. Well written and interesting.

Haber, Carole, and Brian Grattan. *Old Age and the Search for Security: An American Social History.* Bloomington: Indiana University Press, 1993. A brief, informative history of the quest for some form of security for the elderly.

Kirkendall, Richard S. *Social Scientists and Farm Politics in the Age of Roosevelt.* (1966). Reprint. Ames: Iowa State University Press, 1982. Examines the place of agriculture within governmental economic policy embracing social services to its citizens. Initially published by the University of Missouri.

Neuberger, Richard L., and Kelley Loe. *An Army of the Aged, a History and Analysis of the Townsend Old Age Pension Plan.* (1936). Reprint. New York: Da Capo, 1973. Early examination of the Townsend National Recovery Plan, proposed prior to the Social Security Act.

van der Linden, Marcel et al., eds. *Social Security Mutualism: The Comparative History of Mutual Benefit Societies.* New York: Peter Lang, 1996. Detailed account of the origin, growth, and development of social security systems around the world.

SPECIALIZED SOURCES

Altmeyer, Arthur J. *The Formative Years of Social Security.* Madison: University of Wisconsin Press, 1966. Examination of the early years of social security; identifies official documents from 1935 to 1965.

Conkin, Paul K. *FDR and the Origins of the Welfare State.* New York: Crowell, 1967. Brief and interesting treatment of Roosevelt's efforts in pushing through New Deal legislation and security measures.

Douglas, Paul H. *Social Security in the United States: An Analysis and Appraisal of the Federal Social Security Act.* (1936). Reprint. Westport, CT: Greenwood, 1972. Thorough and detailed early analyis of the impact of the social security system in the United States.

Duncan, John I. *A Guide to Expanding Social Services to the Blind Under Title XX of the Social Security Act.* New York: American Foundation for the Blind, 1976. Good example of the manner in which social security has been expanded through the years to embrace the needs of various population groups. Brief guide to benefits.

McKinley, Charles, and Robert W. Frase. *Launching Social Security: A Capture-and-Record Account, 1935–1937.* Madison: University of Wisconsin Press, 1970. Detailed and thorough history of the start-up procedures and emergence of the social security system, with a good exposition on the Social Security Act.

Witte, Edwin E. *The Development of the Social Security Act: A Memorandum on the History of the Committee on Economic Security and Drafting and Legislative History of the Social Security Act.* Madison: University of Wisconsin Press, 1962. Examination of the work of the committee in drafting and submitting the Social Security Act.

BIOGRAPHICAL SOURCES

Morris, Jeffrey B. *The FDR Way.* Minneapolis: Lerner, 1996. Brief easy-to-read description of the life and presidency of FDR, with an emphasis on his important decisions, such as social security.

AUDIOVISUAL SOURCES

Social Security: Mainstream USA. Kent, CT: Creative Arts Television Archive, 1987. Videocassette. 17-minute informative analysis of the system and how it operates.

WORLD WIDE WEB

Social Security History Page. September 1997. http://www.ssa.gov/history/ A mix of material of both general and scholarly interest. Includes a brief history, text of the 1935 law as well as the current law, 1937 rulings of the Supreme Court, and a chronology.

40. Good Neighbor Policy

Since the Spanish-American War, the United States had won the enmity of Latin American nations for its repeated intervention in their affairs. Relations began to improve, however, during the 1920s. President Hoover toured Latin America and in 1930 allowed publication of the Clark Memorandum, which repudiated the Roosevelt Corollary to the Monroe Doctrine. In the 1930s the United States expanded this "policy of the good neighbor." Under President Franklin D. Roosevelt, all troops were withdrawn from Haiti and Nicaragua, the Platt Amendment affecting Cuba was terminated, the temptation to intervene in Mexico, which was nationalizing foreign oil interests, was avoided, and unilateral intervention, except in instances recognized by international law, was officially renounced.

Suggestions for Term Papers

1. Discuss the origins and consequences of the Roosevelt Corollary to the Monroe Doctrine.
2. Discuss U.S. intervention in Latin American affairs from Presidents Theodore Roosevelt to Calvin Coolidge.
3. Compare the Latin American policy of President Herbert Hoover with that of President Franklin D. Roosevelt.
4. What were the consequences of the Good Neighbor Policy?
5. Why did the United States change its Latin American foreign policy from intervention to that of the Good Neighbor?

Suggested Sources: See entry 32 for related items.

REFERENCE SOURCES

A Reference Guide to Latin American History. James D. Henderson et al. Armonk, NY: M. E. Sharpe, 1998. Useful survey of Latin American history providing a descriptive chronology, thematic survey of topics and issues, and over 300 biographical sketches. With maps, photographs, and a bibliography.

GENERAL SOURCES

Cohen, Warren I. *Empire without Tears: America's Foreign Relations, 1921–1933.* New York: Knopf, 1987. Concise description of foreign policy in the years just prior to adoption of the Good Neighbor Policy. Good background material.

Curry, Earl R. *Hoover's Dominican Diplomacy and the Origins of the Good Neighbor Policy.* New York: Garland, 1979. Examination of Latin American policy under Hoover, with the beginnings of Roosevelt's good neighbor approach.

Roosevelt, Franklin D. *Development of United States Foreign Policy.* Washington, DC: U.S. Government Printing Office, 1942. Government publication compiling FDR's addresses, messages, and announcements up to 1942 regarding foreign policy matters, beginning with the announcement of the Good Neighbor Policy in 1933. (See World Wide Web entry.)

SPECIALIZED SOURCES

Fejes, Fred. *Imperialism, Media, and the Good Neighbor: New Deal Foreign Policy and United States Shortwave Broadcasting to Latin America.* Norwood, NJ: Ablex, 1986. Examination of the place of broadcasting to Latin America within the foreign policy structure of the Good Neighbor Policy.

Gellman, Irwin F. *Roosevelt and Batista: Good Neighbor Diplomacy in Cuba, 1933–1945.* Albuquerque: University of New Mexico Press, 1973. Interesting and informative treatment of foreign relations with Cuba during the Batista period.

Green, David. *The Containment of Latin America: A History of the Myths and Realities of the Good Neighbor Policy.* Chicago: Quadrangle Books, 1971. Historical overview of the conditions resulting from implementation of the Good Neighbor Policy in Latin America.

Grow, Michael. *Good Neighbor Policy and Authoritarianism in Paraguay: United States Economic Expansion and Great-Power Rivalry in Latin America during World War II.* Lawrence: Regents Press of Kansas, 1981. Concise, useful examination of the nature of authoritarian politics in Paraguay alongside economic relations with the United States.

Pike, Frederick B. *FDR's Good Neighbor Policy: Sixty Years of Generally Gentle Chaos.* Austin: University of Texas Press, 1995. Detailed treatment of the Good Neighbor Policy, its implementation, and its effects some sixty years later.

Roorda, Eric. *The Dictator Next Door: The Good Neighbor Policy and the Trujillo Regime in the Dominican Republic, 1930–1945.* Durham,

NC: Duke University Press, 1998. Recent examination of the Trujillo years and foreign relations under the Good Neighbor Policy.

Steward, Dick. *Trade and Hemisphere: The Good Neighbor Policy and Reciprocal Trade*. Columbia: University of Missouri Press, 1975. Overview of commerce and economic relations with Latin American countries during the period of the Good Neighbor Policy.

Wood, Bryce. *The Dismantling of the Good Neighbor Policy*. Austin: University of Texas Press, 1985. Good exposition of the decline of the policy with special emphasis on the Argentine situation with Péron.

———. *The Making of the Good Neighbor Policy*. New York: Norton, 1967. Thorough and well-documented examination of the origin and development of the Good Neighbor policy. Extensive bibliographic references.

Woods, Randall B. *The Roosevelt Foreign-Policy Establishment and the "Good Neighbor": The United States and Argentina*. Lawrence: Regents Press of Kansas, 1979. Detailed description of foreign relations with Argentina during World War II.

AUDIOVISUAL SOURCES

History of U.S. Foreign Relations—A Series. Springfield, VA: National Audio-Visual Center, 1979. 4 videocassettes. Docudrama begins with "An Age of Revolutions" and traces the development of American foreign policy through its increasing maturity as a nation. Final volume is "The Road to Interdependence." Each cassette is 30 minutes.

WORLD WIDE WEB

"Addresses and Messages of Franklin D. Roosevelt." *U.S. Foreign Policy Development under FDR*. June 1996. http://www.sunsite.unc.edu/pha/7–2-188/188title.html Printed as Senate Document No. 188 in 1942 (see General Sources entry above), this is a compilation of official source material intended to present the chronological development of foreign policy from 1933 to February 1942. Can click on any of the documents from the table of contents.

41. Pre-Pearl Harbor Debate between Isolationists and Interventionists

As international conflicts and crises erupted during the mid-1930s—the Italian-Ethiopian War, the Spanish Civil War, Germany's reoccupation of the Rhineland, the Munich Pact, Japan's war against China—both neutrality legislation and popular opinion kept the United States aloof. Detachment became more difficult when World War II erupted. The America First Committee spearheaded the drive for continued isolationism, but others, such as the Committee to Defend America by Aiding the Allies, urged differently. Meanwhile, President Franklin D. Roosevelt successfully fought for changes in the neutrality laws, executed a destroyers-for-bases deal with Great Britain, and convinced Congress to pass the Lend-Lease Act. Pearl Harbor ended the isolationist-internationalist debate.

Suggestions for Term Papers

1. Analyze the isolationist movement from the mid-1930s until Pearl Harbor.
2. Discuss the participation of American volunteers in the Spanish Civil War.
3. Discuss the consequences of the Lend-Lease Act.
4. Analyze the debate over foreign policy and the 1940 presidential election.
5. Discuss American fascist organizations and sympathizers in the years before Pearl Harbor.

Suggested Sources: See entry 40 for related items.

REFERENCE SOURCES

The ABC Companion to the American Peace Movement. Christine A. Lunardini. Santa Barbara, CA: ABC-CLIO, 1995. Concentrates on people, organizations, and events attempting to keep the United States out of war or promoting peace during the twentieth century.

Anti-intervention: A Bibliographical Introduction to Isolationism and Pacifism from World War I to the Early Cold War. Justus D. Doenecke. New York: Garland, 1987. Extensive bibliographic coverage of pacifism, neutrality, and foreign relations.

Guide to American Foreign Relations since 1700. Richard Dean Burns, ed. Santa Barbara, CA: ABC-CLIO, 1983. Covers isolationism, manifest destiny, national security, and other social, political, and economic topics.

The Literature of Isolationism: A Guide to Non-Interventionist Scholarship, 1930–1972. Justus D. Doenecke. Colorado Springs: R. Myles, 1972. Identifies writings on pacifism and foreign relations.

GENERAL SOURCES

Chalberg, John C., ed. *Isolationism: Opposing Viewpoints.* San Diego: Greenhaven, 1995. Good topical treatment of pro and con on foreign relations, neutrality, and isolationism in the United States.

Foster, H. Schuyler. *Activism Replaces Isolationism: U.S. Public Attitudes, 1940–1975.* Washington, DC: Foxhall, 1983. Traces the dispute from prewar 1940 to the fall of Vietnam.

Powaski, Ronald E. *Toward an Entangling Alliance: American Isolationism, Internationalism, and Europe, 1901–1950.* Westport, CT: Greenwood, 1991. Good examination of U.S. neutrality issues with Europe for the first half of the twentieth century.

Rossini, Daniela. *From Theodore Roosevelt to FDR: Internationalism and Isolationism in American Foreign Policy.* Staffordshire, UK: Ryburn Publishing/Keele University Press, 1995. Brief examination of foreign relations during the first half of the twentieth century.

SPECIALIZED SOURCES

Guinsburg, Thomas N. *The Pursuit of Isolationism in the United States from Versailles to Pearl Harbor.* New York: Garland, 1982. Provides a detailed examination of U.S. foreign relations between the wars.

Holbe, Paul Sothe, *Isolationism and Interventionism, 1932–1941.* Chicago: Rand McNally, 1967. Sixty-page overview of U.S. foreign relations over the critical nine-year period.

Jonas, Manfred. *Isolationism in America, 1935–1941.* (1966). Reprint. Chicago: Imprint Publications, 1990. Publication treating in depth the critical period before World War II.

Ketchum, Richard M. *The Borrowed Years, 1938–1941: America on the Way to War.* New York: Anchor Books, 1990. The contest between internationalism and isolationism in the prewar years.

Roots, Roger. *Montana's Lost Cause: Isolationism and the Montana Congressional Delegation, 1937–1946.* Big Timber, MT: Sweet Grass, 1997. Recent study of isolationism in the state of Montana.

Schacht, John N., ed. *Three Faces of Midwestern Isolationism: Gerald P. Nye, Robert E. Wood, John L. Lewis.* Iowa City: Center for the Study of the Recent History of the United States, 1981. Collection of papers presented at a conference under the sponsorship of the publisher.

BIOGRAPHICAL SOURCES

Smith, Glenn H. *Langer of North Dakota: A Study in Isolationism, 1940–1959.* New York: Garland, 1979. Good study of Senator William Langer's politics. From the publisher's Modern American History series.

AUDIOVISUAL RESOURCES

Potter, Anthony. *Between the Wars. Return to Isolationism.* Great Neck, NY: 8 videocassettes. Relevant topical treatment is provided in this 8-part series; the first one, *Versailles: The Lost Peace/Return to Isolationism*, is a 60-minute reissue of the original 1978 video by Alan Landsburg Productions.

WORLD WIDE WEB

Churney, Linda J. *America's Wars, 1898–1945.* 1977. http://www.yale.edu/ynhti/curriculum/units/1978/3/78.03.06.x.html   Detailed course guide from the Yale–New Haven Teaching Institute; excellent five-page narrative of prewar U.S. policy as an evolutionary development from the Spanish-American period. Fine outline and good bibliographies for teachers and students.

42. Pearl Harbor (1941)

Japanese-American relations, already strained, deteriorated in July 1941 when Japan declared a protectorate over French Indochina and the United States froze Japanese assets and extended the list of embargoed goods to include oil. Triumphing over their nation's peace faction, Japanese militarists then planned a secret attack on Pearl Harbor, the major U.S. military outpost in the Pacific. Although the United States had broken Japan's secret diplomatic code (the Purple Cipher) and knew of a forthcoming attack somewhere against U.S., British, or Dutch possessions, preparedness at Pearl Harbor proved woefully insufficient. The Japanese attack on December 7, 1941, left 2,400 Americans dead, as well as 150 planes and several battleships destroyed. Congress declared war the following day.

Suggestions for Term Papers

1. Was Japan's attack on Pearl Harbor inevitable?
2. Discuss the decoding of the Purple Cipher and its consequences.
3. Analyze the diplomatic attempts to resolve tensions between Japan and the United States.
4. Discuss why Pearl Harbor was not adequately prepared for an attack.
5. Discuss the effect of the Pearl Harbor attack on the West Coast.

Suggested Sources: See entries 43, 45, 46, and 47 for related items.

REFERENCE SOURCES

The Pacific War Encyclopedia. James F. Dunnigan and Albert A. Nofi. New York: Facts on File, 1998. 2 vols. Detailed history by military experts from multiple perspectives. Treats all aspects, including personalities and African American influences. Dramatic black and white photographs, as well as numerous charts and tables.

GENERAL SOURCES

Costello, John. *Days of Infamy.* New York: Pocket, 1994. New study of declassified materials argues that Admiral Husband E. Kimmel and Lieutenant General Walter C. Short were unjustly blamed for the disasters of Pearl Harbor and the Philippines as well.

Hoyt, Edwin P. *Japan's War: The Great Pacific Conflict.* New York: McGraw-Hill, 1986. Why Japan started the war, why the United States was unprepared, and how Japan's buildup was carried out.

Isserman, Maurice. *World War II.* New York: Facts on File, 1991. From Pearl Harbor to Japan's surrender on the U.S.S. *Missouri*, an accurate, gripping account of the U.S. experience.

SPECIALIZED SOURCES

Beach, Edward L. *Scapegoats: A Defense of Kimmel and Short at Pearl Harbor.* Washington, DC: Naval Institute Press, 1995. Blames the Pearl Harbor disaster on midlevel U.S. intelligence officers rather than the commanding officers.

Clark, Thurston. *Pearl Harbor Ghosts: A Journey to Hawaii Then and Now.* New York: Morrow, 1991. First-person testimony from a cross-section of Japanese, Japanese Americans, native Hawaiians, members of the Caucasian elite, and servicemen stationed at Pearl Harbor on the fateful day.

Clausen, Henry C., and Bruce Lee. *Pearl Harbor: Final Judgment.* New York: Crown, 1992. Places the blame for the attack on key middle-echelon intelligence officers and debunks many of the previous conspiracy theories.

Goldstein, Donald M., and Katherine V. Dillon. *The Pearl Harbor Papers: Inside the Japanese Plans.* Dulles, VA: Brassey's 1993. Details the Japanese plans of the raid with a wide range of political, diplomatic, and military topics.

Honan, William H. *The Untold Story of How Journalist Hector C. Bywater Devised the Plans That Led to Pearl Harbor.* New York: St. Martin's, 1991. Argues that Japanese admiral Yamamoto drew the inspiration for his plan from Bywater's 1925 novel, *The Great Pacific War: A History of the American-Japanese Campaign of 1931–1933.*

Love, Robert W., Jr., ed. *Pearl Harbor Revisited.* New York: St. Martin's 1995. Collection of conference papers on the attack. Part of the Franklin and Eleanor Roosevelt Institute Series on Diplomatic and Economic History.

Prange, Gordon, *At Dawn We Slept: Untold Story of Pearl Harbor.* New York: McGraw-Hill, 1981. Most comprehensive text to date on all aspects of the attack and how the U.S. mission failed to notice the signs of an imminent Japanese attack.

Slackman, Michael. *Target Pearl Harbor.* Honolulu: University of Hawaii Press, 1990. Examines American attitudes toward the Japanese and how those attitudes affected strategy.

Toland, John. *Infamy: Pearl Harbor and Its Aftermath.* New York: Doubleday, 1982. The most complete account of the inquiries into the responsibility for Pearl Harbor and the blame placed on Admiral Kimmel.

Weintraub, Stanley. *Long Day's Journey into War: December 7, 1941.* New York: Truman Talley, 1991. Highly readable narrative as individuals are caught up in the event; nonjudgmental in nature.

Worth, Jr., Roland H. *Pearl Harbor: Selected Testimonies, Fully Indexed, from the Congressional Hearings (1943–1946) and Prior Investigations of the Events Leading Up to the Attack.* Jefferson, NC: McFarland, 1993. Excellent source on the congressional hearings about Pearl Harbor.

BIOGRAPHICAL SOURCES

Hoyt, Edwin P. *Three Military Leaders.* New York: Kodansha, 1993. Studies the careers and military leadership of Japanese admirals Togo and Yamamoto, and General Yamashita.

Raymer, Edward C. *Descent into Darkness: Pearl Harbor, 1941: A Navy Diver's Memoir*. Novato, CA: Presidio, 1996. The story of the salvage efforts on sunken and damaged ships at Pearl Harbor and throughout the Pacific.

AUDIOVISUAL SOURCES

Pearl Harbor: The Eyewitness Story. Wynnwood, PA: Schlessinger/Library Video, 1988. Videocassette. Reenactments, gripping eyewitness stories, and rare historic footage, including captured Japanese war footage in this 70-minute presentation.

WORLD WIDE WEB

"Radio Days—Pearl Harbor." Radio News. November 1996 http:// otr.com/pearl.html Brief narrative and radio report of the attack.

43. Internment of Japanese Americans during World War II (1942–1944)

Japan's attack on Pearl Harbor aggravated existing anti-Japanese sentiment in the United States, particularly on the West Coast, where most Japanese Americans lived and where sabotage and an attack by Japan were most feared. President Roosevelt in February 1942 ordered the evacuation of more than 100,000 Nisei (Japanese born in the United States) and Issei (emigrant Japanese) to internment camps farther east, an action later upheld by the Supreme Court (*Korematsu* v. *United States*, 1944). First forced to sell or entrust their possessions, the internees endured humiliating camp conditions. Nonetheless, many Japanese American youths volunteered for military service. All internment camps were closed by late 1944. In 1983 Congress awarded roughly $20,000 to each internment survivor.

Suggestions for Term Papers

1. Were Japanese Americans a threat to the nation's security after Pearl Harbor?

2. Analyze why the decision was made to intern Japanese Americans.

3. Discuss the reactions, then and now, of Japanese Americans to their internment.

4. Discuss the contributions of Japanese Americans to the war effort.

5. Discuss the opposition to the internment of Japanese Americans.

Suggested Sources: See also entries 42 and 46 for related items.

REFERENCE SOURCES

Encyclopedia of Multiculturalism. Susan Auerbach, ed. New York: Marshall Cavendish, 1994. 6 vols. Comprehensive reference source dealing with all aspects of pluralism, multiculturalism, and ethnology in the United States.

GENERAL SOURCES

Fremon, David K. *Japanese-American Internment in American History.* Springfield, NJ: Enslow, 1996. An easy-to-read and concise book about the roots and ramifications of the decision to imprison Japanese immigrants and Japanese American citizens during World War II.

O'Brien, David J., and Stephen S. Fugita. *The Japanese American Experience.* Bloomington: Indiana University Press, 1991. Studies the history of Japanese Americans and Asians in the United States. Part of the publishers' Minorities in Modern America series.

Takezawa, Yasuko I. *Breaking the Silence: Redress and Japanese American Ethnicity.* Ithaca: Cornell University Press, 1995. Studies Japanese Americans in the Seattle area and how the internment affected their lives and ethnic identity. Part of the publisher's Anthropology of Contemporary Issues series.

SPECIALIZED SOURCES

Baker, Lillian, and Karl R. Bendetsen. *American and Japanese Relocation in World War II Fact, Fiction and Fallacy.* Medford, OR: Webb, 1996. The only book on the relocation of Japanese, Germans, and Italians from West Coast military areas; explains the difference between a relocation center and an internment camp.

Daniels, Roger, and Eric Foner, eds. *Prisoners without Trial: Japanese Americans in World War II.* New York: Hill & Wang, 1993. Explains how and why the incarceration of Japanese Americans occurred during World War II. Part of the publisher's Critical Issue series.

Daniels, Roger, et. al. eds. *Japanese Americans: From Relocation to Redress.* Seattle: University of Washington Press, 1992. Collection of conference papers dealing with the evacuation and relocation of Japanese Americans and reparations.

Hata, Donald, et al. *Japanese Americans and World War II: Exclusion, Internment and Redress.* Wheeling, IL: Harlan Davidson, 1995. The narrative of Japanese Americans and their attempts for redress after World War II.

Hayashi, Ann K. *Face of the Enemy, Heart of a Patriot: Japanese-American Internment Narratives.* New York: Garland, 1995. Heartbreaking tales of Japanese Americans relocated in the internment camps.

Kashima, Tetsuden. *Personal Justice Denied: Report on the Commission on Wartime Relocation and Internment of Civilians.* Seattle: University of Washington Press, 1996. Government report detailing numbers and locations of wartime relocations; also documents civil rights violations and redress under legislation of 1988.

Levine, Ellen. *A Fence Away from Freedom: Japanese Americans and World War II.* New York: Putnam, 1995. The bitter experience of thirty-five Japanese American children who were in the internment camps and their redress under the 1988 Civil Rights Act.

Nishimoto, Richard S., and Lane R. Hirabayashi. *Inside an American Concentration Camp: Japanese American Resistance at Poston, Arizona.* Tuscon: University of Arizona Press, 1995. Part of the Japanese American Evacuation and Resettlement Study by the University of California—an in-depth account of Japanese American work, leisure, and resistance to the policies of the War Relocation Authority.

Okihiro, Gary Y. *Whispered Silences: Japanese Americans and World War II.* Seattle: University of Washington Press, 1996. Haunting photographs, oral histories, and essays from family history and personal accounts of Japanese Americans at various detention camps throughout the West.

Taylor, Sandra C. *Jewel of the Desert: Japanese American Internment at Topaz.* Berkeley: University of California Press, 1994. Explores the impact on the Issei and Nisei of the San Francisco Bay area, with analysis of the associations and institutions that held the group together before the war. Examines the effects of internment on that network and the people who were part of it.

Weglyn, Michi Nishiura. *Years of Infamy: The Untold Story of America's Concentration Camps.* Seattle: University of Washington Press, 1996. One of the most thoroughly documented accounts of Japanese American internment during World War II. Introduction by James Michener.

BIOGRAPHICAL SOURCES

Drinnon, Richard, and Dillon S. Myer. *Keeper of Concentration Camps: Dillon S. Myer and American Racism.* Berkeley: University of California Press, 1987. Interesting biography of the man who was in charge of the relocation camps for Japanese Americans (and earlier ones for Native Americans).

Fiset, Louis. *Imprisoned Apart: The World War II Correspondence of an Issei Couple.* Seattle: University of Washington Press, 1998. The wartime letters of a Japanese American couple during the internment. Part of the publisher's Scott and Laurie Oki Series in Asian American Studies.

Ichihashi, Yamato. Edited by Gordon H. Chang. *Morning Glory, Evening Shadow: Yamato Ichihashi and His Internment Writings, 1942–1945.* Stanford, CA: Stanford University Press, 1996. Biographical narrative of the experiences and writings of the author during his internment. Part of the publisher's Asian America series.

AUDIOVISUAL SOURCES

World War II. Wynewood, PA: Schlessinger Media, 1996. Videocassette. Volume 19 of the 20-part United States History Video Collection. Japanese-American internment is one aspect of the war that is covered in this 35-minute video.

WORLD WIDE WEB

"Links to Other Sites on the Japanese American Internment." *A More Perfect Union: Japanese Americans and the U.S. Constitution.* 1996. http://www.cruzio.com/~sclibs/history/ww2/links.html A lengthy array from the Santa Cruz Public Library of relevant web sites and documents treating every aspect of the internment.

44. The Manhattan Project (1942–1945)

In October 1939 Albert Einstein warned President Roosevelt that German scientists were trying to produce a bomb from atomic energy and that such a weapon in the hands of Adolf Hitler could prove disastrous. Roosevelt agreed and in 1942 launched the top-secret Manhattan Project, which under the command of General Leslie R.

Groves ultimately cost $2 billion and generated the atomic bomb. The first successful atomic chain reaction took place at the University of Chicago; materials for the bomb were produced in Oak Ridge, Tennessee, and Hanford, Washington; the bomb itself was completed and then tested on July 16, 1945, in New Mexico through the efforts of J. Robert Oppenheimer and other scientists.

Suggestions for Term Papers

1. Discuss the origins of the Manhattan Project.
2. Analyze the difficulties in building the atomic bomb.
3. Discuss the contributions of refugee scientists to the Manhattan Project.
4. Compare the contributions of J. Robert Oppenheimer and Leslie R. Groves to the Manhattan Project.
5. What were the reactions of those who witnessed the bomb test at Alamogordo?

Suggested Sources: See entry 49 for related items.

REFERENCE SOURCES

The Atomic Bomb: An Annotated Bibliography. Hans G. Graetzer and Larry M. Browning, Lanham, MD: Scarecrow, 1992. A comprehensive bibliography devoted to the atom bomb.

GENERAL SOURCES

Chappell, John D. *Before the Bomb: How America Approached the End of the Pacific War.* Lexington, KY: University of Kentucky Press, 1996. Examination of public opinion and the ending of the war.

Hales, Peter B. *Atomic Spaces: Living on the Manhattan Project.* Urbana: University of Illinois Press, 1997. The Manhattan Project changed ideas, beliefs, social systems, and racial, sexual, and economic relations; new languages, new diseases, and new forms of American culture were introduced.

Holloway, Rachel L. *In the Matter of J. Robert Oppenheimer: Politics, Rhetoric, and Self-Defense.* New York: Praeger, 1993. Explores the part that rhetoric played in Oppenheimer's removal from government service and shows the interaction between political and scientific terminologies in American discourse.

Kathryn, Ronald L., et al., eds. *The Plutonium Story: The Journals of Professor Glenn T. Seaborg, 1939–1946.* New York: Battelle Press, 1994. Chronicles the research for and discovery of plutonium and its chemistry and production.

Weintraub, Stanley. *The Last Great Victory: The End of World War II, July/ August 1945.* New York: Truman Talley, 1995. Chronicle of events including the Potsdam Conference, the atomic bomb, the campaign against Japan, and postwar diplomacy between Truman and Stalin.

SPECIALIZED SOURCES

Fermi, Rachel, et al. *Picturing the Bomb: Photographs from the Secret World of the Manhattan Project.* New York: H. Abrams, 1995. Published to coincide with the Manhattan Project's fiftieth anniversary. Presents compelling images of America's building of the atom bomb.

Groves, Leslie. *Now It Can Be Told: The Story of the Manhattan Project.* (1962). Reprint. New York: Da Capo, 1975. A detailed and informative account by a key figure in the Manhattan Project.

Hoddeson, Lillian et al., eds. *Critical Assembly: A Technical History of Los Alamos during the Oppenheimer Years, 1943–1945.* Cambridge: Cambridge University Press, 1993. Detailed and thorough examination of two critical years of the Manhattan Project.

Rhodes, Richard. *The Making of the Atomic Bomb.* New York: Simon & Schuster, 1986. Deals with the history of the people and the science that preceded and then made possible the development of the bomb.

Serber, Robert. *The Los Alamos Primer: The First Lectures on How to Build an Atomic Bomb.* Berkeley: University of California Press, 1992. Annotated lectures on how to build an atomic bomb with an introduction by historian Richard Rhodes. Very readable for the lay reader.

BIOGRAPHICAL SOURCES

Ermenc, Joseph J., ed. *Atomic Bomb Scientists: Memoirs, 1939–1945.* Westport, CT: Meckler, 1989. Based on extensive interviews with nine major contributors, including Leslie R. Groves.

Goodchild, Peter. *J. Robert Oppenheimer: Shatterer of Worlds.* Boston: Houghton Mifflin, 1981. Published in conjunction with the BBC television series, a good biographical study of Oppenheimer and his impact.

Larsen, Rebecca. *Oppenheimer and the Atomic Bomb.* Danbury, CT: Franklin

Watts, 1988. Easy-to-read book that covers Oppenheimer's life in a thorough, objective manner, quoting heavily from his memoirs.

Rummel, Jack. *Robert Oppenheimer: Dark Prince.* New York: Facts on File, 1992. Recounts the scientist's interest in atomic theory and explains the scientific and historic developments that influenced his studies and work.

Smith, Alice K., and Charles Weiner, eds. *Robert Oppenheimer: Letters and Recollections.* Cambridge, MA: Harvard University Press, 1980. Provides insight into Oppenheimer, the man and the scientist, through his correspondence and reflections.

York, Herbert F. *The Advisors: Oppenheimer, Teller, and the Superbomb.* (1976). Reprint. Palo Alto, CA: Stanford University Press, 1989. Interesting and revealing biographical history of the two major scientific minds concerned with the atomic and the hydrogen bomb.

AUDIOVISUAL SOURCES

Peeples, Janet, et al. *The Day After Trinity: J. Robert Oppenheimer and the Atomic Bomb.* Santa Monica, CA: Pyramid Films, 1981. 2 videocassettes. 90-minute documentary on the life of Oppenheimer, with emphasis on his role in the development of the atomic bomb.

WORLD WIDE WEB

"Fat Man and Little Boy: Birth of the Atomic Bomb." *American Airpower Heritage Museum Gallery Tour.* February 1996. http://avdig est.com/aahm/tratmgal.html Leads to excellent illustrated narratives on various phases of the Manhattan Project, as well as subsequent developments and decisions regarding the bomb.

45. Women and World War II

Women contributed to wartime efforts in both the military and on the home front. Some 200,000 enlisted for military service, most in either the Women's Army Corps (WAC) or the Women Accepted for Voluntary Emergency Service (WAVES). The number of wartime women workers increased by nearly 7 million, and by 1945 they constituted slightly more than one-third of the industrial labor force. The poster image of Rosie the Riveter became the patriotic icon for these women, who were doing work previously deemed fitting only for men. With the end of the fighting, most women, voluntarily or not, left their wartime positions and returned to private life.

Suggestions for Term Papers

1. Discuss the role of women in the military during World War II.
2. Did wartime industries discriminate against women?
3. Compare the contributions of women in wartime industries during World War II with those during World War I.
4. Discuss the legacy of wartime work for American women.
5. Discuss the contributions of female entertainers to the war effort.

Suggested Sources: See entries 42 and 46 for related items.

REFERENCE SOURCES

Women and the Military: An Encyclopedia. Victoria Sherrow. Santa Barbara, CA: ABC-CLIO, 1996. An outstanding reference source that chronicles both the contributions and difficulties women have experienced within the U.S. military.

SPECIALIZED SOURCES

Colman, Penny. *Rosie the Riveter: Women Working on the Home Front.* New York: Crown, 1995. Describes how society was changed and women's lives transformed when they held "men's" jobs during World War II.

Gruhzit-Hoyt, Olga. *They Also Served: American Women in World War II.* Secaucus, NJ: Birch Lane, 1995. Brief sketches of the various organizations in which women served including the auxiliaries of the services, the American Red Cross, the Women's Air Force Service Pilots, and the Office of Strategic Services.

Keil, Sally V. *Those Wonderful Women in Their Flying Machines: The Unknown Heroines of World War II.* New York: Four Directions Press, 1994. Recounts the story of over 1,000 women pilots who flew in the military as part of the Women's Air Force Service Pilots. From 1942 to 1944, these pilots flew over 60 million miles, and thirty-eight women lost their lives in services.

Larson, C. Kay. *Til I Come Marching Home: A Brief History of American Women in World War II.* Pasadena, MD: Minerva Center, 1995.

Describes the achievements of women who participated in World War II. Previously these stories were buried in newspaper files.

Meyer, Leisa D. *Creating GI-Jane: Sexuality and Power in the Women's Army Corps in World War II.* New York: Columbia University Press, 1996. Recent informative account of the sociological implications of women in the U.S. Army.

O'Brien, Kenneth Paul, and Lynn H. Parsons, eds. *The Home-Front War: World War II and American Society.* Westport, CT: Greenwood, 1995. A collection of essays examining the impact of World War II on Americans as it influenced gender, race, class, and ethnicity. Part of the publisher's Contributions in American History series.

Poulos, Paula N., ed. *A Women's War Too: U.S. Women in the Military in World War II.* Washington, DC: National Archives and Records Administration, 1996. Papers presented at a conference devoted to the examination of the role of women in World War II.

Putney, Martha S. *When the Nation Was in Need: Blacks in the Women's Army.* Blue Ridge Summit, PA: Scarecrow, 1993. Story of the 6,500 black women who served during World War II, as well as the range of roles in which they were employed.

Tomblin, Barbara B. *G.I. Nightingales: The Army Nurse Corps in World War II.* Lexington: University of Kentucky Press, 1996. Informative narrative history of U.S. Army nurses during World War II. Begins with mobilization for war, leading to service in the Pacific, North Africa, Europe, and China-Burma-India and at home.

Weatherford, Doris. *American Women and World War II.* New York: Facts on File, 1990. Social history using personal accounts to examine the diverse roles American women played on the home front and in the military.

Wise, Nancy B., and Christy Wise. *A Mouthful of Rivets: Women at Work in World War II.* San Francisco: Jossey-Bass, 1994. An interesting and revealing collection of the stories of 125 women who took "men's jobs" when they were in the service: welders, truck drivers, factory workers, pilots, and, of course, riveters. The principal author served in the Office of War Information.

Zeinert, Karen. *Those Incredible Women of World War II.* Brookfield, MA: Millbrook Press, 1994. Brief and easy-to-read account of women in wartime; treats pilots, medical personnel, war correspondents, industrial workers, and others.

BIOGRAPHICAL SOURCES

Litoff, Judy B. *Since You Went Away: World War II Letters from American Women on the Home Front.* New York: Oxford University Press,

1991. Revealing collection of correspondence from women to their husbands, sweethearts, and brothers in service.

———. *We're in This War Too: World War II Letters from American Women in Uniform*. New York: Oxford University Press, 1994. Considered to be a valuable addition to World War II history, letters from women in the armed services, and the Red Cross provide insight into training programs, transportation, and war service.

Wingo, Josette D. *Mother Was a Gunner's Mate: World War II in the Waves*. Annapolis, MD: U.S. Naval Institute, 1994. Humorous recollections of the author's training experiences in her eighteen months in the WAVES beginning in 1944.

AUDIOVISUAL SOURCES

The Hidden Army: Women in World War II. Botsford, CT: Filmic Archives, 1995. 3 videocassettes. 53-minutes each cassette. Contains three award-winning documentaries: *The Hidden Army*—how 18 million women meet the war demands on the home front; *Women in Defense*, narrated by Katherine Hepburn and written by Eleanor Roosevelt; and *Army and Navy Nurse P.O.W.s in WWII*, the shocking story of the first women prisoners of war.

WORLD WIDE WEB

Wilson, Barbara A. "Women in World War II." *Women Veterans*. May 1996. http://userpages.aug.com/captbarb/femvets5.html Brief but informative historical treatment and useful link to further information created by a retired air force captain. Click on the captain's home page for coverage of women in various wars.

46. Minorities and World War II

Like women, minorities contributed substantially to wartime efforts. Significant numbers of African Americans, the nation's largest minority group, served in the armed forces, although in segregated units in the army. One million African Americans, two-thirds of them women, worked in wartime industries. Pressured by A. Philip Randolph and others, President Roosevelt in 1941 issued an executive order that forbade discrimination in defense industries and established the Fair Employment Practices Committee (FEPC). Discrimination still occurred. So did major race riots in 1943 in Harlem and Detroit, and in Los Angeles against Latinos (the Zoot-suit riots).

Suggestions for Term Papers

1. Compare the contributions of African Americans who fought in World War II with those who fought in World War I.
2. Discuss the contributions of various minorities to the war effort.
3. Discuss the wartime race riots in Harlem or Detroit, or both.
4. Discuss the Zoot-suit riots.
5. Analyze the consequences of the war for minorities.

Suggested Sources. See entries 42 and 45 for related items.

REFERENCE SOURCES

Blacks in the American Armed Forces, 1776–1983: A Bibliography. Glenn Anthony May. New Haven, CT: Yale University Press, 1995. Comprehensive listing of writings relevant to blacks in the military.

Let Freedom Ring: Documentary History of the Modern Civil Rights Movement. Peter B. Levy, ed. Westport, CT: Greenwood, 1992. Organizes ninety-five documents on every aspect of the civil rights movement from World War II through the 1980s.

Liberty and Equality, 1920–1994. Oscar Handlin and Lilian Handlin. New York: HarperCollins, 1994. 4 vols. The final volume examines the freedom to participate in the country's affairs through the Depression, World War II, the postwar economic boom, and the emergence of the multicultural society. Part of the publisher's Liberty in America: 1600 to the Present series.

GENERAL SOURCES

Cripps, Thomas. *Making Movies Black: The Hollywood Message Movie from World War II to the Civil Rights Era.* New York: Oxford University Press, 1994. Description of the role of blacks in film from the 1940s to the 1960s.

Garcia, Richard A. *Rise of the Mexican American Middle Class: San Antonio, 1929–1941.* College Station, TX: Texas A&M University Press, 1992. Examination of the development of middle-class Mexican Americans prior to World War II.

Lanning, Michael L. *The African-American Soldier: From Crispus Attucks* to *Colin Powell.* Secaucus, NJ: Birch Lane, 1997. Traces the progress and setbacks in achieving racial equality in the U.S. armed forces, as well as African American soldiers' roles in the various wars.

Moskos, Charles, and John Sibley Butler. *All That We Can Be: Black Leadership and Racial Integration the Army Way.* New York: Basic Books, 1996. Details the racial landscape in the U.S. military, particularly the army, the beacon of opportunity for blacks since the Revolutionary War.

O'Brien, Kenneth Paul, and Lynn H. Parsons, eds. *The Home-Front War: World War II and American Society.* Westport, CT: Greenwood, 1995. Revealing general social history of the American home front during the war.

SPECIALIZED SOURCES

Bernstein, Alison R. *American Indians and World War II: Toward a New Era in Indian Affairs.* Norman, OK: University of Oklahoma Press, 1991. Delineates the role of American Indians during the war and the impact on subsequent developments.

Bixler, Margaret T. *Winds of Freedom: The Story of Navajo Code Talkers of World War II.* Darien, CT: Two Bytes, 1995. The role of Navajo Indians in the Pacific campaign. Their code was the only unbroken one of the war.

Brandt, Nat. *Harlem at War: The Black Experience in World War II.* Syracuse, NY: Syracuse University Press, 1996. African American experiences that focus on racial discrimination and segregation in labor battalions and defense plants at home.

Converse, Elliott V., et al. *The Exclusion of Black Soldiers from the Medal of Honor in World War II: The Study Commissioned by the United States Army to Investigate Racial Bias in the Awarding of the Nation's Highest Military Honor.* Jefferson, NC: McFarland, 1997. An examination of the units in which African Americans served and those whose names were submitted, with the goal of documenting any errors in processing and listing all those African Americans who received Distinguished Service Crosses. Seven African Americans were awarded the Medal of Honor based on this study.

Cooper, Charlie, et al. *Tuskegee's Heroes: Featuring the Aviation Art of Roy Lagrone.* Osceola, WI: Motorbooks International, 1996. Examines the story of the brave black pilots of the 332d Fighter Group, trained at Tuskegee Air Force Base in Alabama, who never lost a bomber on any mission.

James, Cyril, et al. *Fighting Racism in World War II.* New York: Pathfinder

Press, 1991. Details the racism African Americans in the military encountered.

Moore, Brenda L. *To Serve My Country, to Serve My Race: The Story of the Only African American WACS Stationed Overseas during World War II.* New York: New York University Press, 1996. Examines the military service of the only African American women to serve overseas, the 688 Central Postal Directory Battalion. Based on interviews with former members.

Wynn, Neil A. *The Afro-American and the Second World War.* New York: Holmes & Meier, 1993. Delineates the role of African Americans in the armed forces and race relations in the United States.

AUDIOVISUAL SOURCES

Tuskegee Airmen. New York: HBO Home Video, 1995. Videocassette. Dramatizes the distinguished exploits of the 332d Fighter Group in a 107-minute film made for cable television.

WORLD WIDE WEB

Papers of the NAACP—Part 13: The NAACP and Labor, 1940–1955. University Publications of America. February 1996. http://www.upapubs.com/guides/naacp13b.htm#scope Fine six-page narrative of NAACP involvement in labor issues regarding fair employment practices and union membership.

47. Invasion of Normandy (D-Day) (1944)

Allied preparations to invade Europe via France began in early 1942. In January 1944 General Dwight D. Eisenhower arrived in Great Britain to take command of this gargantuan effort, Operation Overlord. Having decoyed the Germans into believing that they would invade at Calais some 200 miles northward, the Allies on June 6, 1944, launched the greatest amphibious assault in history on the still very heavily defended beaches of Normandy. Over 5,000 ships ferried and supported more than 150,000 Allied troops who secured the beachheads after fierce fighting that cost them 5,000 casualties. Paris fell to the Allies two months later.

Suggestions for Term Papers

1. Discuss why General Eisenhower was chosen to command Operation Overlord.
2. Discuss the preparations for Operation Overlord.
3. Analyze why Operation Overlord was successful.
4. Discuss the contributions of a prominent American military leader during World War II.
5. Discuss how the Allies deceived the Germans as to where the invasion of France would take place.

Suggested Sources: See entry 48 for related items.

REFERENCE SOURCES

The D-Day Atlas. John Man. New York: Facts on File, 1994. Examines the campaign from both Allied and German perspectives. Clear and comprehensive maps, graphs, and charts, with more than 60 color maps.

The D-Day Encyclopedia. David G. Chandler and James Lawton, Jr., eds. Englewood Cliffs, NJ: Prentice Hall, 1994. Comprehensive, objective treatment of engagements, strategies, officers, statesmen, weapons, treaties, and other topics.

Oxford Companion to World War II. New York: Oxford University Press, 1995. Contains more than 1,700 entries and 300 photographs, diagrams, and maps.

World War II: A Statistical Survey. John Ellis. New York: Facts on File, 1993. Compendium of facts and figures with hundreds of maps, charts, and graphs, including ones for D-Day.

GENERAL SOURCES

Ambrose, Stephen. *Citizen Soldier: The U.S. Army from the Normandy Beaches to the Bulge to the Surrender of Germany, June 7, 1944–May 7, 1945.* New York: Simon & Schuster, 1997. Draws on interviews and oral histories from both sides on the last battles of the war. The sequel to Ambrose's *D-Day* (see below).

SPECIALIZED SOURCES

Ambrose, Stephen. *D-Day, June 6, 1944.* New York: Simon & Schuster, 1994. An excellent and well-written detailed history and memorial tribute; examines individual ordeals on the Normandy beaches.

Astor, Gerald. *June 6, 1944: The Voices of D-Day.* New York: St. Martin's, 1994. Vivid accounts of veterans regarding action on D-Day.

D'Este, Carlo. *Decision in Normandy.* (1983). Reprint. New York: HarperPerennial Books, 1994. An outstanding military history that offers a new perspective on the Allied campaign.

Drez, Ronald, J., ed. *Voices of D-Day: The Story of the Allied Invasion Told by Those Who Were There.* Baton Rouge: Louisiana State University Press, 1994. Distinctive work recording the interviews with 150 surviving veterans.

Eisenhower, Dwight D. *Crusade in Europe.* Baltimore: John Hopkins University Press, 1997. The account of the Allied war plans and the execution of the Normandy invasion and its aftermath by the commander of the Allied forces.

Goldstein, Richard. *America at D-Day: A Book of Remembrance.* New York: Dell, 1994. Recalls the ferocity of the invasion, beginning with the planning by the Allied command for the invasion two years before the landings.

Hastings, Max. *Overlord: D-Day and the Battle for Normandy.* New York: Simon & Schuster, 1984. Excellent treatment by a noted World War II historian.

Kemp, Anthony. *D-Day and the Invasion of Normandy.* New York: Abrams, 1994. An illustrated account of the Allied invasion from both the Allied and German points of view.

Lewis, John, ed. *Eye-Witness D-Day: The Story of the Battle by Those Who Were There.* New York: Carroll & Graf, 1994. Real-life accounts by soldiers and civilians on both sides.

Miller, Russell. *Nothing Less Than Victory: An Oral History of D-Day.* New York: Morrow, 1993. A compilation of personal commentaries about D-Day collected from letters, diaries, memoranda, official reports, and interviews with veterans on both sides.

Omaha Beachhead (6 June–13 June 1944). Washington, DC: Center for Military History, 1984. Official U.S. Army history of the first days of the Normandy invasions, with detailed accounts on the landings and detailed maps.

Wilson, Theodore A. *D-Day, 1944.* Lawrence: University of Kansas Press, 1994. Essays by leading scholars on the invasion of France, covering all aspects of the largest amphibious assault in history.

BIOGRAPHICAL SOURCES

D'Este, Carlo. *Patton: A Genius for War*. New York: HarperCollins, 1995. A detailed biography of Patton's life, with an emphasis on his leadership abilities in war, as well as his assessment of Eisenhower.

Osmont, Marie Louise. *The Normandy Diary of Marie-Louise Osmont, 1940–1944*. New York: Random House, 1994. The author's experiences living in Normandy during World War II.

AUDIOVISUAL SOURCES

D-Day: The Battle That Liberated the World. Wynewood, PA: Schlessinger/ Library Video, 1998. Discusses the most significant military operation of its time, from the Luftwaffe bombardment of the United Kingdom to the mobilization of the American war industry. 52 minutes.

WORLD WIDE WEB

The 50th Anniversary of the Invasion of Normandy—Operation Overlord. 1994. http://www.nando.net/sproject/dday/dday.html Informative web site treating the planning and execution, equipment, and casualty toll. Links to collection of documents and additional photographs.

48. Yalta Conference (1945)

In early February 1945 the three Allied leaders—Roosevelt, Churchill, and Stalin—met at the Black Sea resort of Yalta. There they postponed certain matters, such as the question of postwar German reparations and status, but they did reach some major decisions. The Soviet Union agreed to enter the war against Japan after Germany's defeat and was to receive important territorial concessions in return. The Big Three also agreed to establish a postwar world organization. Most controversial was their understanding to hold free elections in recently liberated Poland, an agreement that the Soviets failed to abide by and later opened Roosevelt to charges of being naive.

Suggestions for Term Papers

1. Discuss how Roosevelt, Churchill, and Stalin regarded one another.

2. Were the Yalta agreements reasonable compromises or a sellout by the Allies?

3. Analyze the consequences of the Yalta Conference.

4. Was the Yalta Conference a significant factor in bringing on the cold war?

5. Discuss why the Polish government question was so controversial.

Suggested Sources: See entries 47 and 52 for related items.

REFERENCE SOURCES

The Cold War, 1945–1991. Benjamin Frankel, ed. Detroit: Gale, 1992. 3 vols. Provides biographical essays and sketches and coverage of major events and themes.

Cold War Chronology: Soviet American Relations, 1945–1991. Kenneth Hill. Washington, DC: Congressional Quarterly, 1993. Begins with V-J Day, September 1, 1945, and ends on December 25, 1991. Includes references to major speeches and many government publications.

GENERAL SOURCES

Dallek, Robert. *Franklin D. Roosevelt and American Foreign Policy, 1932–1945.* NY: Oxford University Press, 1995. The best comprehensive treatment of the subject to date.

Edmonds, Robin. *The Big Three: Churchill, Roosevelt, and Stalin in Peace and War.* New York: Norton, 1991. The best recent work on Allied diplomatic efforts during the war.

Gardner, Lloyd C. *Spheres of Influence: The Great Powers Partition Europe from Munich to Yalta.* Chicago: Ivan R. Dee, 1993. Views territorial arrangements as the key to a durable peace and Yalta as appeasement politics.

Karski, Jan. *The Great Powers and Poland Nineteen-Nineteen to Nineteen Forty-Five: From Versailles to Yalta.* Washington, DC: University Press of America, 1985. A comprehensive history of Poland from the end of World War I to the end of World War II and its relations with the superpowers.

Kimball, Warren F. *Forged in War: Roosevelt, Churchill and the Second World*

War. New York: Morrow, 1997. Details not only the wartime personalities but also the relationship between Great Britain and the United States.

Lane, Ann, and Howard Temperley, eds. *The Rise and Fall of the Grand Alliance, 1941–1945*. New York: St. Martin's, 1996. Studies the reasons for the failure of the Grand Alliance.

Moskin, J. Robert. *Mr. Truman's War: The Final Victories of World War II and the Birth of the Postwar World*. New York: Random House, 1996. A short but thorough history of this eventful period of Truman's presidency, which began under the terms of the Yalta agreement.

Perlmutter, Amos. *FDR and Stalin: A Not So Grand Alliance*. Columbia MS: University of Missouri Press, 1993. A painstakingly researched account that presents Roosevelt as a disinterested spectator who cared only about continued good relations with the Soviet Union after the war.

Reynolds, Dave, et al., eds. *Allies at War: The Soviet, American, and British Experience, 1939–1945*. New York: St. Martin's, 1994. Revealing account of the varied experiences of the Allied superpowers during World War II.

Shogan, Robert. *Hard Bargain: How FDR Twisted Churchill's Arm, Evaded the Law and Changed the Role of the American Presidency*. New York: Scribner's, 1995. Describes the Lend-Lease Act in relation to the American presidency, as well as wartime relations between the two superpowers, and examines the influence of a strong president.

Thurston, Robert W. *Life and Terror in Stalin's Russia, 1923–1941*. New Haven, CT: Yale University Press, 1996. Portrays Stalin as an initiator of and reactor to events; examines the psychology of the Soviet people and demonstration of their support for him.

SPECIALIZED SOURCES

Buhite, Russell D. *Decisions at Yalta: An Appraisal of Summit Diplomacy*. Wilmington, DE: Scholarly Resources, 1986. Issue-by-issue analysis of background, discussions, and agreements of Yalta; faults Roosevelt for his failure to exploit potential strengths and his concessions to Stalin.

Senarclens, Pierre de. *Yalta*. New Brunswick, NJ: Transaction Books, 1988. Brief, informative account of the Yalta Conference and sociopolitical influences.

BIOGRAPHICAL SOURCES

Markovna, Nina. *Nina's Journey: A Memoir of Stalin's Russia and the Second World War*. Washington, DC: Regnery Gateway, 1989. A young girl's recounting of hardships of daily Soviet life in the late 1930s and Stalin's reign of terror and escaped repatriation after World War II.

Miller, Nathan. *FDR: An Intimate History.* New York: Doubleday, 1983. Balanced, readable examination of FDR's life and career, based on secondary sources.

Radzinsky, Edvard. *Stalin: The First In-Depth Biography Based on Explosive New Documents from Russia's Secret Archives.* New York: Anchor, 1996. Excellent biography based on Stalin's personal archives, with emphasis on his early years. Best authoritative biography on Stalin.

AUDIOVISUAL SOURCES

World War II: When Lions Roared. Orland Park, IL: MPI Home Video, 1994. 2 videocassettes. The 186-minute mini series based on the actual words spoken by the Big Three leaders. Includes behind-the-scenes story, triumph, conflict and the price paid by each leader.

WORLD WIDE WEB

Gung, Yu-mei. *Yalta Conference: February 4–11, 1945.* Enola Gay Perspectives. May 1995. http://www.glue.umd.edu/~enola/drop/yalta. html Brief description of outcomes of the conference. With link to full text of the agreements.

49. Atomic Bombs Dropped on Hiroshima and Nagasaki (1945)

Gauging that an invasion of the Japanese home islands could cost perhaps 1 million American and more Japanese casualties, President Truman opted to use the atomic bomb to end the war with Japan. When the latter refused to surrender after a final American warning of "prompt and utter destruction," the B-29 *Enola Gay* on August 6, 1945 dropped an atomic bomb on Hiroshima, destroying the city and killing possibly 100,000 persons. Japan did not surrender, and a second atomic bomb was dropped on Nagasaki on August 9. Five days later, the emperor announced that Japan had surrendered.

Suggestions for Term Papers

1. Discuss the arguments for and against using the atomic bomb to end the war against Japan.

2. Discuss American public reaction to the use of the bomb.

3. Discuss Japanese recollections of the dropping of the atomic bombs.

4. Analyze the controversy concerning the Smithsonian Institution's fifty-year commemorative exhibit of the dropping of the bombs on Japan.

5. Discuss the long-range consequences of using the atomic bomb against Japan.

Suggested Sources: See entry 44 for related items.

REFERENCE SOURCES

Louis L. Snyder's Historical Guide to World War II. Louis L. Snyder. Westport, CT: Greenwood, 1982. A comprehensive collection of articles on major and minor events before, during, and after World War II.

GENERAL SOURCES

Bailey, Janet. *The Good Servant: Making Peace with the Bomb at Los Alamos.* New York: Simon & Schuster, 1995.

Ball, Howard. *Justice Downwind: America's Nuclear Testing Program in the 1950s.* London: Oxford University Press, 1986. Information on nuclear testing in the United States during the early cold war period.

Bethe, Hans A. *The Road from Los Alamos.* New York: Simon & Schuster, 1991. Nontechnical essays that advocate nuclear disarmament, with a focus on weapons research, arms control, and nuclear power. Part of the publisher's Masters of Modern Physics Series.

Burchett, Wilfred. *Shadows of Hiroshima.* New York: Verso, 1983. Covers Germany's nonnuclear program, Potsdam, Los Alamos, and Hiroshima. The author used Morse code to leak the horrors of radiation sickness to the West.

Hafemeister, D. W. *Physics, Technology and the Nuclear Arms Race.* Baltimore: American Institute of Physics, 1983. Describes the development of the atomic bomb and nuclear weaponry.

Hershberg, James G. *James B. Conant: Harvard to Hiroshima and the Making of the Nuclear Age.* Stanford, CA: Stanford University Press,

1995. Written by the number two supervisor building the fission bomb, as well as the main opponent of building the fusion weapon.

Smyth, Henry D. *Atomic Energy for Military Purposes: The Official Report on the Development of the Atomic Bomb under the Auspices of the United States Government, 1940–1945.* (1945). Reprint. Stanford, CA: Stanford University Press, 1989. The original report surveying the history of the bomb from its development through its use against the Japanese.

SPECIALIZED SOURCES

Ferrell, Robert H. *Harry S. Truman and the Bomb: A Documentary History.* Worland, NY: High Plains Publishing, 1996. Examination of his correspondence provides insight into Truman's situation.

Goldstein, Donald M., et al. *Rain of Ruin.* McLean, VA: Brassey, 1995. Endorses the idea that the bomb saved American lives by destroying the two Japanese cities. Contains more than 400 black and white photographs.

Hersey, John. *Hiroshima.* New York: Knopf, 1985. Brings up to date the lives of the six survivors the author covered so brilliantly in 1946; a new edition of a classic work with a final chapter written nearly forty years later.

Leckie, Robert. *Okinawa: The Last Battle of World War II.* New York: Viking, 1995. Covers the controversy over the use of atomic bombs on Japan.

Nagai, Takashi. *The Bells of Nagasaki.* New York: Kodansha America, 1984. The story of a physician and radiologist and his eyewitness account of the tragedy.

Prentice, Ross L. *Atomic Bomb Survivor Data: Utilization and Analysis.* Philadelphia: Society for Industrial and Applied Mathematics, 1984. Information on the survivors of Nagasaki and Hiroshima.

Schull, William J. *Effects of Atomic Radiation: A Half-Century of Studies from Hiroshima and Nagasaki.* New York: Wiley-Liss, 1995. Summarizes the largest and longest medical follow-up study known, as well as an eyewitness account of the pertinent events and findings.

———. *Song among the Ruins.* Cambridge, MA: Harvard University Press, 1990. Documents genetic damage among children of survivors of the atomic bomb. Written under the auspices of the Atomic Bomb Casualty Commission.

Selden, Kyoko, and Mark Selden. *The Atomic Bomb: Voices from Hiroshima and Nagasaki.* Armonk, NY: Sharpe, 1990. An excellent pictorial and text containing novellas, photographs, poetry, memoirs, pictures by survivors, and statements by and about children.

Sherwin, Martin J. *A World Destroyed: Hiroshima and the Origins of the Arms Race.* (1975) Reprint. New York: Vintage, 1987. History of the diplomatic and political circumstances surrounding the development and use of the first atom bomb, with a new introduction and epilogue examining recent developments in the nuclear arms race.

Wyden, Peter. *Day One: Before Hiroshima and After.* New York: Simon & Schuster, 1984. Synthesizes the literature and interviews both the scientists and the survivors.

BIOGRAPHICAL SOURCES

Ferrell, Robert N. *Harry S. Truman and the Bomb: A Documentary History.* Worland, WY: High Plains Publishing, 1996. Insight into the event by one of the leading Truman biographers.

Walker, Samuel J. *Prompt and Utter Destruction: Truman and the Use of Atomic Bombs against Japan.* Chapel Hill: University of North Carolina Press, 1997. Concise, informative account of Truman and his decision to drop the bomb.

AUDIOVISUAL SOURCES

World War II: The War Chronicles Series. New York: A&E Home Video, 1998. 2 videocassettes. The 140-minute Volume 2 treats "The War in the Pacific" from Pearl Harbor to the atomic bombing of Japan; condensed version of the 1983 motion picture by Lou Reda Productions.

WORLD WIDE WEB

Ohba, Mitsuru and John Benson. *A-Bomb WWW Museum.* June 1995. http://www.csi.ad.jp/ABOMB/index.html A project of Hiroshima City University that provides Japanese perspective. Excellent, informative links such as "Introduction: About the A-Bomb" and "The Atomic Bombing of Nagasaki."

50. United Nations Established (1945)

At the time of the Atlantic Charter in 1941, President Roosevelt had voiced the need for a post–World War II international organization. Support for his idea gained momentum, and at the Dumbarton Oaks

Conference in 1944, the United States, Great Britain, the Soviet Union, and China agreed to create the United Nations. The United States and the Soviet Union disagreed on but ultimately compromised their differences regarding the form and functioning of the proposed association. Then, meeting in late April 1945 in San Francisco, delegates from fifty nations signed the charter that created the United Nations.

Suggestions for Term Papers

1. How did the United Nations differ from the League of Nations?
2. Analyze the disputes between the United States and the Soviet Union with regard to the organization and function of the UN.
3. Discuss the long-range consequences of the veto power in the Security Council.
4. How effective has the UN been in resolving international disputes?
5. Discuss the organization and purposes of a specific UN agency.

Suggested Sources: See entry 18 for related items.

GENERAL SOURCES

Baehr, Peter R., and Leon Gordenker. *The United Nations in the 1990s.* 2d ed. New York: St. Martin's, 1994. Examines the likely role of the UN in the future. Part of the Woodrow Wilson School of Public and International Affairs series.

Bailey, Sydney D. *The U.N. Security Council and Human Rights.* New York: St. Martin's, 1994. History of the Security Council and its relationship to human rights issues.

Black, Maggie. *Children First: The Story of UNICEF, Past and Present.* London: Oxford University Press, 1996. About one of the most vital units of the UN and its concern for children worldwide.

Falk, Richard, et al., eds. *The United Nations and a Just World Order.* Boulder, CO: Westview, 1991. Examines the role of the UN in the future world order.

Gakuin, Nagoya. *Diplomatic Discourse: International Conflict at the United Nations: Addresses and Analysis.* Greenwich, CT: Ablex, 1997. Dis-

cusses the international aspects, with emphasis on various conflicts in
which the UN has become involved.

Hamburg, David A. *Sustainable Peace: The Role of the U.N. and Regional
Organizations in Preventing Conflicts.* Lanham, MD: Rowman &
Littlefield, 1997. The role of peacekeeping with UN and regional
groups.

Hoopes, Townsend. *F.D.R. and the Creation of the U.N.* New Haven, CT:
Yale University Press, 1997. Traces the decades from idealism of the
League of Nations through World War II; examines FDR's influence
on postwar diplomacy and development of the UN.

Knipping, Franz. *The United Nations System and Its Predecessors: Basic Documents.* London: Oxford University Press, 1998. Important documents detailing the UN and its workings.

Meisler, Stanley. *United Nations: The First Fifty Years.* New York: Grove,
1995. History and accomplishments of the UN.

Murray, Gilbert. *From the League to U.N.* (1948). Reprint. Westport, CT:
Greenwood, 1988. Brief account of the development of international
organization—the League of Nations to the founding of the UN.

Thakur, Ramesh C. *Past Imperfect, Future Uncertain: The United Nations
at Fifty.* New York: St. Martin's, 1997. Detailed history as well as
observations about the future.

Tomuschat, Christian. *The United Nations at Age 50: A Legal Perspective.*
Cambridge, MA: Kluwer, 1996. Legal examination regarding the
participation of the United Nations in international affairs.

United Nations at Fifty: The Notes for Speakers. New York: UNESCO, 1995.
Reviews the achievements and accomplishments of the past fifty years.

United Nations in the 1990s, a Second Chance? New York: UNESCO, 1992.
Looks at the UN as a permanent diplomatic market for the exchange
of information and views, as well as action on a global basis.

AUDIOVISUAL SOURCES

The Arsenal. Botsford, CT: Filmic Archives, 1973. Traces the development
of the United States as a world power, including Los Alamos, the
United Nations, and the Pentagon. 52 minutes. Part of the America
series, created by Alistair Cooke and produced by BBC and Time
Life Video.

WORLD WIDE WEB

"San Francisco Commemorates UN50: San Francisco and the UN." *United
Nations 50th Anniversary in San Francisco.* May 1995. http://

www.lh.com/un50sf/h/history.htm Brief historical narrative of the founding of the UN.

51. War Crime Trials (1945–1948)

In 1946 the Allies established an international tribunal in Nuremberg to try twenty-one Germans for crimes against humanity and against the acknowledged rules of warfare committed during World War II. After nearly a year, eleven of the defendants received death sentences; seven others received long prison sentences. Beginning in 1945, similar proceedings took place in Japan, where twenty-five wartime figures were tried and convicted, seven of them condemned to execution. In future years, several thousand defendants were to go on trial in various countries, particularly in Asia. While many applauded the effort to bring perpetrators of wartime atrocities to justice, others were opposed, largely on legal grounds.

Suggestions for Term Papers

1. Analyze the arguments for and against holding the post–World War II war crime trials.
2. Compare the war crime trials of Germans and Japanese.
3. Discuss the postwar hunt for escaped prominent Nazis.
4. Discuss the capture, trial, and execution of Adolf Eichmann.
5. Discuss attempts to deny the historical existence of the Holocaust.

REFERENCE SOURCES

Encyclopedia of the Third Reich. Christian Zentner et al., eds. New York: Macmillan, 1991. The definitive reference source for basic data on events in Nazi Germany, as well as strong biographical entries.

Great World Trials: The 100 Most Celebrated and Significant Courtroom Battles in World History. Edward W. Knappman, ed. Detroit: Gale, 1997. Trials of political and historical significance in the twentieth century.

GENERAL SOURCES

Landau, Elaine. *Nazi War Criminals.* New York: Franklin Watts, 1990. Shows the complicity of people, countries, and governments in knowingly sheltering these men.

Lipstadt, Deborah. *Denying the Holocaust: The Growing Assault on Truth and Memory.* New York: Free Press, 1993. Forty years ago, pseudo-historians argued that Hitler never meant to kill the Jews and only a few hundred thousand died in the camps. Today, this irrational idea has become an international movement.

Morin, Isobel V. *Days of Judgment: The World War II War Crimes Trials.* Bridgeport, CT: Millbrook, 1995. Argues that the tribunals at Nuremberg and Tokyo failed to establish the clear standard of international justice needed to prevent history from repeating itself.

Wiesenthal, Simon. *The Sunflower: On the Possibilities and Limits of Forgiveness.* 2d ed. New York: Schocken Books, 1997. Revised and expanded edition of the author's 1976 effort providing personal narratives of the concentration camp experience and philosophical insight.

SPECIALIZED SOURCES

Arnold, James R. *Operation Eichmann: The Truth behind the Pursuit, Capture and Trial of Adolf Eichmann.* New York: Wiley, 1997. The story behind the kidnapping of Eichmann from Brazil by the Israeli Secret Service to Jerusalem to stand trial for war crimes.

Conot, Robert E. *Justice at Nuremberg.* New York: Carroll & Graf, 1984. Story of the trials for major Nazi war criminals.

Gilbert, Gustave M. *Nuremberg Diary.* (1947). Reprint. New York: Da Capo, 1995. Recorded thoughts on the trial of the German war criminals.

Marrus, Michael R. *Nuremberg War Crimes Trial.* New York: St. Martin's, 1997. Recent and explicit descriptive account of the major trials.

Persico, Joseph E. *Nuremberg: Infamy on Trial.* New York: Viking, 1994. Treats the trials' principal issues and gives biographical vignettes and scenes of Nuremberg life.

Taylor, Telford. *Anatomy of the Nuremberg Trials: A Personal Memoir.* Boston: Little, Brown, 1993. A definitive volume covering only the first of the major trials; compelling narrative with excerpts from the trial proceedings.

Tusa, Ann, and John Tusa. *The Nuremberg Trial.* New York: Macmillan, 1984. Clear and highly readable, balanced in its judgments. For those interested in international law, a must read.

BIOGRAPHICAL SOURCES

Levy, Michael. *Wiesenthal File.* Grand Rapids, MI: Eerdman's, 1994. The enthralling story of the most famous Nazi hunter as he searched the world for Nazi war criminals.

Pick, Hella. *Simon Wiesenthal: A Life in Search of Justice.* Boston: Northeastern University Press, 1996. His search for justice for those who died in the Holocaust by finding those who escaped the Nuremberg trials.

Sereny, Gitta. *Albert Speer: His Battle with Truth.* New York: Knopf, 1995. Based on information from Speer's family, friends, and colleagues, as well as Allied advisers after the war. Concludes he was an opportunist who served Hitler, outwitted the justices at Nuremberg, and found favor in postwar West Germany.

AUDIOVISUAL SOURCES

Nuremberg: Tyranny on Trial. New York: A&E, 1995. 50-minute documentary examines the historic trials that tested the principles governing the laws of nations, from the accusations through the executions. Interprets the verdicts and historical impact.

WORLD WIDE WEB

Fray, William C., and Lisa A. Spar. "Nuremberg War Crimes Trials." *The Avalon Project: The International Military Tribunal.* 1996. http://www.yale.edu/lawweb/avalon/imt/imt.htm Complete collection of documents relating to the trials' motions, rules of procedure, indictments, reports, and so forth. Includes documents cited in the official records, including those from the Hague Conventions.

52. Cold War Begins

Allied against a common foe during World War II, the United States and the Soviet Union put aside the differences that had divided them since the Bolshevik Revolution of 1917. The Yalta Conference and questions regarding the future of Germany and the organization of the United Nations brought renewed controversy, however, and in the years immediately following the war, differences hardened into a firm opposition that has been labeled the "cold war." Traditional historians blamed the Soviet Union for the cold war; revisionists either blamed the United States or claimed that both nations shared responsibility.

Suggestions for Term Papers

1. Who was to blame for the cold war: the United States or the Soviet Union?
2. Was the cold war avoidable?
3. Analyze President Truman's cold war policies.
4. Discuss the U.S. containment policy and its consequences.
5. Discuss the cold war as a 1948 presidential election issue.

Suggested Sources: See entries 48, 54, and 56–58 for related items.

REFERENCE SOURCES

The Cold War Encyclopedia. Thomas Parrish. New York: Facts on File, 1994. Over 700 entries, more than 100 photos, and a chronology of forty-five years of history.

The Cold War Reference Guide: A General History and Annotated Chronology, with Selected Biographies. Richard Alan Schwartz. Jefferson, NC: McFarland, 1997. Documents the cold war with chronology and biographies.

Events That Changed America in the Twentieth Century. John E. Findling and Frank W. Thackeray, eds. Westport, CT: Greenwood, 1996. Entries covered include the cold war.

GENERAL SOURCES

Baker, Robert H. *Hollow Victory: The Cold War and Its Aftermath.* New York: St. Martin's, 1998. Traces the history of the cold war, focusing on politics and international imperatives from the final months of World War II to June 1996.

Beschloss, Michael R., et al. *At the Highest Levels: The Inside Story of the End of the Cold War.* Boston: Little, Brown, 1994. Interesting and revealing narrative providing insight into the real story behind the end of the cold war; based on classified documents, transcripts, records, and other material.

Brinkley, Douglas. *Dean Acheson: The Cold War Years, 1953–71.* New Haven, CT: Yale University Press, 1992. Interesting and informative study of the former secretary of state and his operations in diplomacy during the cold war.

Chace, James. *Acheson: The Secretary of State Who Created the American World*. NY: Simon & Schuster, 1988. The book's subtitle underscores the importance the author attributes to his subject.

Fuigiello, Philip J. *American-Soviet Trade in the Cold War*. Chapel Hill: University of North Carolina Press, 1988. Exposition of the application of economic sanctions against the Soviet Union in order to achieve foreign policy objectives.

Ginsburgs, George, et al., eds. *Russia and America: From Rivalry to Reconciliation*. Armonk, NY: Sharpe, 1993. An analysis of relations between the United States and Soviet Union from the advent of the cold war to the present.

Johnson, Robert H. *Improbable Dangers: U.S. Conceptions of Threat in the Cold War and After*. New York: St. Martin's, 1994. Questions why U.S. policymakers regularly exaggerated the Soviet threat during the cold war by examining psychological and political analysis.

Kennedy-Pipe, Caroline. *Stalin's Cold War: Soviet Strategies in Europe*. Manchester, England: Manchester University Press, 1995. Details Stalin's strategies for keeping Eastern Europe under his control while maintaining diplomatic relations with the United States.

Kunz, Diane B. *Butter and Guns: America's Cold War Diplomacy*. New York: Free Press, 1997. Examines the cold war from an economic perspective in terms of the political and diplomatic events.

Kutler, Stanley I. *The American Inquisition: Justice and Injustice in the Cold War*. New York: Hill and Wang, 1984. Informative examination of various incidents regarding the suppression of civil rights with the idea of protecting the national security.

Lindey, Christine. *Art in the Cold War: From Vladivostok to Kalamazoo, 1945–1962*. New York: New Amsterdam, 1991. Interesting comparison of art forms between the West and the Soviet Union; looks at social dissent in the United States and conservative and conformist art in the Soviet Union.

McCormick, Thomas J. *America's Half-Century: United States Foreign Policy in the Cold War and After*. Baltimore: Johns Hopkins University Press, 1995. Examines the development of American leadership in world affairs with increasing militarization and pursuit of goals.

May, Ernest, ed. *American Cold War Strategy*. New York: St. Martin's, 1993. Describes and interprets National Security Council policy in the cold war.

Murphy, David E., et al. *Battleground Berlin: CIA vs. KGB in the Cold War*. New Haven, CT: Yale University Press, 1997. Provides insight into strategies and espionage tactics employed by both the United States and the Soviet Union in German politics.

Schwartz, Richard A. *Cold War Culture: Media and the Arts*. New York: Facts on File, 1997. Describes the influence of the cold war, including books and writers, movies, the press, and television and radio.

Warren, James A. *Cold War: The American Crusade against World Communism 1945–1991*. New York: Facts on File, 1996. Documents the nearly fifty-year crusade with commentary and examination of personalities and issues.

SPECIALIZED SOURCES

Borstelmann, Thomas. *Apartheid's Reluctant Uncle: The United States and Southern Africa in the Early Cold War*. New York: Oxford University Press, 1993. Behind-the-scenes account of U.S. relations with the apartheid government of South Africa.

Herken, Gregg. *The Winning Weapon: The Atomic Bomb in the Cold War, 1945–1950*. Princeton, NJ: Princeton University Press, 1988. Examination of diplomatic history and foreign relations with respect to the atomic bomb.

Senarclens, Pierre de. *From Yalta to the Iron Curtain: The Great Powers and the Origins of the Cold War*. Washington, DC: Berg Publications, 1995. Thorough examination focused on the beginnings of the cold war. Translated from the French.

BIOGRAPHICAL SOURCES

Clarridge, Duane R. *A Spy for All Seasons: My Life in the CIA*. New York: Scribner, 1997. Interesting account of a CIA spy whose early career was shaped by his participation in the cold war.

Kalugin, Oleg. *The First Directorate: My 32 Years in Intelligence and Espionage against the West*. New York: St. Martin's Press, 1994. A personal narrative of a key spymaster for the other side.

McCullough, David. *Truman*. New York: Simon & Schuster, 1992. An excellent and detailed biography of Harry S. Truman. Winner of the Pulitzer Prize.

AUDIOVISUAL SOURCES

American Foreign Policy: Eisenhower and the Cold War. Chicago: Encyclopedia Brittanica, 1981. Videocassette. Details U.S. cold war diplomacy during international crises. 16 minutes.

American Foreign Policy: Truman and Containment. Chicago: Encyclopedia

Brittannica, 1981. Videocassette. Examines the origin of the cold war and containment in postwar years. 16 minutes.

WORLD WIDE WEB

"Revelations from the Russian Archives." *Library of Congress Exhibits.* January 1996. http://lcweb.loc.gov/exhibits/archives/intro.html Collection of images and narratives relating to the Soviet Union. Several segments deal with the cold war; see the "Soviet Union and the United States" section.

53. Jackie Robinson Integrates Major League Baseball (1947)

Segregated from the major leagues, professional African American baseball players participated in the Negro Leagues through World War II. In 1947, Branch Rickey, general manager of the Brooklyn Dodgers, called up Jackie Robinson from the team's minor league farm club in Montreal. A star athlete at UCLA and a World War II serviceman, Robinson stoically accepted jeers and racial epithets and won that year's National League Rookie of the Year award for his athletic achievements. Through his skills and endurance of insults, Robinson, later inducted into baseball's Hall of Fame, broke the color line in baseball.

Suggestions for Term Papers

1. Discuss the origins of Negro League baseball.
2. Discuss the career of a famous Negro League player (e.g., Josh Gibson, "Cool Papa" Bell, Satchell Paige).
3. Discuss the difficulties Robinson faced in his first year in major league baseball and his response.
4. How did Latino players fare with baseball's color line?
5. Discuss public reaction to Robinson's first year in the major leagues.

Suggested Sources: See entry 71 for related items.

GENERAL SOURCES

Brashler, William. *The Story of Negro League Baseball*. New York: Ticknor & Fields, 1994. Concise, easy-to-read, and interesting account of the history of the Negro League, with a focus on Jimmie Crutchfield's career.

Cooper, Michael L. *Playing America's Game: The Story of Negro League Baseball*. New York: Lodestar Books, 1993. Concise, comprehensive, and easy-to-read illustrated history of the Negro League and the men who played in it.

Dixon, Phil, and Pat Hannigan. *The Negro Baseball Leagues: A Photographic History*. Mattituck, NY: Amereon, 1992. Follows Simpson Younger, the first black to play college baseball, to Jackie Robinson's breaking the major leagues' color barrier after World War II and the subsequent death of the Negro Leagues in the mid-1950s.

Margolies, Jacob. *The Negro Leagues: The Story of Black Baseball*. New York: Franklin Watts, 1993. A concise and easy-to-read account examining the history of the Negro League, with highlights of some of the great players.

McKissack, Patricia C., and Frederick McKissack, Jr. *Black Diamond: The Story of the Negro Baseball Leagues*. New York: Scholastic, 1994. An interesting and easy-to-read history of the Negro League and its great heroes.

SPECIALIZED SOURCES

Coombs, Karen M. *Jackie Robinson: Baseball's Civil Rights Legend*. Springfield, NJ: Enslow, 1997. The story of Jackie Robinson and his advent into all-white major league baseball.

Tygiel, Jules. *Jackie Robinson Reader: Perspectives on an American Hero*. New York: NAL/Dutton, 1998. Different viewpoints on Jackie Robinson and his impact.

BIOGRAPHICAL SOURCES

The Biographical Dictionary of Black Americans. New York: Facts on File, 1992. Critical resource on more than 180 African Americans covering all fields of endeavor.

Falkner, David. *Great Time Coming: The Life of Jackie Robinson, from Baseball to Birmingham*. New York: Simon & Schuster, 1995. Complete biography of this all-time baseball great from New York through the civil rights movement.

Porter, David L., ed. *African-American Sports Greats: A Biographical*

Dictionary. Westport, CT: Greenwood, 1995. An excellent article on Jackie Robinson and his contributions to baseball.

Rampersad, Arnold. *Jackie Robinson.* New York: Random House, 1997. Detailed and comprehensive biography of the baseball star from childhood to fame. The author is a university professor and biographer who was given access to Robinson's papers.

Riley, James A. *The Biographical Encyclopedia of the Negro Baseball Leagues.* New York: Carroll & Graf Publishers, 1994. Comprehensive coverage with detailed biographical sketches of the men who played the game.

Robinson, Jackie. *I Never Had It Made: An Autobiography.* Hopewell, NJ: Ecco, 1995. In his own words, the Jackie Robinson story as he saw it; examines the fortunate combination of talent and opportunity.

Robinson, Sharon. *Stealing Home: An Intimate Family Portrait by the Daughter of Jackie Robinson.* New York: HarperCollins, 1997. Intimate portrait of Jackie from his daughter's viewpoint.

Smith, Jessie Carney. *Black Heroes of the 20th Century.* Detroit: Gale, 1997. A compendium of African American achievements over the past 100 years.

Stout, Glenn. *Jackie Robinson: Between the Baselines.* San Francisco: Woodford, 1997. General biography.

AUDIOVISUAL SOURCES

Jackie Robinson Story: 50th Anniversary Collector's Edition. Wynnwood, PA: Schlessinger/Library Video, 1998. Videocassette. 83-minute chronicle of Robinson's life and struggle for fame from UCLA to the big leagues.

WORLD WIDE WEB

"Jackie Robinson." *CMG Worldwide.* 1997. http://www.jackie42.com/ right.html Paragraph description and small picture; leads to biography, photographs, career highlights, and other material.

54. Marshall Plan (1947)

Despite loans from the United States, Western European nations continued to suffer from dire economic problems during the early postwar period. To alleviate these problems and, implicitly, to prevent further inroads by communism, Secretary of State George C. Marshall in his Harvard University commencement speech on June 5, 1947, proposed large-scale aid to all European nations, including the Soviet Union. Ultimately only the noncommunist nations availed themselves of Marshall's proposals, which Congress enacted in 1948 and for which it appropriated more than $12 billion for the period 1948–1951.

Suggestions for Term Papers

1. Discuss the origins of the Marshall Plan.
2. Analyze why the Soviet Union rejected the Marshall Plan.
3. Discuss the American public's reaction to the Marshall Plan.
4. Discuss the consequences of the Marshall Plan for U.S. foreign policy.
5. Compare current aid given to foreign countries with that given under the Marshall Plan.

Suggested Sources: See entries 52 and 55 for related items.

REFERENCE SOURCES

Encyclopedia of the Cold War. Thomas S. Arms. New York: Facts on File 1994. Covers the cold war from the closing days of World War II to the dissolution of the Soviet empire.

GENERAL SOURCES

Brands, H. W. *The Devil We Knew: Americans and the Cold War.* London: Oxford University Press, 1993. Convincingly demonstrates the cost of the cold war to the United States and other nations, in lives, dollars, human rights, and moral principles.

Carew, Anthony. *Labor under the Marshall Plan: The Politics of Productivity and the Marketing of Management Science.* Detroit: Wayne State University Press, 1987. Well-researched study of the interaction between the American labor movement and European labor and management personnel that accompanied the implementation of the Marshall Plan.

Dornbusch, Rudiger, et al., eds. *Postwar Economic Reconstruction and Lessons for the East Today.* Cambridge, MA: MIT Press, 1993. American,

European, and Japanese economists suggest that Eastern Europe today faces many of the same problems faced by Europe and Japan at the end of World War II.

Fromkin, David. *In the Time of the Americans: FDR, Truman, Eisenhower, Marshall, MacArthur—The Generation That Changed America's Role in the World.* New York: Knopf, 1995. Examines the impact of these famous Americans who influenced world affairs.

Woods, Randall B., and Howard Jones. *Dawning of the Cold War: The United States Quest for Order.* Atlanta: Georgia Press, 1991. Argues that perception was the most important reality of the cold war; the Marshall Plan, Truman Doctrine, Berlin airlift, and NATO were all necessary.

SPECIALIZED SOURCES

Bland, Larry I. *The Papers of George Catlett Marshall.* Baltimore: Johns Hopkins, 1981. 3 vols. Covers Marshall's life and career.

Clesse, Armand, and Archie C. Epps. *Present at the Creation: The Fortieth Anniversary of the Marshall Plan.* New York: Harper & Row, 1990. Papers from a 1987 conference to discuss the origins and implementation of the Marshall Plan.

Hogan, Michael J. *The Marshall Plan: America, Britain, and the Reconstruction of Western Europe, 1947–1952.* London: Cambridge University Press, 1987. Examines the most successful peacetime foreign policy carried out by the United States in this century.

Mee, Charles L., Jr. *The Marshall Plan.* New York: Simon & Schuster, 1983. Credits the Marshall Plan with restoration of confidence to Western Europe's governments and entrepreneurs. Well documented and fast paced.

Puryear, Edgar F., Jr. *19 Stars: A Study in Military Character and Leadership.* Novato, CA: Presidio Press, 1997. Excellent study of Marshall's character and his leadership qualities.

Wexler, Imanuel. *The Marshall Plan Revisited: The European Recovery Program in Economic Perspective.* Westport, CT: Greenwood, 1983. Focuses on four economic factors: strong production effort, expansion of foreign trade, the creation and maintenance of internal financial stability, and the development of European economic cooperation.

BIOGRAPHICAL SOURCES

Cray, Ed. *General of the Army: George C. Marshall—Soldier and Statesman.* New York: Norton, 1990. A splendid biography of one of the giant figures of the mid-twentieth century. Thoroughly researched and engagingly written.

National Portrait Gallery Staff. *George C. Marshall: Soldier of Peace.* Baltimore: Johns Hopkins, 1997. Good biography with excellent illustrations.

Pogue, Forrest C. *George C. Marshall: Statesman, 1945–1959.* New York: Viking, 1987. The fourth and final volume of Pogue's monumental study of a man who after years of military accomplishment took on the challenges of the post–World War II world.

Saunders, Alan. *George C. Marshall: A General for Peace.* New York: Facts on File, 1995. Account of the wartime Joint Chiefs of Staff chairman and author of plan that rebuilt Europe after World War II and who won the Nobel Peace Prize.

Stoler, Mark A. *George C. Marshall: Soldier-Statesman of the American Century.* New York: Macmillan, 1989. Extensive biography of Marshall and his role as chief of staff to both Roosevelt and Truman.

WORLD WIDE WEB

Marshall Plan 50th Anniversary Site. 1997. http://www.marshfdn.com/ Operated by the George C. Marshall Foundation, provides valuable links to information. Click on "European Recovery Program," an eleven-page article by Anne M. Dixon.

55. NATO Established (1949)

In June 1948 the Soviet Union blocked U.S., British, and French road access to their zones in Western Berlin. The United States retaliated with a successful airlift that lasted until the Soviets ended their obstruction in May the following year. Before that, however, the Truman administration called for an alliance to resist possible Soviet aggression. The result was the establishment of the North Atlantic Treaty Organization (NATO), signed into agreement on April 4, 1949, by twelve nations. This agreement, which Congress ratified shortly after, stipulated that an attack on any one of its members would be construed as an attack on all.

Suggestions for Term Papers

1. Analyze the Berlin airlift crisis.

2. Did the creation of NATO needlessly heighten cold war tensions, or was it a necessary response to Soviet aggression?

3. Discuss public opposition to the creation of NATO.

4. Analyze the decision to include West Germany in NATO.

5. Discuss whether NATO has fulfilled its purpose and should be disbanded.

Suggested Sources: See entries 52 and 54 for related items.

REFERENCE SOURCES

NATO: An Annotated Bibliography. Phil Williams. New Brunswick, NJ: Transaction, 1994. Detailed annotations about NATO from its beginning to date. Part of the publisher's International Organizations series.

GENERAL SOURCES

Grathwol, Robert P. *American Forces in Berlin: Cold War Outpost, 1945–1994.* Upland, PA: Diane Publishing, 1995. Description of the American military and its fifty-year stint in Berlin.

Heuser, Beatrice. *NATO, Britain, France and the FRG: Nuclear Strategies and Forces for Europe, 1949–2000.* New York: St. Martin's, 1997. Brief histories of nuclear strategies of NATO members, including Britain, France, and West Germany, from the beginning of the cold war.

Kaplan, Lawrence S. *NATO and the United States: The Enduring Alliance.* Upd. ed. New York: Twayne, 1994. Informative account of NATO and its close association with U.S. foreign policy.

Kay, Sean. *NATO and the Future of European Security.* Lanham, MD: Rowman & Littlefield, 1998. Recent examination of NATO's history and a consideration of the future.

Papacosma, S. Victor, and Mary Ann Heiss. *NATO in the Post-Cold War Era: Does It Have a Future?* New York: St. Martin's, 1995. Detailed examination of NATO progress and development; considers implications for the future.

SPECIALIZED SOURCES

Carpenter, Ted G., and Barbara Conry. *NATO Enlargement: Illusions and Reality.* Washington, DC: Cato, 1998. Examines the decision to expand NATO eastward in Europe.

Clemens, Clay. *NATO and the Quest for Post–Cold War Security.* New York: St. Martin's, 1997. Review of NATO's role and future after the cold war.

Davison, W. Phillips. *The Berlin Blockade: A Study in Cold War Politics.* (1957). Reprint. New York: Ayer, 1990. The history of Berlin from 1945 to 1990, including an excellent account of the Berlin airlift.

Giangreco, D. M. *Airbridge to Berlin: The Berlin Crisis of 1948, Its Origins and Aftermath.* Santa Monica, CA: Presidio Press, 1988. Detailed history of the Berlin airlift from its creation to its subsequent impact.

Haydock, Michael D. *City under Siege: The Berlin Blockade and Airlift.* Dulles, VA: Brassey's, 1998. Excellent analysis of the American airlift to Berlin.

Heller, Francis, and John Gillingham. *NATO: The Founding of the Atlantic Alliance and the Integration of Europe.* New York: St. Martin's, 1996. The development of NATO in Europe; informative account of its creation and role on the Continent.

———, eds. *The United States and the Integration of Europe.* New York: St. Martin's, 1992. Emphasizes the prominence of the U.S. role in supporting NATO.

Parrish, Thomas. *Berlin in the Balance, 1945–1949: The Blockade, the Airlift, the First Major Battle of the Cold War.* Reading, MA: Addison-Wesley, 1998. Informative account of the developments and activities leading to the establishment of NATO.

Reed, John A. *Germany and NATO.* Washington, DC: National Defense University, 1995. Germany's foreign policies as they affect the U.S. role in NATO.

Villaume, Poull. *Cement of Fear: The Cold War and NATO until 1961.* Boulder, CO: Westview, 1998. The history of NATO and its role in the cold war from its inception to 1961.

AUDIOVISUAL SOURCES

The Cold War. Wynnwood, PA: Schlessinger/Library Video, 1995. CD-ROM. Covers twentieth-century history, world events, U.S. foreign policy, and international politics between the two superpowers.

WORLD WIDE WEB

NATO—Overview. December 1996. http://www.saclant.nato.int/nato-Overview.html Brief exposition of NATO, with link to the full treaty.

56. Alger Hiss Trials (1949–1950)

In 1948 ex-communist Whittaker Chambers testified to the House Committee on Un-American Activities (HUAC) that during the 1930s he had received secret government papers from Alger Hiss, a State Department official, and had transmitted this material to the Soviet Union. The statute of limitations precluded charges of treason, but the government brought Hiss to trial in 1949 on charges of perjury. That trial resulted in a hung jury; a second trial, undertaken in large part through the prompting of Congressman Richard M. Nixon, resulted in a guilty verdict. Hiss served more than three years in prison but maintained his innocence up to his death in 1996.

Suggestions for Term Papers

1. Compare the arguments for and against the guilt of Alger Hiss.
2. Discuss the role of Richard Nixon in the Hiss trials.
3. Compare the pretrial careers of Hiss and Chambers.
4. Analyze Chambers' transformation from communist to anticommunist.
5. Discuss the origins and activities of HUAC.

Suggested Sources: See entries 52, 57, and 58 for related items.

GENERAL SOURCES

Busch, Francis X. *Guilty Not Guilty? An Account of the Trials of, The Leo Frank Case, The D.C. Stephenson Case, The Samuel Insull Case, The Alger Hiss Case.* Buffalo, NY: W. S. Hein, 1998. Examines the evidence and the conclusions in four notable cases. From the publisher's Notable American Trials series.

Chambers, Whittaker. *Odyssey of a Friend: Whittaker Chambers' Letters to William F. Buckley, Jr., 1954–1961.* New York: Putnam, 1970. Interesting compilation of correspondence between Chambers and Buckley; treats politics and government, communism, Alger Hiss, and other topics.

Fisher, David. *Hard Evidence: How Detectives Inside the FBI's Sci-Crime Lab Have Helped Solve America's Toughest Cases.* New York: Simon & Schuster, 1995. Discusses how the lab has helped solve crimes through forensic evidence; includes Sacco and Vanzetti, Alger Hiss, and JFK assassination.

Morris, Richard B. *Fair Trial: Fourteen Who Stood Accused, from Anne Hutchinson to Alger Hiss.* Rev. ed. New York: Harper & Row, 1967. Interesting and informative examination of fourteen major trials in the United States, ranging from the seventeenth century to Alger Hiss.

O'Reilly, Kenneth. *Hoover and the Un-Americans: The FBI, HUAC, and the Red Menace.* Philadelphia: Temple University Press, 1983. Thorough account of subversive activities in the United States and the government response during the twentieth century.

SPECIALIZED SOURCES

Cooke, Alistair. *A Generation on Trial: U.S.A. vs. Alger Hiss.* (1952). Reprint. Westport, CT: Greenwood, 1982. Detailed account of the Hiss trial and its ramifications.

Levitt, Morton, and Michael Levitt. *A Tissue of Lies: Nixon vs. Hiss.* New York: McGraw-Hill, 1979. Informative examination of communism and subversive activities in the United States, with an emphasis on the Nixon-Hiss encounter and HUAC.

Moore, William H. *Two Foolish Men: The True Story of the Friendship between Alger Hiss and Whittaker Chambers.* Portland, OR: Moorop Press, 1987. Brief examination of the Chambers-Hiss relationship and the nature of national security in fighting communism.

Rappaport, Doreen. *Alger Hiss Trial.* New York: HarperCollins, 1993. Presents the evidence in the controversial case and asks readers to be the judge. Points out issues, strategies, relevant evidence, and so forth.

Tiger, Edith, ed. *In Re Alger Hiss: Petition for a Writ of Error Coram Nobis.* New York: Hill & Wang, 1979–1980. 2 vols. An extensive array of exhibits as well as narrative in support of Hiss's petition to reexamine the case in volume 2.

Zeligs, Meyer A. *Friendship and Fraticide: An Analysis of Whittaker Chambers and Alger Hiss.* New York: Viking, 1967. Detailed account of the friendship between the two men, with an interpretation of its conclusion.

BIOGRAPHICAL SOURCES

Chambers, Whittaker. *Witness.* (1952). Reprint. Chicago: Regnery Gateway, 1984. Detailed autobiography written by Chambers three years after the Hiss trial; best-seller at the time.

Hiss, Alger. *Recollections of a Life.* New York: Seaver, 1988. Focuses only partially on Hiss's avowed innocence and his unsuccessful attempt to establish it legally.

Hiss, Tony. *Laughing Last: Alger Hiss.* Boston: Houghton Mifflin, 1977. Brief biography written thirty years after the trial.

Smith, John C. *Alger Hiss, The True Story.* New York: Holt, Rinehart and Winston, 1976. Detailed biography that claims to present the accurate version of Hiss's career and trial.

Tanenhaus, Sam. *Whittaker Chambers: A Biography.* New York: Random House, 1997. Exhaustive research on Chambers with emphasis on his life after Hiss; examines his political ideas and contempt for liberalism.

Worth, Esme J. *Whittaker Chambers: The Secret Confession.* London: Mazzard, 1993. Brief biography of Chambers with clarification of subversive activities in the United States at the time.

AUDIOVISUAL SOURCES

The Spy Who Broke the Code. Santa Monica, CA: PBS Home Video, 1989. Interesting and informative 60-minute interview with a former spy who sold the USSR information about military codes.

WORLD WIDE WEB

"Alger Hiss, Perjurer." *Detroit News.* December 1996. http://detnews.com/EDITPAGE/9611/20/2edit/2edit.htm Editorial from a conservative newspaper written at the time of Hiss's death.

Navasky, Victor. "Alger Hiss." *The Nation.* December 1996. http://www.thenation.com/issue/961209/1209nava.htm An opposing view from the editor of a liberal journal.

57. Trial of the Rosenbergs (1950–1951)

The existence of a World War II spy ring that had passed along British and American atomic secrets to the Soviet Union came to light when the British government in 1950 arrested Klaus Fuchs, a physicist who had worked on the Manhattan Project. The German-born Fuchs implicated several others, including the Americans Julius and Ethel Rosenberg. His disclosure came shortly after the Soviet Union tested its first nuclear bomb, thereby destroying America's monopoly of atomic weaponry. Found guilty of espionage in 1951, the Rosenbergs were executed two years later, the only spies executed in peacetime in U.S. history.

Suggestions for Term Papers

1. Discuss the discovery and breakup of the atomic spy ring.
2. Should the Rosenbergs have been executed?
3. Discuss public reaction to the verdict and execution of the Rosenbergs.
4. Discuss the long-range consequences of the Rosenberg case.
5. Discuss the role of the FBI in the Rosenberg case.

Suggested Sources: See entries 52, 56, and 58 for related items.

GENERAL SOURCES

Albright, Joseph, and Marcia Kunstel. *Bombshell: The Secret Story of America's Unknown Atomic Spy Conspiracy.* New York: Times Books, 1997. Recent informative account describing the conduct of espionage activities beginning with the Manhattan Project.

Carmichael, Virginia. *Framing History: The Rosenberg Story and the Cold War.* Minneapolis: University of Minnesota, 1993. Reviews the Rosenberg story in terms of history and culture. Part of the publisher's American Culture series.

Garber, Margorie, and Rebecca L. Walkowitz, eds. *Secret Agents: The Rosenberg Case, McCarthyism and Fifties America.* New York: Routledge, 1995. Essays on the 1950s, including the Rosenbergs, J. Edgar Hoover, the bomb, and McCarthyism. Part of the publisher's Culture Work series.

Neville, John F. *The Press, the Rosenbergs and the Cold War.* Westport, CT: Greenwood, 1995. Study of the cold war agenda, with the primary focus on the press coverage of the Rosenbergs' case from 1950 to 1953.

SPECIALIZED SOURCES

Goldstein, Alvin H. *The Unquiet Death of Julius and Ethel Rosenberg.* New York: Lawrence Hill, 1975. Brief exposition of the circumstances regarding the execution of the pair.

Meeropol, Robert, ed. *We Are Your Sons: The Legacy of Ethel and Julius Rosenberg.* 2d ed. Urbana: University of Illinois, 1986. Correspondence of the Rosenbergs to their sons maintaining their innocence of the charges.

Okun, Rob A. *The Rosenbergs: Collected Visions of Artists and Writers.* New York: St. Martin's, 1988. Collection of portraits of the Rosenbergs done by various American artists.

Philipson, Ilene. *Ethel Rosenberg: Beyond the Myths.* New Brunswick, NJ: Rutgers University Press, 1993. Contends that Ethel Rosenberg had no role in passing secrets to Soviets.

Radosh, Ronald, et al. *The Rosenberg File: A Search for Truth.* 2d ed. New Haven, CT: Yale University Press, 1997. With an introduction containing revelations from National Security Agency and Soviet sources; sheds new light on the proceedings.

Rosenberg, Julius, et al. *The Rosenberg Letters: A Complete Edition of the Prison Correspondence of Julius and Ethel Rosenberg.* Robert Meeropol, ed. Hamden, CT: Garland, 1993. The complete and unedited text of all the surviving letters written by the Rosenbergs during their three years in Sing Sing.

Schneir, Walter. *Invitation to an Inquest: A New Look at the Rosenberg-Sobell Case.* New York: Dell, 1968. Detailed examination of the trial and its ramifications published fifteen years after the event.

Sharlitt, Joseph. *Fatal Error: The Miscarriage of Justice That Sealed the Rosenbergs' Fate.* New York: Macmillan, 1989. Indicts the criminal justice system that allowed the Rosenbergs' sentencing and execution. Judge Kaufman presumed that the Rosenbergs gave the Russians the atomic bomb, which led to the Korean War.

Yalkowsky, Stanley. *The Murder of the Rosenbergs.* New York: Crucible Pub., 1990. From a review of the transcripts of the trial, study of the FBI files, and interviews conducted with various personalities, maintains that unconstitutional laws and cruelty led to the Rosenbergs' persecution and execution.

BIOGRAPHICAL SOURCES

Moss, Norman. *Klaus Fuchs: The Man Who Stole the Atom Bomb.* New York: St. Martin's, 1987. Brief biography of the scientist who initiated the Rosenberg inquiry.

Powers, Richard G. *Secrecy and Power: The Life of J. Edgar Hoover.* New York: Free Press, 1987. Well-researched book covering all aspects of Hoover's controversial career from the Red Scare to his retirement. Used previously unknown personal documents, interviews, presidential papers, and FBI files.

Williams, Robert C. *Klaus Fuchs, Atom Spy.* Cambridge, MA: Harvard University Press, 1987. A biographical study of Fuchs; extensive thirty-six-page bibliography.

AUDIOVISUAL SOURCES

American Justice: The Rosenbergs. New York: A&E Home Video, 1993. Videocassette. 50-minute presentation on the espionage trial of Julius and Ethel Rosenberg.

WORLD WIDE WEB

Pizzo, Stephen. The Rosenberg Communiques. *Web Review.* September 1997. http://www.webreview.com/news/natl/rosenberg/index. html Brief overview of the controversy regarding the question of the Rosenbergs' punishment. Especially useful is the link to excerpts from the partially decoded Soviet cables released by the National Security Agency in 1995.

58. McCarthyism (1950–1954)

The cold war brought widespread fear that a communist threat existed from inside the United States as well as from without. Looking for an issue to boost his reelection chances, Joseph R. McCarthy, a Republican senator from Wisconsin, announced in a speech on February 9, 1950, that he had a list containing the names of 205 communists in the State Department. The senator never publicly showed the list, but over the next several years his sensationalistic investigations and hearings intensified the red scare. While some critics spoke out against his tactics and his anti-Democratic political partisanship, he remained popular and powerful until 1954, when his accusations of widespread communism in the U.S. Army backfired, leading to his censure by the Senate.

Suggestions for Term Papers

1. Analyze the origins of McCarthyism.
2. Discuss HUAC's investigation of Hollywood.
3. Analyze the effects of McCarthyism on teachers and professors.

4. How real was the threat of domestic communism at this time?

5. Compare McCarthyism to the Red Scare after World War I.

Suggested Sources: See entries 52, 56, and 57 for related items.

REFERENCE SOURCES

Encyclopedia of the McCarthy Era. William K. Klingaman. NY: Facts on File, 1996. Unique and comprehensive reference of those who were blacklisted as a result of the Senate hearings in the early 1950s.

GENERAL SOURCES

Ewald, William B., Jr. *McCarthyism and Consensus?* Washington, DC: University Press, 1986. Important book on the role of consensus and media treatment.

Fariello, Griffin. *Red Scare: Memories of the American Inquisition.* New York: Norton, 1995. Testimonies of those personally affected by the era of the "second red scare," including persecutors and "friendly" witnesses.

Fried, Richard. *Nightmare in Red: The McCarthy Era in Perspective.* New York: Oxford University Press, 1990. An examination of the anticommunist crusade, as well as a close analysis of Hiss.

Heale, M. J. *McCarthy's Americans: Red Scare Politics in State and Nation, 1935–1965.* Washington, DC: University Press, 1998. Informative history examines the anticommunist movement in the United States from the mid-1930s to the mid-1960s.

Zeinert, Karen. *McCarthy and the Fear of Communism in American History.* Springfield, NJ: Enslow Publishers, 1998. An account of the fear of communism and its impact in propelling McCarthy to the forefront of American politics.

SPECIALIZED SOURCES

Buckley, William F. *McCarthy and His Enemies: The Record and Its Meaning.* (1954). Reprint. Washington, DC: Regnery, 1995. Contemporary account of McCarthy and his battle against subversive activities of communists in the United States.

Cohn, Roy M. *McCarthy: The Answer to "Tail Gunner Joe."* New York: Manor Books, 1977. The story of Joe McCarthy and his fight with communism, written by his close associate.

Landis, Mark. *Joe McCarthy: The Politics of Chaos.* Selinsgrove, PA: Susquehanna University Press, 1987. Challenges McCarthy's character and style through a conceptual analysis derived from the social sciences.

McCarthy, Joseph. *McCarthyism: The Fight for America.* (1952). Reprint. North Stratford, NH: Ayer, 1977. A personal account illustrating McCarthy's debts to his intellectual predecessors and his own contributions to the anticommunist movement.

Rorty, James. *McCarthy and the Communists.* (1954) Reprint. Westport, CT: Greenwood, 1972. Examination of McCarthy and his role in seeking a vendetta against the Communist party of the United States.

Tuck, Jim. *McCarthyism and New York's Hearst Press: A Study of Roles in the Witch Hunt.* Washington, DC: University Press, 1995. Recent analysis that examines the role of the sensationalistic newspaper during the McCarthy era.

BIOGRAPHICAL SOURCES

Flynn, John T. *McCarthy.* New York: Gordon, 1987. Informative and revealing biography of the late senator.

O'Brien, Michael. *McCarthy and McCarthyism in Wisconsin.* Columbia, MO: University of Missouri Press, 1980. Good biography of the senator from Wisconsin and an analysis of Wisconsin politics at the time.

Oshinsky, David M. *A Conspiracy So Immense: The World of Joe McCarthy.* New York: Free Press, 1983. Carefully drawn biography that places McCarthyism in broader context.

Robeson, Paul. *Here I Stand.* (1958). Reprint. Boston: Beacon, 1998. A concise autobiography that celebrates the life of the popular singer who was blacklisted during the McCarthy era. Reissued on the hundredth anniversary of Robeson's birth.

AUDIOVISUAL SOURCES

The McCarthy Years. Beverly Hills, CA: Fox/CBS Video, 1993. Part of the Edward R. Murrow collection, narrated by Walter Cronkite about the late senator from Wisconsin. 113 minutes.

WORLD WIDE WEB

Schrecker, Ellen. *The Impact of McCarthyism.* December 1997. http://www.crocker.com/~blklist/biblio3final.html A clear and comprehensible evaluation of the effects of McCarthyism on the American character.

59. Korean War (1950–1953)

On June 25, 1950, communist North Korea launched an attack across the 38th parallel against South Korea. Viewing this as another instance of Soviet-inspired aggression, the United States convinced the United Nations to repel the invaders. The North Koreans were nearly victorious until General Douglas MacArthur's surprise amphibious assault behind their lines at Inchon. Recrossing the 38th parallel, UN forces (90 percent of them American) pushed to the Manchurian border, only to meet a fierce assault by Communist Chinese troops, who drove them southward. President Truman fired General MacArthur, who wished to enlarge the war, for insubordination. Truce talks, begun in June 1951, lasted two years, at which time the 38th parallel was roughly reestablished as the border between the two Koreas. Americans lost 34,000 dead.

Suggestions for Term Papers

1. Was it necessary for the United States to fight the Korean War?
2. Was President Truman's decision not to ask Congress for a declaration of war justifiable or a misuse of executive power?
3. Discuss the decision to pursue the North Koreans beyond the 38th parallel.
4. Analyze the Truman-MacArthur controversy.
5. Discuss the long-range consequences of the Korean War for the United States.

REFERENCE SOURCES

Historical Dictionary of the Korean War. James Matray, ed. Westport, CT: Greenwood, 1991. Covers prewar events, people, strategies, battles, agendas, diplomatic meetings, and documents.

Korean War Almanac. Harry G. Summers. New York: Facts on File, 1990. Covers key people, specific battles, strategy and tactics, political factors, and effects on the countries involved.

The Korean War: An Annotated Bibliography. Paul M. Edwards, ed. Westport, CT: Greenwood, 1995. An extensive bibliography providing citations to all aspects of the Korean War.

The Korean War: An Encyclopedia. Stan Sandler, ed. Hamden, CT: Garland, 1995. Contains articles on key topics of Korean War, as well as personalities.

GENERAL SOURCES

Lone, Stewart, and Gowan McCormack. *Korea since 1850.* New York: St. Martin's, 1993. History of Korea from the mid-nineteenth century to the present. Good coverage of the Korean War.

SPECIALIZED SOURCES

Bevin, Alexander. *Korea: The First War We Lost.* New York: Hippocrene, 1986. Important study placing the war in context.

Chen, Jian. *China's Road to the Korean War: The Making of the Sino-American Confrontation.* New York: Columbia University Press, 1994. Informative background history providing insight into the reasons behind Chinese involvement in the war.

Fehrenbach, T. R. *This Kind of War: The Classic Korean War History.* (1963). Reprint. Washington, DC: Brassey's, 1994. Detailed early history of the conduct of the war and the lack of preparation on the part of the United States.

James, D. Clayton, and Anne S. Wells. *Refighting the Last War: Command and Crisis in Korea,* 1950–1953. New York: Free Press, 1993. Recent critical examination of the Korean War with respect to its strategies, campaigns, and decision making.

Meador, Daniel J., ed. *The Korean War in Retrospect: Lessons for the Future.* Lanham, MD: University Press, 1998. Compilation of papers presented at a conference examining various aspects of the war and consideration of the future.

Spanier, John W. *The Truman-MacArthur Controversy and the Korean War.* Cambridge, MA: Belknap, 1959. Detailed account of the controversy regarding the civil supremacy over the military.

Stokesbury, James. *A Short History of the Korean War.* New York: Morrow, 1988. Very readable description in narrative style explaining infantry battlefield movements and the air war.

Stone, Isidor F. *The Hidden History of the Korean War, 1950–1951.* (1952). Reprint. Boston: Little, Brown, 1988. Detailed criticism of the first year of the Korean War written at the time by a noted political crusader.

Stueck, William W. *The Korean War: An International History.* Princeton,

NJ: Princeton University Press, 1995. Detailed history of the war and the nature of diplomatic relations.

Tomedi, Rudy. *No Bugles, No Drums: An Oral History of the Korean War.* New York: Wiley, 1993. Personal perspective on the war by a veteran who served in the military.

Whelan, Richard. *Drawing the Line: The Korean War, 1950–1953.* Boston: Little, Brown, 1990. Thorough account on the conduct of the war, with extensive bibliography.

BIOGRAPHICAL SOURCES

Brady, James. *The Coldest War: A Memoir of Korea.* New York: Crown, 1990. A marine lieutenant's account of the Korean War cites the mistakes made in Korea and repeated in Vietnam.

Manchester, William. *American Caesar, Douglas MacArthur, 1880–1964.* New York: Little, Brown, 1978. Detailed, balanced account of a controversial military hero.

Murphy, Edward F. *Korean War Heroes.* Novato, CA: Presidio, 1992. Collective biography of various men who served in the war.

Sauter, Jack. *Sailor in the Sky: Memoirs of an Aircrewman in the Korean War.* Jefferson, NC: McFarland, 1995. Personal account of a veteran airman with photographs and bibliography.

Stephens, Rudolph W. *Old Ugly Hill: A GI's Fourteen Months in the Korean Trenches, 1952–1953.* Jefferson, NC: McFarland, 1995. Personal and graphic reminiscences of Korean war experience.

AUDIOVISUAL SOURCES

Korea, the Forgotten War. Los Angeles: Fox Hills, 1987. Videocassette. In-depth, 92-minute dramatic account of the war that killed more than 50,000 Americans.

WORLD WIDE WEB

Sik, Kim Young. "Korean War History." *Korean War Webs.* November 1997. wysiwyg://9/http:www.kimsoft.com/kr-war.htm Collection of web sites relevant to the Korean War. Click on "Eyewitness: A North Korean Remembers" for the author's historical and partially autobiographical account from the North Korean perspective.

60. *Brown* v. *Board of Education of Topeka, Kansas* (1954)

On May 17, 1954, Chief Justice Earl Warren wrote the unanimous Supreme Court decision in this case that declared segregation in the nation's public schools was illegal. Rejecting the "separate but equal" yardstick handed down by the Court more than a half-century earlier in *Plessy* v. *Ferguson*, the Warren Court accepted the NAACP's argument that "separate" was inherently unequal and thereby undermined the self-esteem of the segregated. The following year, the Court called for implementation of desegregation "with all deliberate speed," but strong southern opposition as well as a disapproving response from President Eisenhower led to little integration until the 1960s.

Suggestions for Term Papers

1. Compare the judicial arguments of *Plessy* v. *Ferguson* and the *Brown* decision.
2. Discuss the roles of the NAACP and Thurgood Marshall in the *Brown* case.
3. Discuss President Eisenhower's response to the *Brown* decision and to segregation in general.
4. Analyze the efforts to desegregate schools in the South in the decade after the *Brown* decision.
5. Discuss the long-range effects of desegregation in the nation's public schools.

Suggested Sources: See entries 9, 64, and 71 for related items.

REFERENCE SOURCES

African American Almanac. L. Mpho Mabunda, ed. Detroit: Gale, 1997.
    An excellent resource for almost any topic on black history.
African American Encyclopedia. Williams, Michael, ed. Tarrytown, NY:
    1993, 8 vols. (6 vols. plus-2 vol. supplement). Extensively covers the

African American experience in the United States from the beginning to the present day.

Civil Rights in America: 1500 to the Present. Detroit: Gale, 1998. 2 vols. Broad coverage of ethnic, minority, and religious groups and the laws, people, events, court cases, and documents.

Encyclopedia of Civil Rights in America. David Bradley and Shelley F. Fishkin, eds. Armonk, NY: Sharpe, 1997. 3 vols. Well-organized reference source on human rights and civil liberties in the United States.

Historic U.S. Court Cases, 1660–1990. John W. Johnson. New York: Garland, 1992. Cases summarized by legal categories. Contains the history of Supreme Court cases from *Plessy* v. *Ferguson* to *Brown* v. *Board of Education.* Also reviews state court cases.

GENERAL SOURCES

Brownell, Herbert. *Advising Ike: The Memoir of Attorney General Herbert Brownell.* Topeka: University of Kansas Press, 1993. Covers Ike, Earl Warren, *Brown* v. *Board of Education*, and the Civil Rights Act of 1957, among others.

Cecelski, David S. *Along Freedom Road: Hyde County, North Carolina, and the Fate of Black Schools in the South.* Chapel Hill: University of North Carolina Press, 1994. Story of desegregation and how two black schools were preserved.

Douglas, Davidson M. *Reading, Writing and Race: The Desegregation of the Charlotte Schools.* Charlottesville: University of Virginia Press, 1995. Looks at school desegregation as a social good in covering the history of desegregation from *Brown* v. *Board of Education* through the 1970s.

Douglas, William O. *The Douglas Letters: Selections from the Private Papers of Justice William O. Douglas.* Melvin Urofsky, ed. Bethesda, MD: Adler & Adler, 1988. Includes letters tracing unroutine decisions such as *Brown* v. *Board of Education* and *Roe* v. *Wade.* The letters cast an interesting light on events such as Douglas's dispute with Frankfurter.

Harrison, Maureen, and Steve Gilbert, eds. *Schoolhouse Decisions of the United States Supreme Court.* San Diego: Excellent Books, 1997. Details significant Supreme Court decisions affecting schools.

Hornsby, Alton. *Chronology of African American History.* 2d ed. Detroit: Gale, 1997. Chronology updated through December 1996 relating the cultural experiences of African Americans.

Lerner, Max. *Nine Scorpions in a Battle: Great Judges and Cases of the Supreme Court.* New York: Arcade Publishing, 1994. A history and analysis of the most influential judges and cases decided by the Supreme Court.

Pratt, Robert A. *The Color of Their Skin: History of School Desegregation in Richmond, Virginia, 1954–1989.* Charlottesville: University of Virginia Press, 1992. Covers racial discrimination in education, in particular, in Richmond, Virginia.

Wexler, Sanford. *The Civil Rights Movement: An Eyewitness History.* New York: Facts on File, 1996. Chronicles the history of the civil rights movement from Frederick Douglass through *Brown* v. *Board of Education* to the present day.

SPECIALIZED SOURCES

Fireside, Harvey, and Sarah Betsy Fuller. *Brown v. Board of Education: Equal Schooling for All.* Springfield, NJ: Enslows Publishing, 1994. A good legal history of the school desegregation cases, including historical context and subsequent legal developments. Part of the publisher's Landmark Supreme Court Cases series.

Martin, Waldo E., Jr. *Brown* v. *Board of Education: A Brief History with Documents.* New York: St. Martin's, 1998. Details the most significant legal decision of the twentieth century, along with other relevant documents.

Orfield, Gary, and Susan Eaton. *Dismantling Desegregation: The Quiet Reversal of Brown* v. *Board of Education.* New York: New Press, 1996. Discusses how Supreme Court rulings in recent years have reversed *Brown* v. *Board of Education* into resegregation as the Supreme Court has chosen the path of judicial avoidance.

Wilson, Paul E. *A Time to Lose: Representing Kansas in Brown v. Board of Education.* Topeka: University of Kansas Press, 1995. Written by the lawyer responsible for upholding the separate-but-equal doctrine as well as the state's defense; examines the evolution of race relations since that time.

BIOGRAPHICAL SOURCES

Davis, Michael D., and Hunter R. Clark. *Thurgood Marshall: Warrior at the Bar, Rebel on the Bench.* New York, Carol Publishing, 1993. About the first African American to serve on the Supreme Court; covers his relationship to other members of the Court, Martin Luther King, Jr., and other notables.

AUDIOVISUAL SOURCES

Separate But Equal. Chicago: Britannica, 1981. 2 videocassettes. 193-minute drama of *Brown* v. *Board of Education* featuring Sidney Poitier as Thurgood Marshall; Burt Lancaster plays John W. Davis, the opposing counsel, and Richard Kiley is Chief Justice Earl Warren, who rallied the Court to the landmark ruling.

WORLD WIDE WEB

Cozzens, Lisa. *Welcome to African American History.* July 20, 1998. http://www.watson.org/~lisa/blackhistory/html Well-developed exposition and description of African American history by a high school teacher. Click on the table of contents providing an overview of the coverage, with *Brown* v. *Board of Education* under the category of "Early Civil Rights Struggle."

61. Montgomery Bus Boycott (1955–1956)

In Montgomery, Alabama, on December 1, 1955, a black woman named Rosa Parks refused to give her bus seat to a white man. Forced from the bus and arrested for disobeying the local segregation ordinance, she contested the matter. Within a few days, the city's African American community instituted a boycott aimed at eradicating the discrimination practiced by the bus company. Led by a young minister, Martin Luther King, Jr., the Montgomery Improvement Association's hugely successful boycott lasted for more than a year. In November 1956, the Supreme Court ruled (*Gayle et al.* v. *Browser*) that the company's segregation policy was illegal. Both the boycott and the Court's decision put an end to Montgomery's segregated municipal transportation system.

Suggestions for Term Papers

1. Discuss Rosa Parks and her contributions to the civil rights movement during the boycott and in later years.
2. Discuss the role of Martin Luther King, Jr., in the boycott.
3. Analyze why the boycott was successful.
4. What effects did the boycott have on segregated transportation elsewhere?
5. Discuss the long-range consequences of the boycott on the civil rights movement.

Suggested Sources: See entries 60, 64, 71, and 73 for related items.

REFERENCE SOURCES

African American Almanac. 7th ed. Mpho Mabunda, ed. Detroit: Gale, 1997. Standard source in the field; contains a range of historical and current information. Treats events such as the bus boycott in Montgomery.

Civil Rights in America: 1500 to the Present. Jay A. Sigler. Detroit: Gale, 1998. 2 vols. Broad coverage of all aspects of the civil rights struggle, with good coverage of events such as the Montgomery bus boycott.

GENERAL SOURCES

Dornfeld, Margaret. *The Turning Tide: From the Desegregation of the Armed Forces to the Montgomery Bus Boycott (1948–1956).* New York: Chelsea House, 1995. Concise history of the civil rights movement over a pivotal eight-year period.

Parks, Rosa, and Gregory J. Reed. *Dear Mrs. Parks: A Dialogue with Today's Youth.* New York: Lee & Low Books, 1996. Correspondence between Mrs. Parks and black youngsters providing answers to their questions, encouragement, and advice.

SPECIALIZED SOURCES

Burns, Stewart, ed. *Daybreak of Freedom: The Montgomery Bus Boycott.* Chapel Hill: University of North Carolina Press, 1997. Compilation of source material on the boycott; provides insight into the nature of segregated public transportation at the time.

Garrow, David J., ed. *The Walking City: The Montgomery Bus Boycott, 1955–1956.* Brooklyn: Carlson Publishing, 1989. Thorough treatment of the boycott with a collection of contributed essays, each examining a separate aspect.

Hughes Wright, Roberta. *The Birth of the Montgomery Bus Boycott.* Southfield, MI: Charro, 1991. Brief examination of the parts played by Rosa Parks and others in the origin of the boycott.

Leventhal, Willy S., ed. *The Children Coming On: A Retrospective of the Montgomery Bus Boycott, and the Oral History of Boycott Participants.* Montgomery, AL: Black Belt Press, 1997. Collection of source documents and interviews prepared in commemoration of the fortieth anniversary of the boycott.

Robinson, Jo Ann G. *The Montgomery Bus Boycott and the Women Who Started It: The Memoir of Jo Ann Gibson Robinson.* Knoxville: Uni-

versity of Tennessee Press, 1987. Good description of the situation
in Montgomery through the personal narrative of a participant.

Siegel, Beatrice. *The Year They Walked: Rosa Parks and the Montgomery Bus Boycott*. NY: Simon & Schuster Children's, 1992. Brief, easy-to-read history of the Montgomery situation and the actions of the participants in the boycott.

BIOGRAPHICAL SOURCES

Friese, Kai. *Rosa Parks: The Movement Organizes*. Englewood Cliffs, NJ: Silver Burdett, 1990. Concise and easy-to-read biography of Rosa Parks and her role in the race relations crisis.

Hull, Mary. *Rosa Parks*. New York: Chelsea House, 1994. A brief and easy-to-read biography of Parks and her pivotal role in creating the boycott.

Parks, Rosa, and Jim Haskins. *Rosa Parks: My Story*. New York: Dial Books, 1992. More detailed biography as related by Parks, but still relatively brief.

AUDIOVISUAL SOURCES

Martin Luther King, Jr.: Montgomery to Memphis. Chicago: Films, Inc. Video, 1970. Videocassette. Comprehensive, 29-minute presentation of King's life from the Montgomery bus boycott to his assassination. Narration by Harry Belafonte and others.

WORLD WIDE WEB

Jones, Ellis M. *The Montgomery Bus Boycott Page*. September 1997. http://socsci.colorado.edu/~jonesem/montgomery.html Contains links to relevant sites and pages such as a periodical article, introductory and biographical information on Rosa Parks, a lesson, and a picture.

62. Elvis Presley and Rock 'n' Roll Music

In the early 1950s disc jockey Alan Freed coined the term *rock 'n' roll* to describe music then known as rhythm and blues (R&B), which was popular primarily among African Americans. Although a few African American R&B singers gained prominence during the decade, it was the white Mississippi-born Elvis Presley who was mainly responsible for the widespread popularity of rock music with white audiences. Many people deplored the sexual suggestiveness of rock 'n' roll, but fully 80 percent of America's television audience viewed Presley's first appearance in 1956 on the *Ed Sullivan Show*.

Suggestions for Term Papers

1. Why did rock 'n' roll became popular during the 1950s?
2. Analyze Elvis Presley's rise to stardom.
3. Analyze the continued popularity of Elvis Presley.
4. Discuss the career of a prominent rock singer or rock group.
5. Discuss opposition to rock 'n' roll.

REFERENCE SOURCES

The Elvis Encyclopedia: The Complete and Definitive Reference Book on the King of Rock and Roll. David E. Stanley and Frank Coffey. Los Angeles: General Publishing, 1994. Extensive treatment of Elvis's life and career written by his stepbrother. More than a biography, it contains over 250 photographs and a detailed chronology. Provides excellent insight.

Elvis Presley: A Bio-Bibliography. Pasty G. Hammontree. Westport, CT: Greenwood, 1985. A detailed examination of Elvis and the Elvis legend through analysis of books, articles, interviews, and other material. Treats his life, career, and impact.

Elvis Presley, a Complete Reference: Biography, Chronology, Concert Lists, Filmography, Discography, Vital Documents, Bibliography, Index. Wendy Sauers, comp. Jefferson, NC: McFarland, 1984. Complete reference volume devoted to the topic; thorough handbook and guide to Elvis.

The Rock and Roll Readers Guide: A Comprehensive Guide to Books by and about Musicians and Their Music. Gary M. Krebs. New York: Billboard Books, 1997. An extensive listing of writings on musicians including Elvis—biographies, magazines, reference works and others.

Rock on Almanac, The First Four Decades of Rock 'n' Roll: A Chronology. 2d ed. Norm N. Nite. New York: HarperPerennial, 1992. Provides a chronology of rock music developments along with discographies and indexes.

Rock On: The Illustrated Encyclopedia of Rock 'n' Roll. Norm N. Nite. New York: Harper, 1982–1985. 3 vols. For informed description of early rock history, see *The Solid Gold Years* (vol. 1) and *The Years of Change, 1964–1978* (vol. 2) by Nite and Ralph M. Newman.

GENERAL SOURCES

Brown, Charles T. *The Rock and Roll Story: From the Sounds of Rebellion to an American Art Form.* Englewood Cliffs, NJ: Prentice-Hall, 1983. Good analysis of the evolution of rock and roll from its roots in slave chants to the 1980s; contains a brief bibliography and discography.

Gillett, Charlie. *The Sound of the City: The Rise of Rock and Roll.* 2d ed. New York: Da Capo, 1996. Describes the development of rock and roll as an urban phenomenon descending from doo-wop and rhythm and blues.

Pielke, Robert G. *You Say You Want a Revolution: Rock Music in American Culture.* (1986). Reprint. Chicago: Nelson-Hall, 1988. Examines the birth of rock and roll as an antiestablishment happening and the first cultural revolution in American society.

Stuessy, Joe, and Scott Lipscomb. *Rock and Roll: Its History and Stylistic Development.* 3d ed. Upper Saddle River, NJ: Prentice-Hall, 1988. A new edition of this popular historical treatment examining the artistic presentation of rock and roll music. Good analysis of musical structures and harmonies.

Ward, Ed, et al. *Rock of Ages: The Rolling Stone History of Rock and Roll.* New York: Rolling Stone/Summit Books, 1986. Detailed, popular version of the history and critical artistry of rock and roll beginning with the Sinatra influences of the 1940s and ending with the time of publication.

Wicke, Peter. *Rock Music: Culture, Aesthetics, and Sociology.* New York: Cambridge University Press, 1990. Concise, serious examination of the place of rock music within contemporary culture; sees it as a product of an industry that has been used by the working class to express itself.

SPECIALIZED SOURCES

Chadwick, Vernon, ed. *In Search of Elvis: Music, Race, Art, Religion.* Boulder, CO: HarperCollins, 1997. Proceedings of the first annual International Conference on Elvis Presley held in 1995 at the University of Mississippi. Numerous contributors examine the many facets and influences (some of which are personal to the writer) surrounding the impact of Elvis.

Doll, Susan M. *Understanding Elvis: Southern Roots vs. Star Image.* New York: Garland, 1998. Considers Elvis's career with respect to his southern roots; examines the early years when his identity shaped the new music, as well as the later years when he was transformed into a movie star and Las Vegas performer.

Plasketes, George. *Images of Elvis Presley in American Culture, 1977–1997: The Mystery Train.* New York: Haworth, 1997. A comprehensive and well-documented exposition of the Elvis influence in the United States. Contains a brief bibliography, discography, and even filmography.

Quain, Kevin, ed. *The Elvis Reader: Text and Sources on the King of Rock'n' Roll.* New York: St. Martin's, 1992. Emphasis on the texts and sources relevant to the study of Elvis; includes essays, articles, excerpts, and filmography.

Rodman, Gilbert B. *Elvis after Elvis: The Posthumous Career of a Living Legend.* New York: Routledge, 1996. An examination of American popular culture and its reluctance to let Elvis die.

Strausbaugh, John. *Reflections on the Birth of the Elvis Faith.* New York: Blast Books, 1995. Examines Elvis as an article of faith of the American scene complete with religious fervor and worship.

BIOGRAPHICAL SOURCES

Gentry, Tony. *Elvis Presley.* New York: Chelsea House, 1994. Brief, easy-to-read biography describing Elvis's rise from poverty to fame and wealth. Good black and white photographs.

Krohn, Katherine E. *Elvis Presley: The King.* Minneapolis: Lerner Publications, 1994. A sixty-four-page biography examining the childhood, career, and legacy of the star. Some photographs.

Moore, Scotty. *That's Alright, Elvis: The Untold Story of Elvis' First Guitarist and Manager, Scotty Moore.* New York: Macmillan, 1998. Rare photographs and interesting text describing the manner in which Elvis transformed popular music.

AUDIOVISUAL SOURCES

Elvis: The Echo That Will Never Die. Orland Park, IL: MPI Home Video, 1986. Videocassette. Various celebrities discuss Elvis and his impact; interesting stories about his rise to fame. 50 minutes.

WORLD WIDE WEB

"Script for January 8, 1997." *Merriam-Webster Word for the Wise.* January 1997. http://www.m-w.com/wftw/1897.htm An interesting analysis of the origin of the phrase "rock and roll" from Merriam-Webster's two-minute radio show.

63. Polio Vaccine Discovered

Poliomyelitis was one of the most feared epidemic diseases of the twentieth century. In 1952 alone, it struck 50,000 Americans, killing more than 3,000 of them. Dr. Jonas E. Salk discovered a vaccine for this crippling disease that could be derived from the inactive virus itself, and in 1955 nearly 2,000 schoolchildren were inoculated with his vaccine. The following year Dr. Albert Sabin perfected an oral vaccine that derived from the live virus. The work of both men led to the rapid decline of the disease.

Suggestions for Term Papers

1. Discuss the prevaccine attempts to combat polio.
2. Discuss Franklin D. Roosevelt's personal battle against polio.
3. Discuss Dr. Jonas Salk's discovery of the first polio vaccine.
4. Discuss Dr. Albert Sabin and the discovery of the oral polio vaccine.
5. Analyze the battle for public vaccination of schoolchildren.

GENERAL SOURCES

Black, Kathryn. *In the Shadow of Polio: A Personal and Social History.* Reading, MA: Addison-Wesley, 1996. An interesting narrative, part biography and part history, of a polio victim and her treatment.

Daniel, Thomas M., and Frederick C. Robbins, eds. *Polio.* Rochester, NY: University of Rochester, 1997. Historical narrative on the fight against polio in the twentieth century.

Gould, Tony. *A Summer Plague: Polio and Its Survivors.* New Haven, CT: Yale University Press, 1995. Detailed history of polio and its victims; recalls the fear of the summer seasons, when polio struck.

Munsat, Theodore, ed. *Post-Polio Syndrome.* Boston: Butterworth-Heinemann, 1991. Brief collection of essays on polio and its complications.

Rogers, Naomi. *Dirt and Disease: Polio before FDR.* New Brunswick, NJ: Rutgers University Press, 1992. Informative history of the disease in the United States. In the Health and Medicine in American Society series.

Sink, Alice E. *The Grit behind the Miracle: A True Story of the Determination and Hard Work behind an Emergency Infantile Paralysis Hospital, 1944–1945, Hickory, North Carolina*. Lanham, MD: University Press of America, 1998. Interesting and informative case history of a polio hospital.

SPECIALIZED SOURCES

Carter, Richard. *Breakthrough: The Saga of Jonas Salk*. New York: Trident, 1966. Detailed examination of the discovery of the polio vaccine.

Klein, Aaron E. *Trial by Fury: The Polio Vaccine Controversy*. New York: Scribner, 1972. Examination of the controversy regarding use of the polio vaccination on the population.

Smith, Jane S. *Patenting the Sun: Polio and the Salk Vaccine*. (1990). Reprint. New York: Anchor/Doubleday, 1991. Good historical account of polio and use of the vaccine in the United States.

BIOGRAPHICAL SOURCES

Bredeson, Carmen. *Jonas Salk: Discoverer of the Polio Vaccine*. Hillside, NJ: Enslow Publishers, 1993. Brief and easy-to-read description of Salk's life and career, including his work on influenza and AIDS.

Curson, Marjorie. *Jonas Salk*. Englewood Cliffs, NJ: Silver Burdett, 1990. Easy-to-read treatment of Salk's work on the polio vaccine. In the publisher's Pioneers in Change series.

Sherrow, Victoria. *Jonas Salk*. New York: Facts on File, 1993. Brief and interesting biographical portrait of the scientist who created the polio vaccine.

Tomlinson, Michael. *Jonas Salk*. Vero Beach, FL: Rourke Publications, 1993. Easy-to-read, brief account of Salk and his pursuit of the polio vaccine.

AUDIOVISUAL SOURCES

A World of Ideas with Bill Moyers: The Science of Hope with Jonas Salk. Santa Monica, CA: PBS Home Video, 1990. Interesting interview with Dr. Salk conducted by Bill Moyers for public television.

WORLD WIDE WEB

" 'Sabin Sundays' Helped Wipe Out Polio." *Insiders' Guide to Cincinnati.*
July 1997. http://insiders.com/cincinnati/sb-healthcare2.htm Interesting description of the period in 1960 when thousands of Cincinnati schoolchildren were administered the vaccine developed by
Sabin, a local physician.

64. Little Rock School Crisis (1957)

In 1957 a federal judge ordered Little Rock, Arkansas, to enroll nine
African Americans in the city's Central High School. Segregationist
Governor Orval Faubus used the National Guard to defy this order.
Pressure from President Eisenhower and another federal court order
convinced Faubus to remove the Guard, but a threatening crowd
forced the African American students to flee the school. This, as well
as rioting in the African American section of the city, caused Eisenhower to deploy the already-nationalized Guardsmen and to send in
U.S. Army troops. The African American students, under military
protection, attended school. Little Rock closed all its public schools
the following year to prevent integration.

Suggestions for Term Papers

1. Compare the roles of Governor Faubus and President Eisenhower
   in the crisis.
2. Discuss public reaction to the crisis.
3. Discuss the defiance of integration in other southern public
   schools.
4. Analyze the role of federal courts in integrating southern public
   schools.
5. Discuss the remembrances of African Americans who enrolled in
   newly integrated schools during the 1950s.

Suggested Sources: See entries 60 and 71 for related items.

REFERENCE SOURCES

Historical Dictionary of School Segregation and Desegregation: The American Experience. Jeffrey A. Raffel. Westport, CT: Greenwood, 1998. Comprehensive dictionary treating issues, topics, and events relevant to the history of school integration, along with the attendant conditions.

GENERAL SOURCES

Adams, Julianne L., and Thomas A. Deblack. *Civil Disobedience: An Oral History of School Desegregation in Fayetteville, Arkansas, 1954–65.* Fayetteville: University of Arkansas Press, 1994. Collection of interviews that provides insight into how Fayetteville became the first southern city to obey the law and accommodate the *Brown* decision.

Berman, Daniel M. *It Is So Ordered: The Supreme Court Rules on School Segregation.* New York: Norton, 1966. Concise examination of legal history regarding the major decisions of the 1950s; provides insight into the conditions under which the Little Rock actions were undertaken.

Blaustein, Albert P., and Clarence C. Ferguson, Jr. *Desegregation and the Law: The Meaning and Effect of the School Segregation Cases.* 2d ed. rev. New York: Vantage, 1962. Detailed exposition of the various school segregation cases and the ensuing results.

Brown, Philip L. *A Century of "Separate But Equal" Education in Anne Arundel County.* New York: Vantage, 1988. Good historical examination of school segregation and discrimination over a long period of time in a Maryland county.

Duram, James C. *A Moderate among Extremists: Dwight D. Eisenhower and the School Integration Crisis.* Chicago: Nelson-Hall, 1981. Revealing and interesting account of Eisenhower and his policies during these momentous years.

Haskins, James, and Jim Haskins. *Separate But Not Equal: The Dream and the Struggle.* New York: Scholastic Trade, 1988. Comprehensive history of the struggle for equal education. Opens with the confrontation at Little Rock, then goes back to the beginnings in the nineteenth century.

Hauser, Pierre. *Great Ambitions: From the "Separate But Equal" Doctrine to the Birth of the NAACP (1896–1909).* New York: Chelsea House, 1995. Easy-to-read background history that provides insight into the conditions that led to the *Brown* decision and eventually to Little Rock action.

SPECIALIZED SOURCES

Beals, Melba P. *Warriors Don't Cry: A Searing Memoir of the Battle to Integrate Little Rock's Central High.* New York: Pocket Books, 1995. Thorough and detailed account of the integration of Central High School by nine brave African American students. The author was one of them and provides a vivid picture of the violence and fear.

Huckaby, Elizabeth. *Crisis at Central High, Little Rock, 1957–58.* Baton Rouge: Louisiana State University Press, 1980. Brief but thorough case study of the developments and activities regarding the Little Rock incident.

O'Neil, Laurie A. *Little Rock: The Desegregation of Central High.* Brookfield, CT: Millbrook, 1994. Brief, easy-to-read but enlightening perspective regarding the struggle and its background. From the publisher's Spotlight on American History series.

Wells, John G. *Time Bomb, The Faubus Revolt: A Documentary—1977 Addendum.* Little Rock: General Publishing, 1977. Describes the Faubus opposition. First published in 1962, this 1977 effort provides concluding commentary.

BIOGRAPHICAL SOURCES

Faubus, Orval. *Down from the Hills.* Little Rock: Pioneer, 1980. Detailed and thorough autobiography describing Faubus's life and career; a second issue was published by Democrat Printing and Lithographing in 1985.

Reed, Roy. *Faubus: The Life and Times of an American Prodigal.* Fayetteville: University of Arkansas Press, 1997. Recent biography on the controversial governor; revealing treatment of segregation issues.

AUDIOVISUAL SOURCES

School Colors. Santa Monica, CA: PBS Home Video, 1994. Videocassette. Up-to-date, insightful, and interesting 143-minute examination of racial issues in Berkeley (CA) high school. Dating, violence, segregation, and other issues are discussed by students along with footage of current conditions.

WORLD WIDE WEB

Rains, Craig. *Little Rock Central High 40th Anniversary.* 1997. http// www.centralhigh57.org/ Site commemorating the fortieth anniversary of the struggle in Little Rock. Fine exposition with links to the event and the history that created it.

65. *Sputnik* (1957)

In October 1957 the Soviet Union launched *Sputnik I,* the first satellite to orbit the earth. The following month it launched into orbit the much larger *Sputnik II,* which carried a dog. Thanks to secret U-2 spy plane forays over the Soviet Union, President Eisenhower did not see this as a threat to American security, but others, who lacked his information, did. As a result, some congressmen and the general public assumed there was a dangerous "missile gap" favoring the Soviets. This fear led to the creation of the National Aeronautics and Space Administration (NASA); the National Defense Education Act to improve instruction in math, science, and foreign languages; and increased funding for the National Science Foundation. In January 1958 the United States put into space its first satellite, *Explorer I.*

Suggestions for Term Papers

1. Discuss public reaction to the launching of *Sputnik* I and *Sputnik* II.
2. Discuss how President Eisenhower responded to *Sputnik.*
3. Compare American and Soviet missile technology at the time of *Sputnik.*
4. Discuss the creation and purposes of the National Aeronautics and Space Administration.
5. Analyze the impact of the National Education Act on American education.

Suggested Sources: See entries 52 and 67 for related items.

REFERENCE SOURCES

The Cambridge Encyclopedia of Space. Michael Rycroft, ed. New York: Cambridge University Press, 1990. Informative reference source providing well-written and authoritative information on all aspects of space travel.

The Encyclopedia of U.S. Spacecraft. Bill Yenne. New York: Exeter/Simon & Schuster, 1985. Treats all U.S. manned and unmanned spacecraft that followed *Sputnik* up to the date of publication.

GENERAL SOURCES

Hansen, James R. *Spaceflight Revolution: NASA Langley Research Center from Sputnik to Apollo.* Washington, DC: National Aeronautics and Space Administration, 1995. Detailed history of the research center that contributed so much to the U.S. space program.

Launius, Roger D. *NASA: A History of the U.S. Civil Space Program.* Malabar, FL: Krieger Publishing, 1994. Concise, interesting, and informative history of NASA from its creation to the present.

————. *NASA and the Exploration of Space: With Works from the NASA Art Collection.* New York: Stewart, Tabori & Chang, 1998. Recent comprehensive illustrated history of space flight.

————, and Howard E. McCurdy, eds. *Spaceflight and the Myth of Presidential Leadership.* Urbana: University of Illinois Press, 1997. Collection of essays by specialists examining the role of the presidency in the U.S. space program; begins with Eisenhower and his reluctance to enter the space race.

Spangenburg, Ray, and Diane Moser. *Opening the Space Frontier.* New York: Facts on File, 1989. Brief but comprehensive overview of the origins and developments of worldwide space flight from its visionary beginnings to the moon landings.

SPECIALIZED SOURCES

Bulkeley, Rip. *The Sputniks Crisis and Early United States Space Policy: A Critique of the Historiography of Space.* Bloomington: Indiana University Press, 1991. Examines the causes of what the author terms "stunning defeat" in the space race when *Sputnik I* and *Sputnik II* were launched.

Clowse, Barbara B. *Brainpower for the Cold War: The Sputnik Crisis and the National Defense Education Act of 1958.* Westport, CT: Greenwood, 1981. Examines the impact of *Sputnik* in propelling support for the first piece of legislation to provide funds for higher education.

Divine, Robert A. *The Sputnik Challenge.* New York: Oxford University Press, 1993. Interesting and revealing account of the national hysteria over the launching of *Sputnik*; Eisenhower was unable to quell the fears that resulted in numerous efforts to remedy the perceived missile gap.

Dow, Peter B. *Schoolhouse Politics: Lessons for the Sputnik Era.* Cambridge, MA: Harvard University Press, 1991. Well-written, seriously researched account of the emergence and ultimate decline of an innovative social science program of study in elementary education with its innovative techniques and emphasis on the scientific method; examines the economic and political controversies in this program founded by the National Science Foundation.

Gurney, Gene, and Clare Gurney. *The Launching of Sputnik, October 4, 1957: The Space Age Begins.* New York: Franklin Watts, 1975. Easy-to-read, concise account of events leading up to the launching of *Sputnik* and its impact.

McDougall, Walter A. *The Heavens and the Earth.* New York: Basic Books, 1985. Interesting account of the early development of the space program relating the major impact of *Sputnik* in setting government goals.

BIOGRAPHICAL SOURCES

Glennan, Thomas K., and J. D. Hunley. *The Birth of NASA: The Diary of T. Keith Glennan.* Washington, DC: NASA History Office, National Aeronautics and Space Administration, 1993. Detailed personal account providing a thorough description of the creation of NASA.

Harford, James. *Korolev: How One Man Masterminded the Soviet Drive to Beat America to the Moon.* New York: Wiley, 1997. Detailed and revealing biography of S. P. Korolev, founder of the Soviet space program, who spearheaded the effort until his death at age fifty-nine in 1966.

AUDIOVISUAL SOURCES

The Class of the 20th Century: 1952–1961. New York: A&E Home Video, 1991. Videocassette. One of six videos in the series examining events of the twentieth century up to 1990; the "1952–1961" coverage treats the race for space, among other important developments. 100 minutes each.

Eyewitness Encyclopedia of Space and the Universe. New York: DK Multimedia, 1996. CD-ROM. Excellent treatment of the space program; includes prints, sound, graphics, video, and animation.

WORLD WIDE WEB

"The Beep Heard Round the World." *Scientific American: Explorations.* October 1997. http://www.sciam.com/explorations/100697sputnik/hall__1.html Good narratives on various aspects surrounding *Sputnik* with leads to additional pages as well as the NASA site commemorating the fortieth anniversary of the event.

66. Golden Age of Television

Although television was invented in the 1920s, it became a staple item in American life and culture only during the 1950s. By the end of that decade, 90 percent of all households owned at least one television set. In many instances, television had radically altered Americans' lifestyles. The quality of programming varied widely, ranging from broad comedy to sporting events and serious drama, and from congressional investigations to quiz shows, one of which, *Twenty One*, proved to be rigged. For all its benefits television seemed to one chairman (Newton Minow) of the Federal Communications Commission (FCC) "a vast wasteland."

Suggestions for Term Papers

1. Was television a golden age or a "vast wasteland" during the 1950s?
2. Discuss the effects of televised congressional hearings during the 1950s.
3. Analyze the effects of television on political life.
4. Compare the federal regulation of television in the 1950s and today.
5. Discuss the effects of television on American education.

REFERENCE SOURCES

Encyclopedia of Television. Horace Newcomb, ed. Chicago: Fitzroy Dearborn, 1998. 3 vols. Comprehensive and serious treatment of television and the television industry; provides biographical sketches, topical essays, and bibliographic references. Won two awards as an outstanding publication.

History of the Mass Media in the United States: An Encyclopedia. Margaret A. Blanchard, ed. Chicago: Fitzroy Dearborn, 1998. Comprehensive coverage of all media (television, radio, newspapers, film, books, magazines, etc.) from the seventeenth century to 1995. Over 475 alphabetically arranged entries, ranging from 500 to 5,000 words.

Total Television: A Comprehensive Guide to Programming from 1948 to the Present. 3d ed. Alex McNeil. New York: Penguin Books, 1991. An alphabetical listing of series with credits, chronological listing of selected special programs and broadcasts, copies of the prime-time schedules for the major networks from 1948 on, lists of Peabody and Emmy Award winners, and listings of top-rated series for each season.

Warner Bros. Television: Every Show of the Fifties and Sixties Episode-by-Episode. Lynn Woolley et al. Jefferson, NC: McFarland, 1985. Based on material drawn from *TV Guide* and press releases, provides descriptions of both obscure and well-known series, along with biographies of performers and illustrations.

GENERAL SOURCES

Goldstein, Fred P. and Stan Goldstein. *Prime-time Television: A Pictorial History from Milton Berle to Falcon Crest.* New York: Crown, 1983. Interesting and informative historical survey of television broadcasting from the "golden age" to the 1980s.

Kisseloff, Jeff. *The Box: An Oral History of Television from 1920 to 1961.* New York: Viking, 1995. Well-written and thorough; based on interviews with 400 television personalities and workers, provides insight into considerations related to economic, technical, and sociopolitical aspects of television.

Minow, Newton, and Craig L. LaMay. *Abandoned in the Wasteland Children, Television, and the First Amendment.* New York: Hill & Wang, 1995. Provides a message similar to that intoned in Minow's 1961 "vast wasteland" speech; sees the ascendancy of commercial greed over public interest as beginning in the 1950s.

SPECIALIZED SOURCES

Marling, Karal A. *As Seen on TV: The Visual Culture of Everyday Life in the 1950s.* Cambridge, MA: Harvard University Press, 1994. Interesting account of pop culture as represented by television of the 1950s; treats such topics as Elvis, Mrs. Eisenhower's fashions, Disneyland, painting by numbers, kitchen appliances, and TV dinners.

Shulman, Arthur, and Roger Youman. *How Sweet It Was: Television, a Pictorial Commentary.* New York: Shorecrest, 1966. Compilation of twenty years of television personalities and trivia with brief commentary and 1,435 photographs.

Sturcken, Frank. *Live Television: The Golden Age of 1946–1958 in New York.* Jefferson, NC: McFarland, 1990. Anecdotal account of the experiment with live television, with an examination of the primary programs and the creative minds behind them.

Wilk, Max. *The Golden Age of Television: Notes from the Survivors.* New York: Delacorte, 1976. Entertaining and interesting work that covers much the same territory as Sturcken's effort above. Treats the early sitcoms, quiz shows, variety shows, and dramatic presentations.

BIOGRAPHICAL SOURCES

Berle, Milton. *B. S. I Love You: Sixty Funny Years with the Famous and the Infamous.* New York: McGraw-Hill, 1988. Autobiography filled with entertaining anecdotes by one of the leading television comedians of the 1950s.

Krampner, Jon. *The Man in the Shadows: Fred Coe and Golden Age of Television.* New Brunswick, NJ: Rutgers University Press, 1997. Interesting biographical account of the exciting life of the director of *Philco Television Playhouse*; provides historical awareness of the rise and decline of live television theater.

Sanders, Coyne S., and Tom Gilbert. *Desilu: The Story of Lucille Ball and Desi Arnaz.* New York: Morrow, 1993. Detailed biography of the husband-wife comedy team of the 1950s.

Whelan, Kenneth. *How the Golden Age of Television Turned My Hair to Silver.* Walker, 1973. Interesting collection of behind-the-scenes stories regarding television production in the 1950s and the author's progressing career, ending up as the director of the *Morning Show*.

AUDIOVISUAL SOURCES

Golden TV: Memories of the '50s. Orland Park, IL: MPI Home Video, 195?. 3 videocassettes. Vintage television vignettes are presented with each 60-minute volume—Jack Benny, Loretta Young, Groucho Marx, Howdy Doody, Cisco Kid, and others.

WORLD WIDE WEB

Rich, Candace. "Variety: The Golden Age of Television." *Fifties Website.* 1996; updated November 1997. http://www.fiftiesweb.com/variety.htm An interesting look at the past with brief treatment given to the shows starring Milton Berle, Ted Mack, Arthur Godfrey, Sid Caesar, and others. Illustrated with small photographs.

67. U-2 Plane Shot Down (1959)

In 1959 relations between the United States and the Soviet Union began to improve, culminating in an agreement to hold a summit meeting in Paris in May 1960 between President Eisenhower and Soviet leader Nikita Khrushchev. Only a few days before, however, the Soviets downed a U-2 American spy plane and produced the plane's pilot, Francis Gary Powers, after Eisenhower had denied the existence of the spy mission. Khrushchev subsequently walked out of the Paris summit conference, but not before denouncing Eisenhower and revoking his earlier invitation for the president to visit the Soviet Union. Powers was exchanged for a Soviet spy in 1962.

Suggestions for Term Papers

1. How important was the U-2 for surveillance of the USSR?
2. Discuss the development and special features of the U-2.
3. Compare how Khrushchev and Eisenhower handled the U-2 incident.
4. Discuss the trial and subsequent life of Francis Gary Powers.
5. Discuss the U.S.'s later use of spy planes.

Suggested Sources: See entry 52 for related items.

REFERENCE SOURCES

Dwight D. Eisenhower, 1890–1969: Chronology, Documents, Bibliographical Aids. Dobbs Ferry, NY: Oceana Publications, 1970. A good listing of references covering all aspects of Eisenhower's career. Somewhat dated.

GENERAL SOURCES

Ambrose, Stephen E., and Richard H. Immerman. *Ike's Spies: Eisenhower and the Espionage Establishment.* Garden City, NY: Doubleday, 1981. Examines Ike's dealing with intelligence and the Secret Service starting with World War II.

Beschloss, Michael R. *May-Day: Eisenhower, Khrushchev and the U-2 Affair.*

New York: Harper & Row, 1986. The fullest account of this celebrated incident, by an adept diplomatic historian.

Bowie, Robert R., and Richard H. Immerman. *Waging Peace: How Eisenhower Shaped an Enduring Cold War Strategy.* New York: Oxford
University Press, 1998. A recent account of the Eisenhower plan for
national security and foreign relations during the critical years of his
terms.

Cook, Blanche W. *The Declassified Eisenhower: A Divided Legacy.* Garden
City, NY: Doubleday, 1981. An examination into the once-secret
considerations and developments in foreign relations and strategies
during the Eisenhower tenure.

Johnson, Miles B. *The Government Secrecy Controversy, a Dispute Involving
the Government and the Press in the Eisenhower, Kennedy, and Johnson
Administrations.* New York: Vantage, 1967. Concise examination of
the increasing awareness of the withholding of government information.

Linden, Carl A. *Khrushchev and the Soviet Leadership, 1957–1964.* (1966).
Reprint. Baltimore: Johns Hopkins University Press, 1983. Provides
insight into the nature of the relationship between Khrushchev and
other top officials in that critical period.

Mayer, Michael S., ed. *The Eisenhower Presidency and the 1950s.* Boston:
Houghton-Mifflin, 1998. Up-to-date examination of the formative
Eisenhower years, providing insight into the situation that would ex-
ist at the time of the U-2 flight.

Tompson, William J. *Khrushchev: A Political Life.* New York: St. Martin's,
1995. Recent examination of politics and government in the Khrushchev years; good insight provided into the man and his manner.

SPECIALIZED SOURCES

Powers, Francis G. *Operation Overflight: The U-2 Spy Pilot Tells His Story
for the First Time.* New York: Holt, 1970. Powers's only book telling
his story of the momentous event.

BIOGRAPHICAL SOURCES

Crankshaw, Edward. *Khrushchev: A Biography.* London: Sphere, 1968.
Good detail and lengthy bibliography.

Medvedev, Roy A. *Khrushchev.* Garden City, NY: Anchor/Doubleday,
1983. Good biography translated from the Russian; examines the
successes and failures of the Khrushchev era.

Parmet, Herbert S. *Eisenhower and the American Crusades.* (1972). Reprint.
New Brunswick, NJ: Transaction Publishers, 1998. Good general bi-

ography providing insight into Eisenhower's life and orientation. From the American Presidents Series.

PERIODICAL ARTICLES

Beschloss, Michael R. "The U-2 Crisis." *US News and World Report*. Pt. 1: "The Spy Flight That Killed Ike's Dream," March 24, 1986, 36–41, 44–45. Pt. 2: "Ike's Nightmare Summit at Paris," March 31, 1986, 34–37. Interesting and informative two-part account of Eisenhower's embarrassment over the incident.

Moser, Don. "The Time of the Angel: The U-2, Cuba, and the CIA." *American Heritage* 28: 4–15 (October 1977). Description of a critical period in U.S.-Soviet relations; use of the U-2 to identify Soviet missiles in Cuba after the Powers incident.

AUDIOVISUAL SOURCES

Francis Gary Powers: The True Story of the U-2 Spy. New York: Worldvision Home Video, 1977. Videocassette. 2-hour television dramatization of the entire event with Lee Majors; based on Powers's recollections.

WORLD WIDE WEB

Garmon, Linda. "Spy in the Sky." *The American Experience*. September 1997.   http//www.boston.com/wgbh/pages/amex/u2/u2.html From the PBS television show. Provides useful brief descriptions and excellent links. One is able to click on the real story, photographs taken by the U-2, declassified information regarding its specifications, and other material.

68. Bay of Pigs Invasion (1961)

Dismayed by Fidel Castro's confiscation of the property of American businesses, his trade agreement with the Soviet Union, and his repressive measures, President Eisenhower in 1960 ordered the CIA to undermine his regime. Newly elected President Kennedy approved the CIA plan but without American airpower to protect the invading force of 1,400 anti-Castro Cubans. The latter landed at the Bay of Pigs on April 17, 1961, but without air support and the expected uprising of the Cuban people, the invasion failed dismally. Fewer than

10 percent of the invaders escaped death or capture. The episode proved a severe embarrassment to President Kennedy and the United States.

Suggestions for Term Papers

1. Discuss why the relationship between the United States and Cuba deteriorated.
2. Analyze President Kennedy's decision to order the invasion.
3. Was the invasion doomed to fail?
4. Discuss the effects of the invasion on America's image in the world.
5. Discuss the CIA attempts to assassinate Castro.

Suggested Sources: See entry 69 for related items.

REFERENCE SOURCES

Encyclopedia of the American Military: Studies of the History, Policies, Institutions and Roles of the Armed Forces in War and Peace. John E. Jessup and Louise B. Ketz, eds. 3 vols. New York: Scribner's Sons, 1994. Detailed, general-purpose encyclopedia for the study of the American military divided into four parts; part 4 examines the military performance from the colonial period to post-Vietnam.

Encyclopedia of U.S. Foreign Relations. Bruce W. Jentleson and Thomas G. Paterson. 4 vols. New York: Oxford University Press, 1997. Comprehensive reference work on U.S. foreign relations; over a thousand articles ranging from 150 to 10,000 words. Provides background on the Cuban situation.

A Guide to Cuban Collections in the United States. Louis A. Perez. Westport, CT: Greenwood, 1991. State-by-state guide to archival resources on collections relating to Cuba; 520 entries indexed by collection and subject.

GENERAL SOURCES

Dickstein, Morris. *Gates of Eden: American Culture in the Sixties.* Cambridge, MA: Harvard University Press, 1997. Interesting examination of the links between culture and politics in the 1960s; analysis of successes and failures, including U.S.-Soviet-Cuban relations.

Drachman, Edward R., et al. *Presidents and Foreign Policy: Countdown to Ten Controversial Decisions.* Albany: State University of New York Press, 1997. Interesting case studies of the background and circumstances regarding ten important presidential decisions, including Kennedy's decision to support the Bay of Pigs invasion.

Paterson, Thomas G. *Contesting Castro: The United States and the Triumph of the Cuban Revolution.* New York: Oxford University Press, 1995. A thorough and detailed examination of U.S. foreign relations from the 1950s; sees the United States as ignorant and arrogant in dealing with various situations.

Perez, Louis A. *Essays on Cuban History: Historiography and Research.* Gainesville: University of Florida Press, 1995. Collection of essays examining the history and politics of Cuba; includes examination of U.S.-Cuban relations and the effects of the Cuban revolution.

SPECIALIZED SOURCES

Bissell, Richard M., Jr., et al. *Reflections of a Cold Warrior: From Yalta to the Bay of Pigs.* New Haven, CT: Yale University Press, 1996. The now-deceased lead author had served as head of the CIA Covert Operations; his failure to assess the Bay of Pigs operation halted his career rise.

Higgins, Trumbull. *The Perfect Failure: Kennedy, Eisenhower, and the CIA at the Bay of Pigs.* New York: Norton, 1987. Examines the blunders that accompanied the Bay of Pigs invasion.

Lynch, Grayston L. *Decision for Disaster: Betrayal at the Bay of Pigs.* Washington, DC: Brassey's, 1998. Recent examination of the incident; seen from the perspective of the Cuban participants.

Persons, Albert C. *Bay of Pigs: A Firsthand Account of the Mission by a U.S. Pilot in Support of the Cuban Invasion Force in 1961.* Jefferson, NC: McFarland, 1990. Primary source of the action; good summary of political scene.

BIOGRAPHICAL SOURCES

Giglio, James N. *The Presidency of John F. Kennedy.* Lawrence, University of Kansas Press, 1991. Balanced examination of Kennedy's presidency that faults him for his unproductive relations with Congress but not for his decisions on the Bay of Pigs or Cuban missile crisis.

Salinger, Pierre D. *John F. Kennedy, Commander in Chief: A Profile in Leadership.* New York: Penguin, 1997. Firsthand account of Kennedy's relationship with the military—from the Bay of Pigs through Laos, the Cuban missile crisis, and the space program.

AUDIOVISUAL SOURCES

Bay of Pigs. New York: Cinema Guild, 1973. Videocassette. 103-minute documentary of invasion; includes actual documentary footage and reenactments.

WORLD WIDE WEB

Elliston, Jon. "The Bay of Pigs Invasion." ParaScope, Inc. (1996). http://www.parascope.com/articles/1296/bayofpigs.htm Special report provides historical overview of the invasion and the events leading up to it, as well as sources and documents.

69. Cuban Missile Crisis (1962)

Fearing a U.S. military invasion following the Bay of Pigs fiasco, Cuba convinced the Soviet Union to install missiles on the island. In mid-October 1962, the Kennedy administration, having discovered the construction of sites capable of launching offensive missiles against the United States, debated the proper course of action. The president opted for a quarantine of Cuba. Nuclear war loomed large as Soviet vessels approached the waiting American ships, but after intensive negotiations Premier Khrushchev ordered the Soviet ships to turn back and promised to remove Soviet missiles and bombers in exchange for an American pledge not to invade Cuba and to remove U.S. missiles from Turkey.

Suggestions for Term Papers

1. Discuss how the United States discovered the existence of the missiles.
2. Discuss the Kennedy administration's debate over what to do about the missiles.
3. Analyze Soviet-American negotiations and the resolution of the crisis.
4. Discuss public reaction to the crisis.
5. Did President Kennedy manage the crisis skillfully or dangerously?

Suggested Sources: See entry 68 for related items.

REFERENCE SOURCES

The Kennedy Tapes: Inside the White House during the Cuban Missile Crisis.
Ernest R. May and Philip D. Zelikow, eds. Cambridge, MA: Belknap
Press of Harvard University Press, 1997. Collection of tape tran-
scripts from the Kennedy files.

The Secret Cuban Missile Crisis Documents. Central Intelligence Agency.
Washington, DC: Brassey's, 1994. Collection of documents relating
to the Cuban missile crisis; released by the CIA.

GENERAL SOURCES

Bostdorff, Denise M. *The Presidency and the Rhetoric of Foreign Crisis.* Columbia: University of South Carolina Press, 1994. Interesting comparison of the political oratory of six presidents—three Democrats
and three Republicans—when each was faced with a different crisis
from 1962 (Cuban missile crisis and Kennedy) to 1983 (Grenada
and Reagan).

SPECIALIZED SOURCES

Blight, James G., and David A. Welch. *On the Brink: Americans and Soviets
Reexamine the Cuban Missile Crisis.* New York: Hill and Wang,
1989. After more than twenty-five years, both sides again consider
the crisis and its implications.

———. *The Shattered Crystal Ball: Fear and Learning in the Cuban Missile
Crisis.* Savage, MD: Rowman & Littlefield, 1990. A retrospective of
the fearful conditions in 1962.

Brugioni, Dino A. *Eyeball to Eyeball: The Inside Story of the Cuban Missile
Crisis.* New York: Random House, 1991. Detailed, authoritative, and
thorough description of the entire event.

Chayes, Abram. *The Cuban Missile Crisis: International Crises and the Role
of Law.* (1974). Reprint. Lanham, MD: University Press of America,
1987. A brief examination of legal implications, published under the
auspices of the American Society of International Law.

Detzer, David. *The Brink: Cuban Missile Crisis, 1962.* New York: Crowell,
1979. Good examination of political maneuvering during the missile
crisis.

Divine, Robert A. *The Cuban Missile Crisis.* 2d ed. New York: M. Wiener
Publishing, 1988. Description with analysis of the Cuban missile crisis and the outcomes.

Finkelstein, Norman H. *Thirteen Days/Ninety Miles: The Cuban Missile Crisis.* New York: J. Messner, 1994. Brief overview of the thirteen-day crisis.

Fursenko, A. A., and Timothy Naftali. *One Hell of a Gamble: Khrushchev, Castro, and Kennedy, 1958–1964.* New York: Norton, 1997. Detailed account of the dangerous game of brinkmanship in foreign relations played by the principals in this drama.

Garthoff, Raymond L. *Reflections on the Cuban Missile Crisis.* Washington, DC: Brookings Institution, 1989. Informative reexamination of the crisis published by the Washington think tank.

Gow, Catherine H. *The Cuban Missile Crisis.* San Diego: Lucent Books, 1997. Examines all aspects regarding the confrontation in brief and easy-to-read fashion.

Gribkov, A. I., and William Y. Smith. *Operation ANADYR: U.S. and Soviet Generals Recount the Cuban Missile Crisis.* Chicago: Edition Q, 1994. A retrospective analysis of the crisis by high-ranking military officials.

Hilsman, Roger. *The Cuban Missile Crisis: The Struggle over Policy.* Westport, CT: Praeger, 1996. Well-written account providing insight into the nature of the confrontation over foreign policy and the crisis.

Medland, William J. *The Cuban Missile Crisis of 1962: Needless or Necessary?* New York: Praeger, 1988. Critical review and analysis of the government position during the crisis.

Nathan, James A. *The Cuban Missile Crisis Revisited.* New York: St. Martin's 1992. A recent retrospective and analysis of the crisis.

Pope, Ronald R., ed. *Soviet Views on the Cuban Missile Crisis: Myth and Reality in Foreign Policy Analysis.* Washington, DC: University Press of America, 1982. Interesting and revealing analysis of foreign relations between the two countries during the time; uses government source documents.

Thompson, Robert S. *The Missiles of October: The Declassified Story of John F. Kennedy and the Cuban Missile Crisis.* New York: Simon & Schuster, 1992. Revealing study of Kennedy and his response during the crisis.

White, Mark J. *The Cuban Missile Crisis.* Hampshire, UK: Macmillan, 1996. Detailed examination of the crisis with analysis of events.

AUDIOVISUAL SOURCES

American Foreign Policy: Kennedy and Confrontation. Chicago: Britannica Films, 1981. Videocassette. 16-minute presentation that includes the crisis. From the American Foreign Policy series.

WORLD WIDE WEB

Fourteen Days in October: The Cuban Missile Crisis. August 1997. http://
hyperion.advanced.org/11046 A well-designed site that is valuable
in the amount of information it contains and is noteworthy for its
organization. One may click on "Introduction," "Crisis Center,"
"Briefing Room," "Recon Room," etc. Illustrated material provided.

70. John F. Kennedy Assassinated (1963)

In an effort to heal local party factionalism and boost his own stand-
ing for the next year's election, President Kennedy visited Texas in
November 1963. While passing through Dallas in his motorcade, he
was fatally shot on November 22 by Lee Harvey Oswald. Oswald, in
turn, was shot while in police custody by Jack Ruby. The nation was
profoundly shocked and grieved by the president's murder. A special
investigating commission headed by Chief Justice Earl Warren subsequently decided that Oswald had acted alone in the assassination.
Nevertheless, many people, then and since, believed that a conspiracy
had existed.

Suggestions for Term Papers

1. Discuss why Dallas was considered dangerous for Kennedy to visit
   and why he visited there.
2. Compare the findings of the Warren Commission Report with
   those of various conspiracy theories.
3. Compare the actual assassination with what has been depicted in
   fiction and film.
4. Discuss the 1979 House of Representatives committee investigation of the assassination.
5. Discuss the effects of the Kennedy assassination on American life.

GENERAL SOURCES

Baden, Michael M., and Judith A. Hennessee. *Unnatural Death: Confessions of a Medical Examiner.* New York: Random House, 1989. Interesting narrative examining the untimely deaths of various notables; (e.g., Kennedy, Belushi, Presley).

DeLoach, Cartha. *Hoover's FBI: The Inside Story by Hoover's Trusted Lieutenant.* Washington, DC: Regnery Publishing, 1995. Comprehensive narrative of the FBI and its powerful head; interesting account of the Kennedy assassination's effect.

Lindop, Edmond. *Assassinations That Shook America.* New York: Franklin Watts, 1992. Concise, easy-to-read account of major assassinations in the United States; describes assassins and their motives. Treats Kennedy and his brother as well as King, Garfield, McKinley, and others.

SPECIALIZED SOURCES

Bishop, Jim. *The Day Kennedy Was Shot.* (1968). Reprint. New York: Gramercy, 1998. The popular classic work covering in detailed fashion the events of that day.

Callahan, Bob. *Who Shot JFK?* New York: Simon & Schuster, 1993. Similar to Hurt's work (see below) in its willingness to accept various theories regarding the assassination.

Fonzi, Gaeton. *The Last Investigation.* Emeryville, CA: Thunder's Mouth, 1993. Holds that the investigation was deliberately misdirected to investigate organized crime. Written by a former House investigator.

Groden, Robert J. *The Killing of a President: The Complete Photographic Record of the JFK Assassination.* New York: Viking Studio, 1994. More than 600 photographs of the participants, the event, and the outcome.

Hampton, Wilborn. *Kennedy Assassinated!: The World Mourns.* New York: Scholastic, 1997. Fascinating account of the assassination written by a reporter at the UPI office in Dallas at the time of the tragedy. Brief and easy to read.

Hurt, Henry. *Reasonable Doubt: An Investigation into the Assassination of John F. Kennedy.* New York: H. Holt, 1986. Examination of various alternative theories regarding the assassination and the possibility that some may have validity; similar to Callahan's effort (see above).

Nechiporenko, Oleg M. *Passport to Assassination.* New York: Carol Publishing, 1993. By a former agent and operative who met Oswald; takes a firm position against any conspiracy theory involving the Soviet Union.

Newman, John. *Oswald and the CIA.* New York: Carol & Graf, 1995. A reexamination of the controversy regarding the assassination; includes an interpretation of Oswald's distribution of pro-Castro handbills in New Orleans.

Scott, Peter D. *Deep Politics and the Death of JFK.* (1993). Reprint. Berkeley: University of California Press, 1996. Views the assassination as part of a conspiracy; sees the fruit companies as a major culprit due to their concern about spreading communist influence.

Sloan, Bill. *JFK: Breaking the Silence.* Dallas: Taylor Publishing, 1993. Supports conspiracy theories; describes views and observations of twelve people.

United States. Warren Commission. *The Warren Commission Report: The Official Report of the President's Commission on the Assassination of President John F. Kennedy.* (1964). Reprint. Stamford, CT: Longmeadow, 1993. The most recent reprint of the full report of the commission's inquiry, providing a detailed examination of the events that led up to and followed the assassination.

BIOGRAPHICAL SOURCES

Manchester, William R. *One Brief Shining Moment: Remembering Kennedy.* Boston: Little, Brown, 1983. Personal portrait of Kennedy the man; provides a rejoinder to his critics. Good anecdotes.

Posner, Gerald L. *Case Closed: Lee Harvey Oswald and the Assassination of JFK.* New York: Random House, 1993. Detailed description of Oswald's life and his unhappiness with any political system; discredits claims of those who favor a conspiracy theory.

AUDIOVISUAL SOURCES

Who Killed JFK: Facts Not Fiction. Beverly Hills: CBS/Fox Video, 1992. Videocassette. 75-minute presentation examining the assassination with interviews of important personalities; hosted by Dan Rather from a CBS telecast.

WORLD WIDE WEB

McAdams, John. The Kennedy Assassination Home Page. August 1997. http://mcadams.posc.mu.edu/home.htm Great site for Kennedy assassination buffs; contains brief descriptions of all phases and theories along with links to featured articles. Subject index.

71. Martin Luther King, Jr., and the Civil Rights Movement

The Reverend King's initial notable involvement with civil rights came with his leadership of the Montgomery bus boycott in 1955–1956. In 1957 he formed the Southern Christian Leadership Conference (SCLC) and launched peaceful demonstrations against segregation in the South, notably in Birmingham (1963) and Selma (1965) Alabama. The latter, which met with violent resistance, helped the passage of the Voting Rights Act (1965). The March on Washington, D.C., in August 1963, an event that drew 250,000, was the high point of King's career. The following year he received the Nobel Peace Prize. Later he denounced the war in Vietnam and led peaceful protest marches in the North. He was assassinated on April 4, 1968, in Memphis, Tennessee.

Suggestions for Term Papers

1. Analyze Dr. King's philosophy and use of nonviolence.
2. Discuss the effects of the Selma, Alabama, protest on the civil rights movement.
3. Discuss the effect of media coverage on the civil rights movement.
4. Discuss African American opposition to Dr. King's philosophy and tactics.
5. Analyze the achievements and failures of Dr. King.

Suggested Sources: See entries 9, 60, 61, and 72–73 for related items.

REFERENCE SOURCES

The ABC-CLIO Companion to the Civil Rights Movement. Mark Grossman. Santa Barbara, CA: ABC-CLIO, 1994. Useful alphabetically arranged reference source treating issues, events, and personalities.

Black/White Relations in American History: An Annotated Bibliography. Leslie V. Tischauser. Blue Ridge Summit, PA: Scarecrow, 1997. Comprehensive bibliography of black-white relations in the United States since 1945.

Encyclopedia of African-American Civil Rights: From Emancipation to the Present. Charles D. Lowery and John F. Marszalek, eds. Westport, CT: Greenwood, 1992. Well-written source of information on personalities, legislation, print media, events, and other items; more than 800 entries by numerous contributors.

The Encyclopedia of Civil Rights in America. David Bradley and Shelley F. Fishkin, eds. Armonk, NY: Sharpe Reference, 1997. 3 vols. Comprehensive collection of nearly 700 alphabetically arranged entries treating all aspects of the civil rights movement in the United States (e.g., personalities, historical events and eras, economics, education, culture, landmark court cases).

Facts on File Encyclopedia of Black Women in America. Darlene C. Hine, ed. New York: Facts on File, 1997. Contains eleven volumes, each devoted to a different area of endeavor (business, education, social activism, etc.). Profiles of more than 1,000 African American women over the past 400 years.

Historical Dictionary of the Civil Rights Movement. Ralph E. Luker. Blue Ridge Summit, PA: Scarecrow, 1996. Over 300 entries.

Let Freedom Ring: Documentary History of the Modern Civil Rights Movement. Peter B. Levy, ed. Westport, CT: Praeger, 1992. Collection of ninety-five documents (speeches, sermons, essays, court cases, etc.). Contains the words of influential personalities such as King and Malcolm X and also of less well-known civil rights workers.

GENERAL SOURCES

Goings, Kenneth W., and Raymond A. Mohl, eds. *The New African American Urban History.* Thousand Oaks, CA: Sage, 1996. Revealing and informative collection of essays by different scholars treating a variety of topics related to blacks in the urban environment from slavery days to 1964.

Mann, Robert. *The Walls of Jericho: Lyndon Johnson, Hubert Humphrey, Richard Russell, and the Struggle for Civil Rights.* New York: Harcourt Brace, 1996. Compelling analysis of the civil rights struggle examining the lives of three U.S. senators and four presidents whose careers affected the movement.

Washington, James M., ed. *A Testament of Hope: The Essential Writings of Martin Luther King, Jr.* San Francisco: Harper & Row, 1986. Useful and comprehensive collection of King's writings—sermons, speeches, essays, interviews, and excerpts from his books. Good critical interpretation and commentary.

SPECIALIZED SOURCES

Albert, Peter J., and Ronald Hoffman, eds. *We Shall Overcome: Martin Luther King, Jr., and the Black Freedom Struggle*. (1990). Reprint. New York: Da Capo, 1993. Popular history of King and the struggle for civil rights.

Bullard, Sara. *Free at Last: A History of the Civil Rights Movement and Those Who Died in the Struggle*. New York: Oxford University Press, 1993. Concise and easy-to-read history of the movement for civil rights, with emphasis on the period from 1954 (school desegregation) to 1968 (King's assassination).

Carson, Clayborne, ed. *The Movement: 1964–1970*. Westport, CT: Greenwood, 1993. Compiled by the staff of the King Papers Project; collection of papers, documents, and other material providing excellent insight into the nature of the civil rights movement.

———, et al., eds. *The Eyes on the Prize Civil Rights Reader: Documents, Speeches, and Firsthand Accounts from the Black Freedom Struggle, 1954–1990*. Rev. ed. New York: Viking, 1991. Produced in conjunction with a PBS television series; comprehensive collection of relevant primary source material. (See the Williams work below.)

Levine, Michael L. *African Americans and Civil Rights: From 1619 to the Present*. Phoenix: Oryx, 1996. Interesting history of the civil rights struggle and overview of laws and customs. Contains biographical sketches and a glossary. Part of the publisher's Social Issues in American History series.

Levy, Peter B. *The Civil Rights Movement*. Westport, CT: Greenwood, 1998. Provides narrative history, biographical sketches, and annotated bibliography. Topical chapters contain primary documents. Part of the publisher's Guides to Historic Events of the Twentieth Century series.

McKissack, Patricia, and Frederick McKissack. *The Civil Rights Movement in America: From 1865 to the Present*. 2d ed. Danbury, CT: Children's Press, 1991. Well-written and readable revised edition of a classic work; contains photographs, and excellent narrative.

Patterson, Charles. *The Civil Rights Movement*. New York: Facts on File, 1995. Examination of major events beginning with *Brown* v. *Board of Education* in 1954 to the early 1970s. Similar in scope and coverage to the Bullard work above.

Posner, Gerald. *Killing the Dream: James Earl Ray and the Assassination of Martin Luther King, Jr.* New York: Random House, 1998. Latest theory on the assassination; published on the thirtieth anniversary of King's death.

Riches, William T. M. *The Civil Rights Movement: Struggle and Resistance.* New York: St. Martin's, 1997. Chronological account of all aspects of the civil rights struggle; examines organizations, personalities, and strategies.

Wexler, Sanford. *The Civil Rights Movement: An Eyewitness History.* New York: Facts on File, 1993. Readable accounts from a variety of people witnessing a variety of events, with emphasis on the 1950s and 1960s. Part of the publisher's Eyewitness History series.

Williams, Juan. *Eyes on the Prize: America's Civil Rights Movement 1954–1965.* New York: Viking, 1987. Illustrated well-written textual narrative to accompany the PBS series of the same name. See Carson source book above.

BIOGRAPHICAL SOURCES

Branch, Taylor. *Parting the Waters: America in the King Years, 1954–63.* New York: Simon & Schuster, 1988. Excellent, detailed, and thorough account of the life and times of the civil rights leader beginning with the early years of the King family ministry to focus on the critical period between the Montgomery bus boycott and the Kennedy assassination; continued by *Pillar of Fire* (see next entry).

——. *Pillar of Fire: America in the King Years, 1963–65.* New York: Simon & Schuster, 1998. Recently published second volume in the historical biography that provides an in-depth look at the two years following the Kennedy assassination (see previous entry).

Jakoubek, Robert. *Martin Luther King, Jr.* New York: Chelsea House, 1989. Concise and easy-to-read but informative biography of King and the civil rights movement; contains a chronology as well as a bibliography.

Lane, Mark, and Dick Gregory. *Murder in Memphis: The FBI and the Assassination of Martin Luther King.* (1977). Reprint. New York: Thunder's Mouth, 1993. One of the first works to raise questions about the accepted version of the killing. Originally published under the title of *Code Name Zorro.*

Powledge, Fred. *We Shall Overcome: Heroes of the Civil Rights Movement.* New York: Scribner's Sons, 1993. Begins with a brief history of the movement for civil rights and leads into collective biography of ten relatively unknown individuals who dared to oppose prevailing societal inequities.

Smith, Jessie C., ed. *Black Heroes of the 20th Century.* Detroit: Visible Ink, 1997. Collective biography of modern black Americans who have had significant impact.

Thompson, Julius E. *Percy Greene and the Jackson Advocate: The Life and*

Times of a Radical Conservative Black Newspaperman, 1897–1977.
Jefferson, NC: McFarland, 1994. Interesting brief biography of an
outspoken critic of the radical left.

Washington, Linn. *Black Judges on Justice: Perspectives from the Bench.* New
York: New Press/Norton, 1994. Collective biography of fourteen
African American judges; survey of their lives, careers, and philo-
sophical positions, with example rulings.

AUDIOVISUAL SOURCES

Friedman, Thomas. "Dr. Martin Luther King, Jr.: A Historical Perspective."
Biography. New York: A&E Home Video, 1994. 1-hour television
presentation of King's life; film footage, photographs, and narration.

WORLD WIDE WEB

Grossman, Wendy. "The Voting Rights Act: 30 years Later." *The Chronicle
Online.* 1997. http://www.chronicle.duke.edu/chronicle/95/11/
15/s08TheVoting.html Four-page narrative written for the *Duke
University Chronicle* in 1995 on the impact of the Voting Rights Act
and its current interpretation.

72. The 1960s Counterculture

Alienated from parental values and by the Vietnam War and racism,
large numbers of youths, mostly middle class and educated, abandoned mainstream American culture during the late 1960s. Similar
in ways to the Beats of the 1950s, these "hippies," as they were
called, turned to rock and folk music, drugs, and promiscuous sex to
flaunt society's and their parents' teachings. Denouncing materialism
and life's complexities, some established simple urban or rural com-
munes. In August 1969 more than 500,000 peacefully celebrated the
counterculture at a huge rock festival in Woodstock, New York, but
a similar concert a few months later in Altamont, California, was
marred by violence. The counterculture, but not all its values, dwin-
dled rapidly after the early 1970s.

Suggestions for Term Papers

1. Compare the Beats and the hippies.

2. Analyze the popularity of a counterculture singer or musical group.

3. Would the counterculture have existed without the war in Vietnam?

4. Compare the Woodstock and Altamont music festivals as symbols of the counterculture.

5. Analyze the legacy of the counterculture to American life.

Suggested Sources: See entries 71, 73, 75, and 77 for related items.

REFERENCE SOURCES

The ABC-CLIO Companion to the 1960s Counterculture in America. Neil A. Hamilton. Santa Barbara, CA: ABC-CLIO, 1997. Excellent treatment of personalities, events, themes, and issues associated with the counterculture movement; alphabetically arranged.

GENERAL SOURCES

Burner, David. *Making Peace with the 60s.* Princeton, NJ: Princeton University Press, 1996. Good survey of the troubled decade as the author examines the splintering and breakdown of liberalism; interesting perspective on the counterculture.

Casale, Anthony M., and Philip Lerman. *Where Have All the Flowers Gone? The Fall and Rise of the Woodstock Generation.* Kansas City: Andrews and McMeel, 1989. Revealing examination of the baby boom generation and social conditions from the 1960s on.

Francese, Carl, and Richard S. Sorrell. *From Tupelo to Woodstock: Youth, Race, and Rock-and-Roll in America, 1954–1969.* 2d ed. Dubuque, IA: 1995. Interesting survey of social history and popular culture of the 1960s.

Weiner, Rex, and Deanne Stillman. *Woodstock Census: The Nationwide Survey of the Sixties Generation.* New York: Viking, 1979. Report of the nature of the attitudes, perceived conflicts, and radicalism of the time.

SPECIALIZED SOURCES

Chepesiuk, Ron. *Sixties Radicals, Then and Now: Candid Conversations with Those Who Shaped the Era.* Jefferson, NC: McFarland, 1995. Excellent insight into 1960s radicalism provided through conversations with former hippies and protesters some thirty years later.

Goldstein, Richard. *Reporting the Counterculture.* Boston: Unwin Hyman, 1989. Concise account of journalism and mass media coverage of the counterculture during the 1960s and 1970s.

Graubard, Mark. *Campustown in the Throes of the Counterculture (1968–1972).* Minneapolis, MN: Campus Scope, 1974. Detailed examination of the political activity of students and faculty during the frenzied period.

Guinness, Os. *The Dust of Death: The Sixties Counterculture and How It Changed America Forever.* Wheaton, IL: Crossway Books, 1994. Thorough survey of the counterculture and Christianity and their impact on the American character.

Hoffman, Abbie, et al. *Vote!* New York: Warner Paperback Library, 1972. Written by Hoffman and Jerry Rubin, two of the leading voices of dissent; exposition of social conditions of the time.

Horowitz, David et al., eds. *Counterculture and Revolution.* New York: Random House, 1972. Compilation of extracts and selections from the works of the major voices (Cleaver, Rubin, Leary, Hayden, and others).

Kaiser, Charles. *1968 in America: Music, Politics, Chaos, Counterculture, and the Shaping of a Generation.* New York: Weidenfeld & Nicolson, 1988. Interesting examination of that pivotal year by one of that generation; sees positive aspects of the nonconformity while criticizing Eugene McCarthy.

Laffan, Barry. *Communal Organization and Social Transition: A Case Study from the Counterculture of the Sixties and Seventies.* New York: P. Lang, 1997. A university study of communal living among adherents of the subculture.

Perry, Paul, et al. *On the Bus: The Complete Guide to the Legendary Trip of Ken Kesey and the Merry Pranksters and the Birth of the Counterculture.* New York: Thunder's Mouth, 1990. Provides insight into that trip. With forewords by Hunter S. Thompson and Jerry Garcia.

Whitmer, Peter O., and Bruce VanWyngarden. *Aquarius Revisited: Seven Who Created the Sixties Counterculture That Changed America.* New York: Macmillan, 1987. More of a social history than a biography of the major literary figures: Burroughs, Ginsberg, Kesey, Leary, Mailer, Robbins, and Thompson.

Hippies and Yippies

Feigelson, Naomi. *The Underground Revolution: Hippies, Yippies, and Others.* New York: Funk & Wagnalls, 1970. Brief contemporary exposition of the hippie movement in the United States.

Miller, Timothy. *The Hippies and American Values.* Knoxville: University of Tennessee Press, 1991. Concise examination of hippie social morality and its relationship to American values and traditions.

Stein, David L. *Living the Revolution: The Yippies in Chicago.* Indianapolis: Bobbs-Merrill, 1969. Concise, focused account of the riots during the 1968 Democratic National Convention.

Feminism and Sexuality

Echols, Alice. *"Daring to be Bad": Radical Feminism in America, 1967–75.* Minneapolis: University of Minnesota Press, 1989. Focused history of women's liberation and the radical movement examining the various positions of its adherents and controversies within its ranks.

Harrison, Cynthia. *On Account of Sex: The Politics of Women's Issues, 1945–1968.* Berkeley: University of California Press, 1988. Clear, lucid historical overview of the progressive development of the women's movement beginning with the Truman administration.

Ryan, Barbara. *Feminism and the Women's Movement: Dynamics of Change in Social Movement Ideology and Activism.* New York: Routledge, 1992. Survey of the history of the women's movement with particular emphasis on the period following 1970.

Woodstock

Curry, Jack. *Woodstock: The Summer of Our Lives.* New York: Weidenfield & Nicolson, 1989. Interesting and enlightening treatment of the Woodstock Festival in 1969 and its impact on those who attended.

Makower, Joel. *Woodstock: The Oral History.* New York: Doubleday, 1989. Detailed account of the Woodstock Festival.

Spitz, Bob. *Barefoot in Babylon: The Creation of the Woodstock Music Festival, 1969.* New York: Norton, 1989. Detailed record of the planning and promotion of the monumental event.

BIOGRAPHICAL SOURCES

Horowitz, David. *Radical Son: A Generational Odyssey.* New York: Free Press, 1997. A searing indictment of New Left politics and the counterculture by a former leading New Left figure.

Rubin, Jerry. *Growing Up at Thirty-Seven.* New York: M. Evans/Lippincott,

1976. Brief autobiography of the radical career of the young Jerry Rubin.

Sloman, Larry. *Steal This Dream: Abbie Hoffman and the Counterculture Revolution against America*. New York: Doubleday, 1998. Recent biographical study of the noted radical; useful social history of the time.

AUDIOVISUAL SOURCES

Sixties Headlines. Orland Park, IL: MPI Home Video, 1990. Videocassette. 30-minute survey of the momentous events, including assassinations, the moon landing, Vietnam, and the Beatles.

WORLD WIDE WEB

Counterculture of the Sixties. June 1996. http://www.fred.net/nhhs/ html3/culture.htm Brief illustrated overview of the chaotic period; excellent link to listing of relevant web sites treating all phases of the movement.

73. Black Power Movement

Although the majority of African Americans supported the peaceful tactics and goals of integration voiced by the Reverend Martin Luther King, Jr., some turned to threatened or actual violence to achieve civil rights or even separatism. Such leaders of the Student Non-Violent Coordinating Committee (SNCC) as Stokely Carmichael and H. Rap Brown preached defiance and black nationalism, as did the Black Muslims, who denounced Christianity as a slave religion. The Black Panthers, led by such radicals as Bobby Seale and Huey Newton, publicly carried weapons and became involved in shoot-outs with law officials. Malcolm X, a Black Muslim who became the most famous advocate of black power, was assassinated in 1965 after breaking with the Muslims' leader, Elijah Muhammad.

Suggestions for Term Papers

1. Analyze the achievements and failures of the black power movement.

2. Discuss the origins of the Black Muslims.

3. Compare the philosophy and tactics of Martin Luther King, Jr., and Malcolm X.

4. Discuss the legacy of Malcolm X.

5. Compare the black nationalism movement of the 1960s with that of the 1920s.

Suggested Sources. See entries 71 and 72 for related items.

REFERENCE SOURCES

African American Encyclopedia. Michael W. Williams, ed. Tarrytown, NY: Marshall Cavendish, 1993–1997. 8 vols. Comprehensive reference set covering the history and heritage of African Americans from their African roots to the present time. Articles range in size from 1,250 to 5,000 words, providing insight into issues, events, personalities, and developments.

Dictionary of Race and Ethnic Relations. Rev. ed. Ellis Cashmore. New York: Routledge, 1996. Comprehensive examination of the changes in perspective regarding black-white relations. Such events as the O. J. Simpson trial have polarized the population along racial lines.

Encyclopedia of African-American Culture and History. Jack Salzman et al., eds. New York: Macmillan, 1996. 5 vols. Treats a wide variety of topics and issues, including black power; includes coverage of personalities, themes, and events.

GENERAL SOURCES

Cleaver, Eldridge. *Soul on Ice.* New York: McGraw-Hill, 1968. Classic work of the sixties; collection of letters, essays, and reflections that Cleaver wrote while in prison.

King, Richard H. *Civil Rights and the Idea of Freedom.* New York: Oxford University Press, 1993. Clearly written account of the civil rights movement in the 1960s; good insight into the conflict between Martin Luther King and the more radical black power advocates.

Patterson, Charles. *The Civil Rights Movement.* New York: Facts on File, 1997. Concise history of the movement with emphasis on its origins, personalities, and development; includes an examination of the Black Panthers and other radical reformers.

SPECIALIZED SOURCES

Carmichael, Stokely, and Charles V. Hamilton. *Black Power: The Politics of Liberation in America.* (1967). Reprint. New York: Vintage Books, 1992. Contemporary examination of the political elements involved in the black power struggle by one of the leading advocates of the time.

Franklin, V. P. *Black Self-Determination: A Cultural History of African-American Resistance.* 2d ed. Brooklyn: Lawrence Hill Books/Independent Publishers Group, 1992. Brief, comprehensive account of black cultural development and establishment of identity.

Haines, Hubert H. *Black Radicals and the Civil Rights Movement, 1954–1970.* Knoxville: University of Tennessee Press, 1988. Concise examination of the role and influence of radical black power advocates and their influence in helping moderates attain their goals.

Haskins, James. *Power to the People.* New York: Simon & Schuster, 1997. Current historical perspective of the Black Panther party; good photographs aid the comprehension of the party's rationale at time of origin, the program shifts, and the conflicts within and without.

McCarthy, John T. *Black Power Ideologies.* Philadelphia: Temple University Press, 1992. Begins with detailed history of black protest, then focuses on black power ideologies of the 1960s and 1970s.

Marsh, Clifton E. *From Black Muslims to Muslims: The Resurrection, Transformation, and Change of the Lost-Found Nation of Islam in America, 1930–1995.* 2d ed. Blue Ridge Summit, PA: Scarecrow, 1996. An informative treatment of the rise, fall, and rebirth of the oldest black nationalist organization in the United States.

Van Deburg, William L. *New Day in Babylon: The Black Power Movement and American Culture, 1965–1975.* Chicago: University of Chicago Press, 1992. Good introductory account of the movement and its activities during a critical period of its development.

BIOGRAPHICAL SOURCES

Clegg, Andrew, III. *The Life and Times of Elijah Muhammad.* New York: St. James, 1997. Recent examination of the long-time leader of the Nation of Islam; uses FBI files and family records and recollections.

Gallen, David, ed. *Malcolm X: As They Knew Him.* New York: Ballantine, 1996. Interesting collection of interpretations provided by such people as Maya Angelou, James Baldwin, Robert Penn Warren, and Alex Haley. Full coverage of seven interviews with Malcolm.

Gates, Henry L. *Colored People: A Memoir.* New York: Knopf, 1994. The author's story of his childhood and youth in Piedmont, West Virginia; good presentation of black culture, significant events, and belief systems.

Hilliard, David. *This Side of Glory: The Autobiography of David Hilliard and the Story of the Black Panther Party.* Boston: Little, Brown, 1993. Interesting and thorough biographical account of one of the important personalities connected with the party.

Karim, Benjamin, et al. *Remembering Malcolm.* (1992). Reprint. New York: Ballantine, 1996. Insight provided into Malcolm's life and philosophy told to writers by one of his close associates.

Malcolm X. *The Autobiography of Malcolm X.* (1965). Reprint. New York: Ballantine, 1992. As told to Alex Haley, the most widely read and influential book of the black power movement.

Pearson, Hugh. *The Shadow of the Panther: Huey Newton and the Price of Black Power in America.* Reading, MA: Addison-Wesley, 1994. In-depth biography of Huey Newton and the Black Panthers, with a fifty-page bibliography.

AUDIOVISUAL SOURCES

Black Panthers: Huey Newton/Black Panther Newsreel. Chicago: International Historic Films, 1968. Videocassette. 53-minute treatment of the rally to free Huey Newton with enumeration of the ten-point plan offered by Bobby Seale.

Strickland, William. *Malcolm X: Make It Plain.* Orland Park, IL: MPI Home Video, 1995. Videocassette. 136-minute treatment of Malcolm's life using film footage and interviews. Narrated by Alfre Woodard.

WORLD WIDE WEB

Coombs, Norman. "Black Power." *Black Excellence in World History.* January 1997. http://www.csusm.edu/Black_Excellence/pg_b_Power.html An eight-page segment drawn from Coombs's *The Immigrant Heritage of America Black Power* (Twayne Press, 1972) and reconstructed for the web as *Black Experience in America.*

74. Vietnam War

Both Presidents Eisenhower and Kennedy feared that a communist takeover of South Vietnam would cause other Southeast Asian countries also to fall to communism, in domino fashion. Nonetheless, a

large-scale commitment to defend South Vietnam from its communist Vietcong and North Vietnam enemies only came under President
Johnson. By the end of 1967, more than 500,000 Americans were
in South Vietnam. With no victory in sight and with bitter antiwar
protests dividing the nation, Johnson refused to seek reelection. The
war ended under his successor, President Nixon, in 1973. American
casualties included 58,000 dead, more than 300,000 wounded, and
2,500 missing in action. In 1975 South Vietnam fell to the Vietcong
and North Vietnamese.

Suggestions for Term Papers

1. Analyze U.S. involvement in Vietnam under Presidents Eisenhower and Kennedy.
2. Analyze why the United States did not win the war.
3. Discuss the role of the media in presenting the war to audiences
   at home.
4. Compare the treatment of Vietnam War opponents with the treatment of those who opposed World War I or World War II.
5. Discuss the remembrances of Vietnam veterans.

Suggested Sources: See entries 72, 75, 79, 80, and 84 for related items.

REFERENCE SOURCES

Atlas of American History. 3d ed. Robert H. Ferrell and Richard Natkiel.
New York: Facts on File, 1993. Well-constructed work that combines
illustrations with useful maps. Excellent treatment of Vietnam War
and other wars in its coverage from 1498 to 1992.

Dictionary of the Vietnam War. James S. Olson, ed. Westport, CT: Greenwood, 1988. Alphabetical arrangement of entries describing events,
places, and personalities, as well as motion pictures, novels, and other
relevant topics. Even-handed, relatively unbiased.

Encyclopedia of the Vietnam War. Stanley J. Kutler, ed. New York: Scribner's
Sons, 1996. Comprehensive reference source of the war; coverage
includes personalities, events, issues, and battles. Contains maps and
illustrations. Extensive bibliographic essay and useful appendixes.

Vietnam Documents: American and Vietnamese Views of the War. George
Katsiaficas, ed. Armonk, NY: M. E. Sharpe, 1992. Well-balanced mix

of American and Vietnamese source documents; helpful commentaries by key historical figures.

GENERAL SOURCES

Faas, Horst, and Tim Page. *Indochina Requiem: Images from Vietnam, Cambodia, and Laos Remembered.* New York: Random House, 1997. Moving tribute to photographers who died making the pictures that comprise this volume. Excellent collection of wartime photos.

Simons, Geoff. *Vietnam Syndrome: The Impact on US Foreign Policy.* New York: St. Martin's, 1997. General investigation of the effects of the loss of the war on foreign relations; examines the history of racial genocide beginning with the eighteenth century and ends with comparison to El Salvador and Iraq.

SPECIALIZED SOURCES

Baker, Mark. *NAM.* New York: Morrow, 1981. Vivid description of frightening and sometimes horrifying experiences and memories of combat; based on interviews with anonymous veterans.

Dicks, Shirley. *From Vietnam to Hell: Interviews with Victims of Post-Traumatic Stress Disorder.* Jefferson, NC: McFarland, 1990. Excellent insight into the agony of war, by veterans and their families.

Ehrhardt, W. D. *In the Shadow of Vietnam: Essays, 1977–1991.* Jefferson, NC: McFarland, 1991. Collection of writings from a variety of periodicals from the period following the war; moving, emotional, and some clever.

Elwood-Akers, Virginia. *Women War Correspondents in the Vietnam War, 1961–1975.* Blue Ridge Summit, PA: Scarecrow, 1988. Informative treatment of the contribution of women journalists covering the war from its beginning to its end.

Herr, Michael. *Dispatches.* New York: Knopf, 1978. The author's reports of the fears, suffering, and constant agony of victims and participants.

Isserman, Maurice. *The Vietnam War.* New York: Facts on File, 1992. Up-to-date, brief history from the beginning in 1965 to the aftermath. Part of the publisher's America at War series.

Karnow, Stanley. *Vietnam: A History.* New York: Viking, 1983. Comprehensive popular history by a correspondent for *Vietnam: A Television History* aired on PBS. Well illustrated with good coverage of precolonial and colonial periods.

Kent, Deborah. *The Vietnam War: "What Are We Fighting For?"* Hillside, NJ: Enslow, 1994. Easy-to-read, concise account of the conflict. Part of the American War series.

Mangold, Tom, and John Penycate. *The Tunnels of Cu Chi*. New York: Random House, 1985. Fascinating account of the efforts to eliminate tunnel spaces, chambers, and crawl spaces that served the enemy in storing supplies and hiding troops.

McMaster, H. R. *Dereliction of Duty: Lyndon Johnson, Robert McNamara, the Joint Chiefs of Staff, and the Lies That Led to Vietnam*. New York: HarperCollins, 1997. Detailed examination of the political manipulations and dishonest dealings of government leaders.

McNamara, Robert S., and Brian VanDeMark. *In Retrospect: The Tragedy and Lessons of Vietnam*. New York: Times Books, 1995. By the secretary of defense, a pivotal figure in the Kennedy and Johnson administrations; his detailed history is both compelling and controversial.

Moore, Harold G., and Joseph L. Galloway. *We Were Soldiers Once . . . and Young: Ia Drang, the Battle That Changed the War in Vietnam*. New York: Random House, 1992. Provides the perspective of fighting men on both sides. Moore served as battalion commander and Galloway as war correspondent during this first major battle (1965).

Parker, James E., Jr. *Last Man Out*. Camden, SC: John Culler, 1996. Enlightening narrative of a CIA operative who was the last American to leave the country; reports the lack of understanding at all levels of decision making.

Pimlott, John. *Vietnam: The Decisive Battles*. New York: Macmillan, 1990. Provides description, analysis, and graphic representation through maps, illustrations, and diagrams of seventeen major battles.

Prochnau, William. *Once upon a Distant War: Young War Correspondents and the Early Vietnam Battles*. New York: Times Books, 1995. Popular account of young reporters (Sheehan, Halberstam, etc.) and their attempts to uncover the truth in the early Vietnam period at the time of the advisers.

Terry, Wallace. *Bloods: An Oral History of the Vietnam War by Black Veterans*. New York: Random House, 1984. The words and recollections of twenty veterans treating all aspects of the conflict. Written by a *Time* reporter.

Werner, Jayne, and Luu Doan Huynh, eds. *The Vietnam War: Vietnamese and American Perspectives*. Armonk, NY: M. E. Sharpe, 1993. Interesting and informative treatment on various aspects of the war, with good coverage of the communist perspective.

Westheider, James E. *Fighting on Two Fronts: African Americans and the Vietnam War*. New York: New York University Press, 1997. Brief, revealing account of race relations in the armed forces during the Vietnam War; looks at racial violence and increased radicalism.

BIOGRAPHICAL SOURCES

Ehrhart, W. D. *Passing Time: Memoir of a Vietnam Veteran against the War.* Jefferson, NC: McFarland, 1989. Considered one of the best Vietnam autobiographies; vivid and compelling.

Hodgins, Michael C. *Reluctant Warrior.* New York: Fawcett Columbine, 1997. Personal narrative of a platoon leader's war experiences until the time of U.S. withdrawal.

Mason, Robert C. *Chickenhawk.* New York: Viking, 1983. Story of a helicopter pilot; treats the air war, brutalities, and frustrations of everyday life and its toll on his health and well-being.

Miller, Merle. *Lyndon: An Oral Biography.* New York: Putnam, 1980. Compelling work describing Johnson's frustrations, reactions, and despair over the Vietnam situation and his decision not to seek reelection.

AUDIOVISUAL SOURCES

Vietnam: A Television History. Wilmette, IL: Films, Inc., 1983–1987. 13 videocassettes, each running from 60 to 120 minutes. Emmy-award winning television series tracing the entire war, beginning with its roots (1946–1954) and ending with the legacies it left.

WORLD WIDE WEB

"Tapes Show LBJ's Doubts about Vietnam." *CNN Interactive.* October 1997. http://www.cnn.com/US/9610/15/lbj.doubts/index.html Brief sound bytes provided from tapes recording President Johnson's discomfort with the handling of Vietnam. There is a lead to the CNN story (Oct. 12, 1996) as well as links to several related sites.

75. Great Society Programs (1965–1968)

Delivering the commencement address at the University of Michigan on May 22, 1964, President Lyndon B. Johnson spoke of a "Great Society" for America. Ranging beyond the parameters of President Kennedy's New Frontier, Johnson pledged a war against poverty and the attainment of social justice for all. More than sixty Great Society programs ensued. Such "war on poverty" measures as the Job Corps, VISTA, Medicare, and Medicaid emerged, as did further civil rights laws, laws to help the nation's impoverished inner cities and rural regions, its imperiled environment, and its educational system. Critics complained of the Great Society's cost, especially in the light of the war in Vietnam, and the empowerment it gave the national government.

Suggestions for Term Papers

1. Compare the aims and achievements of the Great Society with those of the New Deal.
2. To what extent did the Great Society solve the nation's problems?
3. Analyze the opposition to the Great Society programs.
4. Discuss the successes and failures of an important Great Society program.
5. Discuss the effects of the Great Society on the nation's educational system.

Suggested Sources: See entry 35 for related items.

GENERAL SOURCES

Beschloss, Michael R., ed. *Taking Charge: The Johnson Whitehouse Tapes, 1963–1964.* New York: Simon & Schuster, 1997. Collection of transcriptions from LBJ's first year in office; fascinating insight into the manner of a political power wielder and the development of his programs.

Butterfield, Roger P. *The American Past: A History of the United States from Concord to the Great Society.* New York: Simon & Schuster, 1976. Comprehensive illustrated history with over 1,100 pictures (photographs, paintings, cartoons, etc.) that provide insight into events and personalities.

Silver, Harold. *An Educational War on Poverty: American and British Policy-Making, 1960–1980.* New York: Cambridge University Press, 1991. Comparative examination of U.S. and British social conditions and educational policies during the critical twenty-year period.

SPECIALIZED SOURCES

Kaplan, Marshall, and Peggy L. Cuciti, eds. *The Great Society and Its Legacy: Twenty Years of U.S. Social Policy.* Durham, NC: Duke University

Press, 1986. Brief survey history of social conditions and government policies during the 1960–1980 period.

Katz, William L. *The Great Society to the Reagan Era, 1964–1990.* Austin, TX: Raintree Steck-Vaughn, 1993. Concise, easy-to-read account of social conditions, with particular attention to minorities, women, race relations, and civil rights.

Unger, Irwin. *The Best of Intentions: The Triumphs and Failures of the Great Society under Kennedy, Johnson, and Nixon.* New York: Doubleday, 1996. Informative critique of the social policies designed to provide assistance and alleviate hardship during the period spanning the administrations of three presidents.

Vatter, Harold G., and John F. Walker, eds. *History of the U.S. Economy since World War II.* Armonk, NY: M. E. Sharpe, 1995. Good and readable collection of articles treating issues, events, and developments over the past fifty years.

War on Poverty

Gillette, Michael L. *Launching the War on Poverty: An Oral History.* New York: Twayne, 1996. Detailed account of politics and government during the period when the war on poverty was begun; includes interviews with politicians.

Haveman, Robert H. *Poverty Policy and Poverty Research: The Great Society and the Social Sciences.* Madison: University of Wisconsin, 1987. Informative account relating the nature of research done on poverty and social policy regarding economic assistance.

Katz, Michael B. *The Undeserving Poor: From the War on Poverty to the War on Welfare.* New York: Pantheon Books, 1989. Examination of the poor and the difference in treatment given them under the Great Society compared to succeeding administrations.

Pilisuk, Marc, and Phyllis Pilisuk, eds. *How We Lost the War on Poverty.* New Brunswick, NJ: Transaction Books, 1973. Critical examination of the way the war has been waged and social policy regarding economic assistance that emerged.

Quadagno, Jill S. *The Color of Welfare: How Racism Undermined the War on Poverty.* New York: Oxford University Press, 1994. Informative account of the manner in which racial intolerance eroded the structure of economic assistance policies.

Zarefsky, David. *President Johnson's War on Poverty: Rhetoric and History.* Tuscaloosa: University of Alabama Press, 1986. Focused historical treatment of the period in which LBJ declared war on poverty and enacted legislation.

Medicare and Medicaid

David, Sheri I. *With Dignity: The Search for Medicare and Medicaid.* Westport, CT: Greenwood, 1985. Brief and informative history of the creation of Medicare and Medicaid.

Feder, Judith M., and John Holahan. *Financing Health Care for the Elderly: Medicare, Medicaid, and Private Health Insurance.* Washington, DC: Urban Institute, 1979. Examination of the state of health care for the aged; addresses costs and financing.

Greenfield, Margaret. *Medicare and Medicaid: The 1965 and 1967 Social Security Amendments.* (1968). Reprint. Westport, CT: Greenwood, 1983. Description and exposition of the legislation that provided the basis for health care for the aged.

BIOGRAPHICAL SOURCES

Andrew, John A. *Lyndon Johnson and the Great Society.* Chicago: Ivan R. Dee, 1998. Recent, brief political biography of LBJ describing the economic and social policies initiated during his administration.

Dallek, Robert. *Flawed Giant: Lyndon Johnson and his Times, 1961–1973.* New York: Oxford University Press, 1998. Monumental biography examining the life and character of LBJ from the time of his vice presidency until his death four years after he left office as president.

Schulman, Bruce J. *Lyndon B. Johnson and American Liberalism: A Brief Biography with Documents.* Boston: Bedford Books/St. Martin's, 1995. Examination of the life and career of LBJ within the perspective of a liberal political agenda.

Solberg, Carl. *Hubert Humphrey: A Biography.* New York: Norton, 1984. Detailed biographical account of the leading liberal who served as LBJ's vice president.

AUDIOVISUAL SOURCES

"LBJ: A Biography." *The American Experience.* Santa Monica, CA: PBS Home Video, 1991. Videocassette. Excellent 4-hour television presentation examining LBJ's entire career; the third of four parts, "We Shall Overcome," examines the Great Society and the increasing problem of Vietnam.

WORLD WIDE WEB

"Johnson Came Out Guns Blazing in His 'War on Poverty.' " *CNN Interactive.* October 1997. http://www.cnn.com/US/9610/18/

lbj.tapes.pt4/index.html Similar to the coverage given to world wide web item in entry 74; brief narrative with sound bytes to relevant taped commentary. Links to related stories and sites.

76. Student Radicalism during the 1960s

During the 1960s the nation's college enrollment more than doubled, to nearly 8 million. By no means were all students radicals, but many did embrace radical causes and the counterculture. In their opposition to traditional values and current policies, some turned to New Left organizations like the Students for a Democratic Society (SDS) or, in fewer instances, to the violence-minded groups such as the Weathermen. Beginning with the Free Speech Movement at the University of California at Berkeley in 1964, campus protests proliferated. Opposition to the war in Vietnam and to racism at home were dominant protest themes, which waned only in the 1970s.

Suggestions for Term Papers

1. Analyze the goals, activities, and consequences of SDS.
2. Why did so many middle-class students become radicals during the 1960s?
3. Discuss a major student disruption at a college campus during the 1960s.
4. Discuss the short- and long-range results of student radicalism during the 1960s.
5. Discuss what has become of leading student radicals since the 1960s.

Suggested Sources: See entries 71–74, 77, 82, and 84 for related items.

REFERENCE SOURCES

Encyclopedia of the American Left. Mary Jo Buhle et al., eds. Hamden, CT: Garland, 1990. Informative reference tool providing good coverage of aspects, personalities, topics, and issues relevant to leftist social and political thought.

Voices from the Underground. Ken Wachsberger, ed. Tempe, AZ: Mica, 1993. 2 vols. Extensive treatment of the underground press during the 1960s and 1970s. Volume 1 contains essays describing twenty-six newspapers written by their editors, and volume 2 is a directory of resources on the topic.

GENERAL SOURCES

Anderson, Terry H. *The Movement and the Sixties.* New York: Oxford University Press, 1996. Detailed history of the radical movement beginning with student civil rights protests in 1960 through the American Indian engagement at Wounded Knee in 1973.

Aronowitz, Stanley. *The Death and Rebirth of American Radicalism.* New York: Routledge, 1996. Brief historical examination of the flowering and decline of the radical movement; considers the prospects for a rebirth of radicalism.

Berman, Paul. *A Tale of Two Utopias: The Political Journey of the Generation of 1968.* New York: Norton, 1996. An interesting and unique, albeit questionable, parallel between the American student revolt of 1968 with the Czech revolt against communism in the Prague Spring of 1989. By a writer for the *New Yorker.*

DeBenedetti, Charles, and Charles Chatfield. *An American Ordeal: The Antiwar Movement of the Vietnam Era.* Syracuse, NY: Syracuse University Press, 1990. Detailed and comprehensive history of the antiwar movement as it developed in the United States following the Korean conflict through the war in Vietnam.

Garfinkle, Adam. *Telltale Hearts: The Origins and Impact of the Vietnam Antiwar Movement.* New York: St. Martin's, 1997. Critical and somewhat controversial interpretation of the antiwar movement as being counterproductive to ending the war in successful fashion and resulting in more lives lost.

Kleidman, Robert. *Organizing for Peace: Neutrality, the Test Ban, and the Freeze.* Syracuse, NY: Syracuse University Press, 1993. Revealing account of the history of peace movements in the United States beginning with the 1930s; provides analysis of the dynamics of peace campaigns.

Lee, Martin A., and Bruce Schlain. *Acid Dreams: The CIA, LSD, and the Sixties Rebellion.* New York: Grove, 1985. Informative social history of the frenzied decade examining the general state of dissent and drug abuse by youth.

Small, Melvin. *Covering Dissent: The Media and the Anti-Vietnam War Movement.* New Brunswick, NJ: Rutgers University Press, 1994. Concise examination of media treatment given to the antiwar movement between 1965 and 1971; provides details regarding column lines, length, placement, and inclusion of illustrations as appeared in several major newspapers and magazines.

Wells, Tom. *The War Within: America's Battle over Vietnam*. Berkeley: University of California Press, 1994. Examines the efforts by the Johnson and Nixon administrations to counter the antiwar movement; credits the movement with bringing the war to an end. Complementary to the DeBenedetti and Chatfield work (above).

Witcover, Jules. *The Year the Dream Died: Revisiting 1968 in America*. New York: Warner Books, 1997. A look at the student rebellion, among other topics revisited some thirty years later by the author, a political columnist for the *Baltimore Sun*. Detailed month-by-month chronological treatment.

SPECIALIZED SOURCES

Davis, James K. *Assault on the Left: The FBI and the Sixties Antiwar Movement*. Westport, CT: Praeger, 1997. Brief, informative account of FBI counterintelligence activities and its questionable infiltration, disruption, and neutralization of student antiwar protests.

Farber, David R. *Chicago '68*. Chicago: University of Chicago Press, 1988. Interesting account of the protest at the Democratic National Convention; provides views of police and Daley aides, as well as protesters.

Gitlin, Todd. *The Sixties: Years of Hope, Days of Rage*. New York: Bantam Books, 1987. Detailed, readable, and informative history of radical student politics and emergence of the New Left by the former president of SDS.

Heineman, Kenneth J. *Campus Wars: The Peace Movement at American State Universities in the Vietnam Era*. New York: New York University Press, 1993. Unique focus on the dissent at the less prestigious "children of working class" universities such as Kent State, Michigan State, and Pennsylvania State; analysis of faculties, student bodies, and communities.

Levine, Lawrence W. *The Opening of the American Mind: Canons, Culture, and History*. Boston: Beacon, 1996. Brief, solid examination of American pluralism and higher education as it has developed from the legacy of the 1960s; sees favorable results from student rioting and dissent.

Miller, Jim. *Democracy Is in the Streets: From Port Huron to the Siege of Chicago*. (1987). Reprint. Cambridge, MA: Harvard University Press, 1994. A good complement to the Gitlin work above; revealing examination of the founding of SDS and the schism with the traditional anticommunist liberal left.

Rosenblatt, Roger. *Coming Apart: A Memoir of the Harvard Wars of 1969.* Boston: Little, Brown, 1997. Concise account of a situation at Harvard in which radical SDS students occupied University Hall and were forcibly removed by police. The author was a young professor at the time and reflects on the time and the various personalities on campus.

BIOGRAPHICAL SOURCES

DeLeon, David, ed. *Leaders from the 1960s: A Biographical Sourcebook of American Activism.* Westport, CT: Greenwood, 1994. Collection of biographies on the lives, careers, and accomplishments of eighty-six individuals ranging from liberal to radical.

AUDIOVISUAL SOURCES

Berkeley in the Sixties. Santa Monica, CA: PBS Home Video, 1990. Videocassette. Interesting, 117-minute presentation of the rise and fall of the protest movement by fifteen campus activists, who describe their activities and the general frenzy of the period.
Making Sense of the Sixties. Santa Monica, CA: PBS Home Video, 1991. 6 videocassettes. Series of 1-hour presentations providing images and interviews from the decade beginning with the seeds of origin of its radical dissent and ending with its legacies.

WORLD WIDE WEB

Schutze, Jim. "Chicago Shudders at Memories of Violence in '68." *Houston Chronicle Interactive.* October 1997. http://www.chron.com/content/chronicle/nation/96/08/25/memories.html Informative article providing background on conditions leading to student radicalism and the confrontation in Chicago during the Democratic National Conventions.

77. National Organization for Women (NOW) Founded (1966)

The civil rights movement spawned other protest movements during the 1960s, including those of women. Betty Friedan's best-selling *The Feminist Mystique* (1963) concluded that women, contrary to popular opinion, were not content with domesticity or with their unequal status if they worked in the marketplace. In 1966 Friedan founded NOW, whose membership grew within two years from a few hundred to 175,000. The organization supported, among other items, a constitutional equal rights amendment and abortion. It also gave rise to more radical feminist movements, which went beyond NOW's original goals.

Suggestions for Term Papers

1. Discuss Betty Friedan's contributions to the feminist movement.
2. Compare the goals of NOW when it was established with its current goals.
3. Analyze the opposition, both male and female, to NOW.
4. Compare the ideas and goals of NOW with those of radical feminist groups.
5. Analyze the successes and failures of NOW.

Suggested Sources: See entries 72, 77, 88, and 89 for related items.

REFERENCE SOURCES

The ABC-CLIO Companion to Women in the Workplace. Dorothy Schneider and Carl J. Schneider. Santa Barbara, CA: ABC-CLIO, 1993. Comprehensive treatment of personalities, organizations, events, and developments regarding the employment of women in the United States. Alphabetically arranged entries.

GENERAL SOURCES

Bouchier, David. *The Feminist Challenge: The Movement for Women's Liberation in Britain and the USA.* New York: Schocken Books, 1983. Relatively brief but informative history of feminism in both the United Kingdom and the United States.

Bradshaw, Jan, ed. *The Women's Liberation Movement.* New York: Pergamon, 1982. Essays on women's liberation throughout Europe; final essay on the North American feminist tradition.

Davis, Flora. *Moving the Mountain: The Women's Movement in America since 1960.* Simon & Schuster, 1991. Detailed and informative history of the women's movement of the 1960s and its progressive development to the present time.

Hewlett, Sylvia A. *A Lesser Life: The Myth of Women's Liberation in America.* New York: Morrow, 1986. Description of the social and economic inequities that gave rise to the feminist movement in the United States.

Hogeland, Lisa M. *Feminism and Its Fictions: The Consciousness-Raising Novel and the Women's Liberation Movement.* Philadelphia: University of Pennsylvania Press, 1998. Examination of twentieth-century American fiction and its relationship to feminism.

Linden-Ward, Blanche, and Carol H. Green. *American Women in the 1960s: Changing the Future.* New York: Twayne of Macmillan, 1993. Detailed historical survey of the momentous decade, treating all aspects and issues that spurred the women's movement.

Lunardini, Christine A. *Women's Rights.* Phoenix: Oryx, 1996. A brief, readable description of the history of the struggle for women's rights in the United States. Part of the publisher's Social Issues in American History series.

Morgan, Robin, comp. *Sisterhood Is Powerful: An Anthology of Writings from the Women's Liberation Movement.* New York: Random House, 1970. A good compilation of essays by leading advocates of women's rights and feminism in the United States during the pivotal period.

SPECIALIZED SOURCES

Carabillo, Toni, et al. *Feminist Chronicles, 1953–1993.* Los Angeles: Women's Graphics, 1993. An excellent focus on the origin and development of NOW along with a broader treatment of feminist activity since the publication of Simone de Beauvoir's *The Second Sex* in 1952.

DuPlessis, Rachel B., and Ann Snitow, eds. *Live from Feminism: Memoirs of Women's Liberation.* New York: Crown, 1998. A most recent examination of feminism in the twentieth-century United States.

Florer, John H. *Now: The Formative Years; The National Effort to Acquire Federal Action on Equal Employment Rights for Women in the 1960s.* Springfield, VA: NTIS, 1972. Government document examining the pivotal period of the struggle for equal employment opportunity for women.

Friedan, Betty. *The Feminine Mystique.* (1964). Reprint. Norton, 1997. The landmark publication of the feminist movement that served as the model for NOW's philosophy. The latest reprint of several issued since its initial publication.

Hernandez, Aileen. *The First Five Years: 1966–1971*. Chicago: National Organization for Women, 1971. The official history of NOW, published by the organization.

BIOGRAPHICAL SOURCES

Henry, Sondra. *Betty Friedan, Fighter for Women's Rights*. Hillside, NJ: Enslow Publishers, 1990. Easy-to-read, concise biography of the celebrated activist and chief founder of NOW. Part of the publisher's Contemporary Women series.

Horowitz, Daniel. *Betty Friedan and the Making of the Feminine Mystique: The American Left, the Cold War, and Modern Feminism*. Amherst: University of Massachusetts Press, 1998. Recent and revealing biographical study that provides insight into the development of feminism and political influence.

Ireland, Patricia. *What Women Want*. New York: Dutton, 1966. An informative autobiography of a NOW leader explaining the needs of women as represented by formation of NOW, its struggles, and its subsequent achievements.

PERIODICAL ARTICLES

National NOW Times: Official Journal of the National Organization for Women (NOW). Washington, DC: NOW, 1977–. Replaced *Do It Now* as the official publication. Contains articles on both historical and current developments.

AUDIOVISUAL SOURCES

NOW's 20th Anniversary Show. Los Angeles: Peg Yorkin Productions, 1986. Videocassette. Interesting and informative 120-minute tribute to NOW; contains brief historical treatment but emphasis on current awareness.

Teach Women's History. Arlington, VA: Feminist Majority Foundation, 1995. Videocassette, with teacher's guide and soft-cover book. A powerful 120-minute video edition of *The Feminist Chronicles*; recorded in 1986 and relates the history of NOW and feminism.

WORLD WIDE WEB

The National Organization for Women (NOW) Home Page. July 1997. http://now.org/ The home page with a detailed index to related leads and sites to actions, issues, and general information. The lead to history provides a three-page overview with various links.

78. American Indian Movement (AIM) Founded (1968)

During the 1950s and the 1960s, the plight of American Indians, or Native Americans, as some preferred, remained abysmal, with rates of unemployment, alcoholism, and suicide far surpassing those of any other national group. The Johnson administration earmarked increased federal funds to fight their impoverishment, but some Native Americans, alienated by current and past grievances, established the American Indian Movement in 1968. Espousing "red power," they staged well-publicized protests that included the occupation of Alcatraz Island in 1969, a sit-in demonstration at the Bureau of Indian Affairs in 1972, and a confrontation with authorities in 1973 at Wounded Knee, South Dakota, that left one Native American dead.

Suggestions for Term Papers

1. How effective has AIM been in improving conditions for Native Americans?
2. Compare the aims, methods, and effectiveness of the red power movement with those of the black power movement.
3. Discuss the changes in the perception of Native Americans and their problems by non–Native Americans since the 1960s.
4. Compare the events at Wounded Knee in 1974 with those that took place in 1890.
5. Discuss the extent to which the problems of Native Americans have been ameliorated since the 1960s.

Suggested Sources: See entries 72 and 73 for related items.

REFERENCE SOURCES

The ABC-CLIO Companion to the Native American Rights Movement. Mark Grossman. Santa Barbara, CA: ABC-CLIO, 1996. Comprehensive source treating persons, legislation, organizations, and events; entries in alphabetical order with many illustrations.

American Indians. Harvey Markowitz, ed. Pasadena, CA: Salem, 1995. 3 vols. Fully illustrated source on American Indian history and culture from ancient times to the present. Outstanding Reference Source Award in 1995. Part of the Ready Reference series.

American Indian Studies: A Bibliographic Guide. Phillip M. White. Englewood, CO: Libraries Unlimited, 1995. Treats a variety of sources on Native Americans: directories, handbooks, encyclopedias, periodicals, computer databases, and others. Outstanding Academic Book Award for 1995.

Encyclopedia of American Indian Civil Rights. James S. Olson et al., eds. Westport, CT: Greenwood, 1997. Most comprehensive, up-to-date coverage of American Indian civil rights issues; over 600 entries (personalities, issues, court cases, etc.).

The Encyclopedia of Native America. Trudy Griffin-Pierce. New York: Viking, 1995. Easy-to-understand, comprehensive treatment of Native American topics, issues, and tribal groups; epilogue treats contemporary topics such as the rise of AIM.

Encyclopedia of North American Indians. D. L. Birchfield, ed. Tarrytown, NY: Marshall Cavendish, 1997. 11 vols. Comprehensive treatment of Native American history, religion, spirituality, and tribal customs; fine biographical sketches and alphabetically arranged access.

Encyclopedia of North American Indians. Frederick E. Hoxie. Boston: Houghton Mifflin, 1996. Award-winning source of information on Native American culture, history, and customs.

Native America in the Twentieth Century: An Encyclopedia. Mary B. Davis et al., eds. New York: Garland, 1994. Award-winning source providing excellent narratives, bibliographies, and illustrations of contemporary issues and personalities.

Native American Political Systems and the Evolution of Democracy: An Annotated Bibliography. Bruce E. Johansen, comp. Westport, CT: Greenwood, 1996. Recent bibliography identifying articles and books on the origin and development of Native American politics and governance; good background for understanding contemporary issues.

Native American Resurgence and Renewal: A Reader and Bibliography. Robert N. Wells, Jr. Blue Ridge Summit, PA: Scarecrow, 1994. Provides documentation listing writings from the past two decades treating recent educational reform, cultural advance, and economic development.

Native Americans: A Reference Guide. Barry Pritzker. Santa Barbara, CA:

ABC-CLIO, 1998. 2 vols. Comprehensive reference source treating history, culture, and current status of the Native American population.

Reference Encyclopedia of the American Indian. 7th ed. Barry T. Klein. Santa Barbara, CA: ABC-CLIO, 1995. Contains extensive listings of organizations, events, and programs, with excellent detailed bibliographic listings and references.

Timelines of Native American History. Susan Hazen-Hammond. New York: Berkley, 1996. Chronology includes brief descriptions of major events; begins with the Pleistocene period and ends in 1997.

GENERAL SOURCES

Deloria, Vine, and Clifford M. Lytle. *American Indians, American Justice.* Austin: University of Texas Press, 1983. Fascinating historical account of treatment accorded American Indians in U.S. courts of law.

Matthiesen, Peter. *In the Spirit of Crazy Horse.* (1983) Reprint. New York: Viking, 1991. Thorough and detailed account of the Lakota Indians' struggle with the U.S. government from the time of Custer, with emphasis on events in the 1970s. Censorship struggles prevented access to this work in 1981.

Olson, James Stuart, and Raymond Wilson. *Native Americans in the Twentieth Century.* Provo, UT: Brigham Young University Press, 1984. Concise examination of twentieth-century developments regarding government relations with the Indians.

Prucha, Francis P. *American Indian Treaties: The History of a Political Anomaly.* Berkeley: University of California Press, 1994. Detailed and informative history of treaty making from the Revolutionary War to 1871; describes the process during different historical periods. Concluding chapter treats current treaty rights activism.

Streissguth, Tom. *Wounded Knee 1890: The End of the Plains Indian Wars.* New York: Facts on File, 1998. Good background information of the original tragedy based on firsthand accounts from soldiers, reporters, Indians, and others. Part of the publisher's Library of American Indian History series.

Thompson, William N. *Native American Issues.* Santa Barbara, CA: ABC-CLIO, 1996. Handbook providing awareness of contemporary political issues along with biographical sketches, chronology, and bibliography.

SPECIALIZED SOURCES

Bordewich, Fergus M. *Killing the White Man's Indian: The Reinventing of Native Americans at the End of the Twentieth Century.* New York:

Doubleday, 1996. Detailed account of the changing ethnic identity of Native Americans in this century.

Eagle, Adam Fortunate, et al. *Alcatraz! Alcatraz! The Indian Occupation of 1969–1971*. Berkeley, CA: Heyday Books, 1992. Interesting, informative, and concise account of the notable event from one of its planners; excellent photographs and commentary.

Johnson, Troy, et al., eds. *American Indian Activism: Alcatraz to the Longest Walk*. Urbana: University of Illinois Press, 1997. Well-developed narrative detailing the activism of Native Americans during the twentieth century.

Sayer, John W. *Ghost Dancing the Law: The Wounded Knee Trials*. Cambridge, MA: Harvard University Press, 1997. Detailed account of the court trials of Dennis Banks and Russell Means following Wounded Knee; reveals the strategy of AIM in using the courts as a forum.

Smith, Paul C., and Robert A. Warrior. *Like a Hurricane: The Indian Movement from Alcatraz to Wounded Knee*. New York: New Press, 1996. Well-written, authoritative description of events from 1969 to 1972, a significant period of dissent and resistance for American Indians.

Stern, Kenneth S. *Loud Hawk: The United States versus the American Indian Movement*. Norman: University of Oklahoma Press, 1994. Interesting story of the longest pretrial case ever; Kenny Loud Hawk and five other AIM members were arrested in 1975, and the case ended in 1988.

Weston, Mary Ann. *Native Americans in the News: Images of Indians in the Twentieth Century Press*. Westport, CT: Greenwood, 1996. Examination of press coverage and public opinion as it relates to Native Americans.

BIOGRAPHICAL SOURCES

Johansen, Bruce E., and Donald A. Grinde. *The Encyclopedia of Native American Biography: Six Hundred Life Stories of Important People from Powhatan to Wilma Mankiller*. New York: H. Holt, 1997. Comprehensive collective biography of Native Americans from all historical periods; good coverage of contemporary figures from AIM.

Malinowski, Sharon. *Notable Native Americans*. Detroit: Gale, 1995. Award-winning biographical reference source; treats more than 265 outstanding Native Americans from all periods of history and all fields of endeavor.

AUDIOVISUAL SOURCES

Native American Cultures in the U.S.A. Olathe, KS: RMI Media Productions, 1992. 2 videocassettes. Part 1 treats history, rights, treaty disputes, land problems; part 2 examines controversy over burial sites and remains. Provides insight into some of the issues that have created a rift with government authorities. 120 minutes.

WORLD WIDE WEB

Dill, Jordan S. "American Indian Movement." *First Nations*. September 1997. http://dickshovel.netgate.net/AIMIntro.html Issue oriented and informative, with many links and leads to relevant activities, events, and concerns. Contains a seven-page history of AIM, along with indications of the rift with the editorship of *Indian Country Today*.

NativeWeb. 1994. http://www.nativeweb.org/ The other leading web site on Native American culture and activities, with many links to information on various subjects, geographic regions, and issues.

79. Tet Offensive (1968)

On January 31, 1968, the Vietcong broke the Vietnamese lunar new year (Tet) truce with a powerful offensive against U.S. and South Vietnamese forces. Three dozen South Vietnamese provincial capitals came under attack, as did the American embassy in Saigon. Ultimately the offensive was repulsed, with huge communist casualties, but the perception that the war was being won was shattered. Domestic antiwar sentiment surged. On March 31, a few weeks after he had won only a narrow New Hampshire primary victory, President Johnson announced that he would not seek a second term of office.

Suggestions for Term Papers

1. Analyze why the Tet offensive was a military victory but a psychological defeat for the United States and South Vietnam.
2. Discuss the effect of the Tet offensive on the American public.
3. Discuss Senator Eugene McCarthy's challenge to President Johnson's nomination for a second term and the New Hampshire primary.

4. Discuss the short- and long-range consequences of the Tet offensive.

5. Was the Tet offensive the turning point of the Vietnam War?

Suggested Sources: See entries 74, 75, and 80 for relevant items.

REFERENCE SOURCES

Vietnam War Almanac. Harry G. Summers, Jr. New York: Facts on File, 1985. Provides an encyclopedic listing of topics along with informative narrative; Tet offensive is described and interpreted. Highly recommended for its accurate perspective.

GENERAL SOURCES

Bergerud, Eric M. *Red Thunder, Tropic Lightning: The World of a Combat Division in Vietnam.* Boulder, CO: Westview, 1993. Narrative of an American combat division known for its high mortality rate that earned honors during the Tet offensive; based on eyewitness accounts and observations of division soldiers.

Davidson, Phillip B. *Vietnam at War: The History, 1946–1975.* Novato, CA: Presidio, 1988. Detailed and thorough history of regional warfare from the French period through the end of the Vietnam War. The author was chief of military intelligence during the Tet offensive.

Herring, George C. *America's Longest War: The United States and Vietnam, 1950–1975.* 3d ed. New York: McGraw-Hill, 1996. Excellent narrative of the war. A popular text for college classes, with informative treatment of all major battles.

Warren, James A. *Portrait of a Tragedy: America and the Vietnam War.* New York: Lothrop, Lee, & Shepard, 1990. Concise, informative, and comprehensive examination of the war; important events such as the Tet offensive are clearly reported and interpreted.

SPECIALIZED SOURCES

Gilbert, Marc J., and William Head. *The Tet Offensive.* Westport, CT: Praeger, 1996. Fine collection of essays and opinion pieces from both sides on the nature of the Tet offensive, the reasoning behind it, and its impact.

Rice, Earle. *The Tet Offensive.* San Diego: Lucent Books, 1996. Easy-to-read and concise account of the planning, execution, and conclusion of the hostility.

Spector, Ronald H. *After Tet: The Bloodiest Year in Vietnam.* New York: Free Press, 1993. Thorough analysis of the period following the Tet offensive, along with President Johnson's decision not to seek reelection.

Wills, Charles. *The Tet Offensive.* Englewood Cliffs, NJ: Silver Burdett, 1989. Brief, easy-to-read description of the large-scale assault and its impact on the war.

Wirtz, James J. *The Tet Offensive: Intelligence Failure in War.* Ithaca, NY: Cornell University Press, 1991. Authoritative examination of the Tet offensive, its strategic deployment, and the American failure to prepare for the assault.

BIOGRAPHICAL SOURCES

Colvin, John. *Giap-Volcano Under Snow: Vietnam's Celebrated General Giap, Victor at Dien Bien Phu and Mastermind of the Tet Offensive.* New York: Soho/Farrar, Straus & Giroux, 1996. Informative examination of the life and career of the general; insight into the political situation.

Macdonald, Peter. *Giap: The Victor in Vietnam.* New York: Norton, 1993. Interesting biography of the major strategist in military planning; excellent military history of the decisive battles.

Tripp, Nathaniel. *Soldier, Son: Memoir of a Platoon Leader.* South Royalton, VT: Steerforth/National Book Network, 1997. Vivid personal narrative of the ground war in the months following the Tet offensive; doubt, courage, commitment, and mixed feeling of home and family, along with disturbing realizations of the military situation.

Zaffiri, Samuel. *Westmoreland: A Biography of General William C. Westmoreland.* New York: Morrow, 1994. Probing examination of the man and the problems he faced; good examination of the Tet offensive.

AUDIOVISUAL SOURCES

Vietnam. Beverly Hills, CA: CBS/Fox Video, 1986. 5 videocassettes. Thorough and compelling survey of the entire war in 10 hours, hosted by Walter Cronkite. Volume 4 is "Dateline Saigon/The Tet Offensive." Newsreel footage and on-the-spot reporting.

WORLD WIDE WEB

"Vietnam Online." *The American Experience.* June 1997. http://www. pbs.org/wgbh/pages/amex/vietnam/index.html Another of the fine PBS television presentations is featured here, with a lead to the script from the Tet offensive, among others from this thirteen-part series.

80. My Lai Massacre (1968)

In March 1968 an American platoon killed more than 200 unarmed Vietnamese men, women, and children in the coastal hamlet of My Lai. The massacre remained unacknowledged until late 1969, when an American reporter, Seymour Hersh, broke the story. Lieutenant William Calley, the leader who had ordered his troops to shoot the Vietnamese villagers, went on trial, as did other members of the platoon who had been involved in the killings and subsequent cover-up. A U.S. Army court-martial convicted only Calley, whom it sentenced to life imprisonment for murder. The sentence was subsequently reduced to ten years, and Calley received a pardon in late 1974.

Suggestions for Term Papers

1. Discuss how the My Lai massacre was uncovered.
2. Was Lieutenant Calley justifiably court-martialed, and did he receive a fair sentence?
3. Discuss popular reaction to the My Lai massacre and Lieutenant Calley's subsequent court-martial.
4. Discuss U.S. courts-martial during the Vietnam War.
5. Compare U.S. courts-martial during the Vietnam War with those during World War II.

Suggested Sources: See entries 74, 75, and 79 for relevant items.

REFERENCE SOURCES

Dictionary of the Vietnam War. James S. Olson, ed. Westport, CT: Greenwood, 1988. Alphabetical arrangement of entries describing events, places, and personalities, as well as motion pictures, novels, and other relevant topics; even-handed, relatively unbiased approach. Good section on atrocities.

Encyclopedia of the Vietnam War. Stanley I. Kutler, ed. New York: Scribner's, 1996. Comprehensive reference source of the war; treats personalities, events, issues, and battles. Contains maps, illustrations, an extensive bibliographic essay, and useful appendixes. Informative segment on My Lai.

GENERAL SOURCES

Kamm, Henry. *Dragon Ascending: Vietnam and the Vietnamese.* New York: Arcade/Little, Brown, 1996. Good general comparative description of prewar and postwar Vietnam. Examines My Lai.

Kelman, Herbert C., and V. Lee Hamilton. *Crimes of Obedience: Toward a Social Psychology of Authority and Responsibility.* New Haven, CT: Yale University Press, 1989. Written by social psychologists who investigated the conditions under which subordinates have committed immoral or illegal acts in response to orders, including My Lai.

Marrin, Albert. *America and Vietnam: The Elephant and the Tiger.* New York: Viking, 1992. Critical of antiwar dissent. Places more emphasis on the atrocities committed by the Vietnamese, though briefly acknowledges certain U.S. war crimes such as My Lai.

Olson, James S., and Randy Roberts. *Where the Domino Fell: America in Vietnam, 1945–1990.* New York: St. Martin's, 1991. Comprehensive account of U.S. involvement in Vietnam dating back to the close of World War II; balanced picture, although the My Lai incident arouses the authors' emotions.

Plaster, John L. *SOG: The Secret Wars of America's Commandos in Vietnam.* New York: Simon & Schuster, 1997. An excellent account of heroism and valor to counter the negative images of My Lai. Written by a member of a special forces group created to rescue downed airmen behind enemy lines.

Westheider, James E. *Fighting on Two Fronts: African Americans and the Vietnam War.* New York: New York University Press, 1997. Examines discrimination in the military, which creates a mixed identity for those who would battle and commit atrocities against other nonwhite populations.

Wilson, James R. *Landing Zones: Southern Veterans Remember Vietnam.* Durham, NC: Duke University Press, 1990. Examines the regional aspects of the military in a series of interviews with people of varied rank, race, and loyalties.

SPECIALIZED SOURCES

Bilton, Michael, and Kevin Sim. *Four Hours in My Lai: The Soldiers of Charlie Company.* New York: Viking, 1992. Thorough treatment of the incident based on eyewitness accounts from soldiers and survivors; good assessment of its impact and outcomes. Drawn from a documentary film made for public television.

Hersh, Seymour M. *Cover-up*. New York: Vintage Books, 1972. Details of the incident and the attempt to conceal it from the American public by the journalist who broke the original story.

———. *My Lai 4: A Report on the Massacre and Its Aftermath*. New York: Random House, 1970. Concise account of My Lai; first book on the topic.

Olson, James S., and Randy Roberts. *My Lai: A Brief History with Documents*. New York: St. Martin's, 1998. Concise and informative history of the event and its cover-up. Contains seventy primary documents, photographs, glossary, a chronology, and an interpretive essay.

BIOGRAPHICAL SOURCES

Hodgins, Michael C. *Reluctant Warrior*. New York: Fawcett/Ballantine, 1977. Clearly written and vivid description of the life of a patrol leader and platoon commander. Provides insight into the challenges of a lieutenant like Calley in killing the enemy and keeping his troops alive.

Hammer, Richard. *The Court Martial of Lt. Calley*. New York: Coward, McCann & Geoghegan, 1971. One of several biographies on Calley that were published in 1971; examines his career and trial.

AUDIOVISUAL SOURCES

Vietnam: A Television History. Richmond, VA: Time-Life Video, 1983. 7 videocassettes. Thorough examination of the Vietnam conflict, each 1 hour long. See volumes 4 and 5 for 1968 coverage.

WORLD WIDE WEB

"Vietnam Online." *The American Experience*. June 1997. http://www. pbs.org/wgbh/pages/amex/vietnam/trenches/index.html The web page of a fine presentation of the PBS television series. This index provides a number of good entry points to the war. Click on "The My Lai Massacre" for a two-page description.

81. *Apollo 11* and the Moon Landing (1969)

After the Soviet Union launched a cosmonaut into space in April 1961, President John F. Kennedy responded by pledging to land an American on the moon by decade's end. Project Mercury and Project Gemini preceded Project Apollo 1, which took the lives of three astronauts in a fire. Then followed several Apollo flights in preparation for landing a man on the moon and returning him to earth. On July 20, 1969, *Apollo 11* carried Neil A. Armstrong, Edwin E. ("Buzz") Aldrin, and Michael Collins through space; they landed on the moon's Sea of Tranquility in their lunar module, *Eagle*. The first human to walk on the moon, Captain Armstrong radioed that he had taken "one small step for man, one giant leap for mankind."

Suggestions for Term Papers

1. Discuss the effect on the United States of the Soviet Union's launching a man into space.
2. Did the United States need an accelerated moon landing program, or should it have spent those funds on other needs?
3. Discuss the technological progress that was necessary to land a man on the moon.
4. Discuss the contributions of Project Mercury and Project Gemini to the moon landing.
5. Discuss the short- and long-range consequences of the *Apollo 11* flight.

Suggested Sources: See entry 65 for related items.

REFERENCE SOURCES

America in Space: An Annotated Bibliography. Russell R. Tobias. Pasadena, CA: Salem, 1991. Thorough bibliography of writings on astronautics in the space age.

GENERAL SOURCES

Chaikin, Andrew. *A Man on the Moon: The Voyages of the Apollo Astronauts.* New York: Viking, 1994. Detailed, popular, and accurate general history of the Apollo flights; served as the basis for the excellent HBO miniseries, *From the Earth to the Moon.*

Collins, Michael. *Liftoff: The Story of America's Adventure in Space.* New York: Grove, 1988. Collins, one of the *Apollo 11* astronauts, provides firsthand knowledge of American success in conquering space.

Gurney, Gene. *Americans into Orbit: The Story of Project Mercury.* New York: Random House, 1965. Interesting, easy-to-read, and informative history of the project designed to investigate space exploration and moon flight.

————. *Americans to the Moon: The Story of Project Apollo.* New York: Random House, 1970. Similar to the above entry, this work examines the preparation, development, and flights of *Apollo 1* to *Apollo 12.*

Kaufmann, James L. *Selling Outer Space: Kennedy, the Media, and Funding for Project Apollo, 1961–1963.* Tuscaloosa: University of Alabama Press, 1994. Concise account of the political and media rhetoric in creating public support for the Apollo project.

Kelly, Fred. *America's Astronauts and Their Indestructible Spirit.* Blue Ridge Summit, PA: AERO, 1986. General assessment of the determination and conviction of those responsible for pushing the space program. Foreword by Buzz Aldrin.

Knight, David C., comp. and ed. *American Astronauts and Spacecraft: A Pictorial History from Project Mercury through Project Apollo.* New York: Franklin Watts, 1972. Fine collection of photographs depicting the critical years of space exploration.

Sullivan, Walter, ed. *America's Race for the Moon: The New York Times Story of Project Apollo.* New York: Random House, 1962. *New York Times* reports on the development and implementation of Project Apollo.

SPECIALIZED SOURCES

Aldrin, Buzz, and Malcolm McConnell. *Men from Earth.* New York: Bantam Books, 1989. Aldrin's own story and interpretation of the project and the men who made his flight to the moon possible.

———— (Edwin E.), and Wayne Warga. *Return to Earth.* New York: Random House, 1973. Aldrin's first account of the successful project.

Booker, Peter J., et al. *Project Apollo: The Way to the Moon.* New York: American Elsevier Publishing, 1969. One of the earliest publications of the successful project outcomes.

Kennedy, Gregory P. *Apollo to the Moon.* New York: Chelsea House Publishers, 1992. Concise and easy-to-read summary of the project and its success. Introduction by Michael Collins.

BIOGRAPHICAL SOURCES

Cox, Donald W. *America's Explorers of Space: Including a Special Report on Project Apollo*. Maplewood, NJ: Hammond, 1969. Concise collective biography of the astronauts in the American space program; published the same year as the *Apollo 11* flight.
Dunham, Montrew. *Neil Armstrong: Young Flyer*. New York: Aladdin Paperbacks, 1996. Recent, easy-to-read biography of Armstrong's childhood.
Kramer, Barbara. *Neil Armstrong: The First Man on the Moon*. Springfield, NJ: Enslow Publishers, 1997. A recent and easy-to-read biography that describes Armstrong's accomplishments.

AUDIOVISUAL SOURCES

Apollo 11: Man's 1st Moon Landing. JEF Films, 1973. Videocassette. 30-minute presentation. Available for free loan from the NASA Lyndon B. Johnson Space Center. Telephone number, 281–483–0123.
One Small Step for Man. Los Angeles: Bennett Marine Video/MPI, 1984. Videocassette. 60-minute examination of all Apollo flights, with an emphasis on the moon landing.

WORLD WIDE WEB

Tuttle, Michael J. "Apollo Manned Space Program." *APOLLO Manned Missions*. January 1997. http://www.nasm.edu/APOLLO/ Patches from all seventeen Apollo flights are displayed and serve as icons to information about each of them. Details of the *Apollo 11* flight are treated in a brief narrative with a few small photographs, and several relevant links.

82. Earth Day Observed (1970)

Fears that industrial and urban wastes were creating vast environmental problems were generally muted during the 1960s, despite dire warnings from environmentalists such as Rachel Carson, whose *Silent Spring* (1962) drew attention to the dangers stemming from pesticides. By decade's end, however, environmental concerns had attracted widespread attention. On Earth Day in April 1970, hundreds of thousands throughout the nation demonstrated or attended teach-ins to protest the assault on the planet's ecology and to call for government action. That same year, Congress created the Environmental Protection Agency (EPA) and passed the Clean Air and Clean Water acts. Earth Day has remained an annual celebration.

Suggestions for Term Papers

1. Analyze the contributions of Rachel Carson or another prominent modern conservationist to environmental awareness.
2. Compare the celebration of Earth Day 1970 with current Earth Day celebrations.
3. Compare the most important environmental concerns of 1970 with those of today.
4. Compare the celebration of Earth Day in the United States with similar celebrations elsewhere.
5. Discuss how Earth Day is or is not celebrated in your own locale.

Suggested Sources: See entry 83 for relevant items.

REFERENCE SOURCES

The ABC-CLIO Companion to the Environmental Movement. Mark Grossman. Santa Barbara, CA: ABC-CLIO, 1994. Treats alphabetically themes, personalities, issues, and events. Good coverage of Earth Day. Part of the publisher's series.

GENERAL SOURCES

Carson, Rachel. *Silent Spring.* (1962). Reprint. Boston: Houghton Mifflin, 1994. The landmark work that first pointed out the need for ecological considerations in the use of pesticides; launched the environmental movement.

Daly, Herman E., and Kenneth N. Townsend, eds. *Valuing the Earth: Economics, Ecology, Ethics.* Cambridge, MA: MIT Press, 1993. Up-to-date examination of the major issues surrounding the controversy over the environment.

Freeman, Martha, ed. *Always Rachel: The Letters of Rachel Carson and Do-*

rothy Freeman, 1952–1964. Boston: Beacon, 1995. Compilation of correspondence between the two environmentalists; good insight into their thoughts and actions.

Gore, Albert. *Earth in the Balance: Ecology and the Human Spirit.* Boston: Houghton Mifflin, 1992. Important work by the vice president that examines the importance of protecting the environment through public policy.

Oelschlager, Max, ed. *After Earth Day: Continuing the Conservation Effort.* Denton, TX: University of North Texas, 1992. Papers from a conference on conservation that treat environmental policy and the importance of ecology.

Santos, Miguel A. *Managing Planet Earth: Perspectives on Population, Ecology, and the Law.* New York: Bergin & Garvey, 1990. On existing legal and societal issues of environmental protection.

Tokar, Brian. *Earth for Sale: Reclaiming Ecology in the Age of Corporate Greenwash.* Boston: South End Press, 1997. Up-to-date treatment of environmentalism and the green movement with respect to public policy.

SPECIALIZED SOURCES

Earth Day—the Beginning: A Guide for Survival. New York: Bantam Books, 1970. Early source of information on Earth Day and its ramifications for the future; compiled by the staff of what was to become the Environmental Action Coalition.

Gardner, Robert, and Sharon L. Holm. *Celebrating Earth Day: A Sourcebook of Activities and Experiments.* Brookfield, CT: Millbrook, 1992. Published in commemoration of Earth Day for the purpose of providing environmental education for youngsters.

Ladd, Everett C., and Karlyn H. Bowman. *Attitudes toward the Environment: Twenty-Five Years after Earth Day.* Washington, DC: AEI Press, 1995. Concise investigation of current public opinion regarding environmental protection and public policy.

Lowery, Linda. *Earth Day.* Minneapolis: Carolrhoda Books, 1991. Concise and easy-to-read account of Earth Day 1970 and 1990, and the activities drawing attention to pollution and its effects on natural resources.

BIOGRAPHICAL SOURCES

Brooks, Paul. *Speaking for Nature: How Literary Naturalists from Henry Thoreau to Rachel Carson Have Shaped America.* (1980). Reprint. San Francisco: Sierra Club Books, 1983. Interesting collective biography of naturalists who have been influential through their writings.

Lear, Linda J. *Rachel Carson: Witness for Nature.* New York: H. Holt, 1997. The most recent biography of Carson; lengthy and detailed examination of her life and career.

McCay, Mary A. *Rachel Carson.* New York: Twayne Publishers, 1993. Brief account of Carson's life, writing, and accomplishments. Part of Twayne's United States Authors series.

Shulman, Jeffrey, and Teresa Rogers. *Gaylord Nelson: A Day for the Earth.* Frederick, MD: Twenty-First Century Books, 1992. Brief, easy-to-read treatment of the senator most responsible for environmental awareness and the creation of Earth Day.

AUDIOVISUAL SOURCES

The Earth Day Special. Burbank, CA: Warner Home Video, 1990. Videocassette. 95-minute television special with a host of stars acting out environmental sketches.

WORLD WIDE WEB

"Earth Day—The Real Story." *Official Earth Trustee Site.* May 1997. http://www.themesh.com/eday.html The site is in honor of John McConnell, father of Earth Day and promoter of the Earth Trustee Concept. Excellent leads to "History of Earth Day" as well as current issues.

83. Environmental Protection Agency (EPA) Created (1970)

Public awareness of destructive environmental practices and health hazards due to industrial pollution accelerated during the 1960s. Shortly after the celebration of Earth Day 1970, President Richard M. Nixon signed into law a measure that created the Environmental Protective Agency. Although the president balked at spending money that Congress appropriated, the EPA brought numerous suits throughout the 1970s against polluters and raised public consciousness about such problems as acid rain and carbon monoxide emissions from automobiles. Some, however, resented the EPA for imposing allegedly needless rules and restrictions on businesses. During the presidency of Ronald Reagan, the EPA suffered from neglect and public scandals involving some high-ranking personnel.

Suggestions for Term Papers

1. Discuss the extent to which the EPA has or has not solved environmental problems.
2. Analyze the Three Mile Island (Pennsylvania) nuclear crisis of 1979 or the Love Canal (New York) pollution crisis of the early 1970s.
3. Discuss the efforts of industry to regulate itself with respect to environmental concerns.
4. Analyze the decline of the EPA during the Reagan presidency.
5. Compare the major concerns of the EPA in the 1970s with its most important current concerns.

Suggested Sources: See entry 82 for relevant items.

REFERENCE SOURCES

Conservation and Environmentalism: An Encyclopedia. Robert Paehlke, ed. New York: Garland, 1995. Some 500 articles with bibliographies, divided into twelve categories, contributed by nearly 250 scholars. Good coverage of the EPA.

The Environmental Encyclopedia and Directory 1998. 2d ed. Detroit: Europa/Gale, 1998. Comprehensive manual providing explanations of terms, organizations, publications, programs, projects, personalities, and other topics.

Gale Environmental Sourcebook: A Guide to Organizations, Agencies and Publications. 2d ed. Detroit: Gale, 1994. Provides brief, descriptive information on more than 9,000 organizations, services, products, and other areas.

GENERAL SOURCES

Baarschers, William H. *Eco-Facts and Eco-Fiction: Understanding the Environmental Debate.* New York: Routledge, 1996. Effective explanation of environmentalism and the need to address it. Good bibliography.

Borrelli, Peter, ed. *Crossroads: Environmental Priorities for the Future.* Washington, DC: Island Press, 1989. Describes current developments in environmentalism; contains essays from twenty environmentalists representing the opinions of different organizations and groups.

Cairncross, Frances. *Costing the Earth: The Challenge for Governments, the Opportunities for Business.* Boston: Harvard Business School, 1993. Clearly written advocacy for governmental intervention in cooperation with business interests. Examples are provided from the United States, United Kingdom, and other nations.

Ehrlich, Paul R., and Ann H. Ehrlich. *Betrayal of Science and Reason: How Anti-Environmental Rhetoric Threatens Our Future.* Washington, DC: Island Press, 1997. A rebuttal to the "misstatements" of scientific findings by authors angered by attempts to minimize the seriousness of environmental problems.

Gottlieb, Robert. *Forcing Spring: The Transformation of the American Environmental Movement.* Washington, DC: Island Press, 1993. Traces the history of environmentalism from the 1890s to its gradual emergence as a powerful political force in shaping national policy.

Hall, Bob, and Mary L. Kerr. *1991–1992 Green Index: A State by State Guide to the Nation's Environmental Health.* Washington, DC: Island Press, 1991. An evaluation of the environmental conditions of all fifty states based on more than 250 indicators. Published under the auspices of the Institute for Southern Studies.

Ladd, Everett C. *Attitudes toward the Environment: Twenty-five Years after Earth Day.* Washington, DC: AEI Press, 1995. A fifty-five-page survey of public opinion on the importance of preserving the environment and fighting pollution.

Nash, Roderick F., ed. *American Environmentalism: Readings in Conservation History.* Rev. ed. New York: McGraw-Hill, 1990. Contains excellent documents relevant to an understanding of the basis of environmental policy. A revision of the second edition of *The American Environment* (1976).

Oelschlager, Max, ed. *After Earth Day: Continuing the Conservation Effort.* Denton: University of North Texas Press, 1995. Collection of sixteen essays on all aspects of the nation's conservation activity, focusing on the impatience of cooperation among all parties in developing realistic solutions.

Rogers, Michael D., ed. *Business and the Environment.* New York: St. Martin's, 1995. Proceedings of a workshop held in Spain to identify ways in which industrial processes could be improved to benefit the environment. The first chapter treats the greening of American industry.

Stefoff, Rebecca. *The American Environmental Movement.* New York: Facts on File, 1995. Broad and sweeping history of environmental activism in the United States with emphasis on nineteenth- and twentieth-century efforts and personalities.

Wildavsky, Aaron. *But Is It True? A Citizen's Guide to Environmental Health and Safety Issues.* Cambridge, MA: Harvard University Press, 1995. A detailed examination of the overstated past risks and "scares" in our society (saccharin, DDT, asbestos, cranberries, etc.) in stating his minority-view conclusion that environmental threats are overly publicized.

SPECIALIZED SOURCES

Landy, Marc K., et al. *The Environmental Protection Agency: Asking the Wrong Questions from Nixon to Clinton.* New York: Oxford University Press, 1994. A detailed analysis of environmental policymaking failures of the EPA in seeking to implement its programs based on broad policy issues such as reduction of cancer to a statistical percentage rather than actually improving the quality of life.

Mintz, Joel. *Enforcement at the EPA: High Stakes and Hard Choices.* Austin: University of Texas Press, 1995. First comprehensive history of the enforcement of standards by the EPA, written by an EPA official. Contains firsthand information on and evaluation of its success.

AUDIOVISUAL SOURCES

The Earth at Risk Environmental Series. Momence, IL: Baker & Taylor, 1993. 10 videocassettes. An examination of important contemporary issues (acid rain, clean air, global warming, etc.) from a variety of perspectives. 30 minutes each.

WORLD WIDE WEB

The U.S. EPA's 25th Anniversary Report: 1970–1995. March 1997. http://www.epa.gov/oppe/25year/ The EPA web site. Click on "Twenty-five Years of Environmental Progress at a Glance" for a good over-view of achievements.

84. Kent State Killings (1970)

In March 1969, President Nixon ordered the secret bombing of communist Vietnamese supply lines in neutral Cambodia. In April the following year, he publicly announced that troops would be sent into that neutral country. Incensed that the Vietnam War was widening, college students angrily demonstrated. As a result, seventy-five of the nation's colleges ended their spring semester prematurely. At Kent State University in Ohio, antiwar students burned an ROTC building. Sent to the campus by Ohio's governor, James Rhodes, to establish order, nervous National Guardsmen on May 4 fired on protesters, killing four and wounding nine others. The event exacerbated tensions within the country.

Suggestions for Term Papers

1. Analyze President Nixon's handling of the Cambodian bombings and invasions.

2. Discuss whether it was necessary to call in the National Guard at Kent State.

3. Analyze public reaction to the Kent State shootings.

4. Compare the Kent State violence with the killing and shooting of protesting students at Jackson State (Mississippi) on May 14, 1970.

5. What were the short- and long-range consequences of college protests during the Vietnam War era on American education?

Suggested Sources: See entries 74 and 75 for related items.

GENERAL SOURCES

Morrison, Joan, and Robert K. Morrison. *From Camelot to Kent State: The Sixties Experience in the Words of Those Who Lived it.* New York: Times Books, 1987. Informative survey of the 1960s, with good background information.

Peterson, Richard E., and John A. Bilorusky. *May 1970: The Campus Aftermath of Cambodia and Kent State.* Berkeley, CA: Carnegie Foundation, 1971. Brief report sponsored by the Carnegie Foundation on Higher Education examining the political activity of college students following the Kent State killings.

Shawcross, William. *Sideshow: Kissinger, Nixon, and the Destruction of Cambodia.* Rev. ed. New York: Simon & Schuster, 1987. Detailed description and analysis of U.S. politics regarding the Vietnam conflict and the bombing of Cambodia.

United States. President's Commission on Campus Unrest. *The Report of the President's Commission on Campus Unrest; Including Special Reports: The Killings at Jackson State, the Kent State Tragedy.* New York: Arno, 1970. The detailed special report examining the tragedies of student unrest and demonstration.

Viorst, Milton. *Fire in the Streets: America in the 1960s.* New York: Simon & Schuster, 1979. Detailed account of the troubled decade that witnessed growing radicalism, militancy, and violence in civil protest demonstrations.

SPECIALIZED SOURCES

Bills, Scott L., ed. *Kent State/May 4: Echoes Through a Decade.* Kent, OH: Kent State University Press, 1988. Memorial narrative describing student attitudes and the 1970 riot.

Eszterhas, Joe, and Michael D. Roberts. *Thirteen Seconds: Confrontation at Kent State.* New York: Dodd, Mead, 1970. Informative account of the event by leading film writer, Joe Eszterhas (*Basic Instinct, Jade*).

Gordon, William A. *Four Dead in Ohio: Was There a Conspiracy at Kent State?* (1990). Reprint. Laguna Hills, CA: North Ridge Books, 1995. Recent exposition of the Kent State riots, including the causes.

Grant, Ed, and Mike Hill. *I Was There: What Really Went On at Kent State.* Lima, OH: C.S.S. Publishing, 1974. Written from the perspective of a former Ohio National Guardsman; brief description and interpretation.

Hensley, Thomas R., and Jerry M. Lewis. *Kent State and May 4th: A Social Science Perspective.* Dubuque, IA: Kendall/Hunt, 1978. Interesting and informative examination of the event, providing an interpretation of societal considerations.

———, et al. *The Kent State Incident: Impact of Judicial Process on Public Attitudes.* Westport, CT: Greenwood, 1981. Examination of public opinion on the judicial process with respect to the handling of the Kent State riot.

Kelner, Joseph, and James Munves. *The Kent State Coverup.* New York: Harper & Row, 1980. Interesting account of the Kent State tragedy from the perspective of ten years after.

Michener, James A. *Kent State: What Happened and Why.* New York: Random House, 1971. Written in the typical Michener style, providing detailed description and analysis; published just one year after the event.

Payne, J. Gregory. *Mayday, Kent State.* Dubuque, IA: Kendall/Hunt, 1981. Brief overview and treatment of the motion picture.

Sorvig, Kim. *To Heal Kent State: A Memorial Meditation.* Philadelphia: Worldview, 1990. A memorial history written twenty years after the event, in tribute to those who died.

Stone, I. F. *The Killings at Kent State: How Murder Went Unpunished.* New York: Vintage Books, 1971. Examines the details of the event and furnishes the secret summary of the FBI findings. By the noted political writer.

Taylor, Stuart, et al. *Violence at Kent State, May 1 to 4, 1970: The Students' Perspective.* New York: College Notes & Texts, 1971. Brief compilation of student interpretations of the event.

Tompkins, Phillip K., and Elaine V. B. Anderson. *Communication Crisis at Kent State: A Case Study.* New York: Gordon & Breach, 1971. Interesting case history of the tragic event and the failures in administrative communication with students and others.

Warren, Bill, ed. *The Middle of the Country: The Events of May 4th As Seen by Students and Faculty at Kent State University.* New York: Avon, 1970. A firsthand report that is one of the earliest publications on the riot.

AUDIOVISUAL SOURCES

Kent State. Universal City, CA: Universal Studios Home Video, 1981. Videocassette. 120-minute television presentation with Ellen Barkin examining the tragic events of Kent State.

WORLD WIDE WEB

Payne, J. Gregory, Ph.D. *Mayday: Kent State.* July 1995. http://grace. it.emerson.edu/acadepts/CS/policom/kentstate/MAYDAY/   A thoughtful but nonevaluative narrative of the event and its aftermath, adapted from the 1981 paperback text. Appendixes include speeches of both President Nixon and Governor Rhodes.

85. Watergate Scandal (1972–1974)

Bent on hindering Democrats in the forthcoming 1972 elections, several persons working for the Committee to Re-Elect the President (CREEP) were arrested before they could break into Democratic headquarters in Washington's Watergate building complex. Repeated efforts to cover up the affair failed over the next two years. Various administration officials admitted their involvement, and President Nixon reluctantly handed over secretly taped White House conferences. The tapes, however, revealed an eighteen-minute erasure, and in early August the House Judiciary Committee voted to recommend impeachment. Nixon resigned office on August 9, 1974, but was pardoned two months later by his successor, Gerald R. Ford. Ultimately twenty-nine persons were convicted of crimes related to the Watergate scandal.

Suggestions for Term Papers

1. Did the Watergate scandal show that the judicial system worked, or did it destroy public faith in government?
2. Analyze President Nixon's handling of the Watergate incident.
3. Discuss the "Saturday Night Massacre" of October 20, 1973.
4. Should President Ford have pardoned ex-president Nixon?
5. Discuss the long-range effects of Watergate on American life.

Suggested Sources: See entry 95 for related items.

GENERAL SOURCES

Crowley, Monica. *Nixon in Winter: Off the Record Reflections on the State of the World, the Scandals of Washington, and Life in and out of the Political Arena.* New York: Random House, 1998. Reflections by the former president, on Watergate among other things. The sequel to the author's *Nixon off the Record* (1996).

Firestone, Bernard J., and Alexej Ugrinsky, eds. *Gerald R. Ford and the Politics of Post-Watergate America.* Westport, CT: Greenwood, 1993. 2 vols. Collection of papers on the period following Watergate. Of interest is "The Nixon-Ford Relationship" and "In Defense of President Ford's Pardon of Richard M. Nixon." Prepared under the auspices of Hofstra University.

Friedman, Leon, and William F. Levantrosser, eds. *Cold War Patriot and Statesman.* Westport, CT: Greenwood, 1993. A balanced examination of politics and government during the Nixon years. Prepared under the auspices of Hofstra University.

Garment, Suzanne. *Scandal: The Culture of Mistrust in American Politics.* (1991). Reprint. New York: Anchor Books, 1992. Examines the presence of scandal in American politics through the years; its full bloom was Watergate.

Greene, John R. *The Limits of Power: The Nixon and Ford Administrations.* Bloomington: Indiana University Press, 1992. Brief, informative study of the politics and governance in the years embracing the Nixon-Ford period.

Lawson, Don. *Famous Presidential Scandals.* Hillside, NJ: Enslow Publishers, 1990. Easy-to-read account of four major scandals; good description of the Watergate affair.

Marty, Myron A. *Daily Life in the United States, 1960–1990.* Westport, CT: Greenwood, 1997. Recent examination of a pivotal period, including civil rights movement, Vietnam, and Watergate.

Riebling, Mark. *Wedge.* New York: Knopf, 1994. Detailed historical account of the friction between the FBI and the CIA; speculates that this friction led to Kennedy's assassination and Watergate.

Ryan, Halford R., ed. *Oratorical Encounters: Selected Studies and Sources of Twentieth-Century Political Accusations and Apologies.* Westport, CT: Greenwood, 1988. Analysis and examination of important speeches and oratory. Of interest is the treatment of Nixon and the Watergate scandal, and Ford and the Nixon legacy.

Williams, Robert. *Political Scandals in the United States.* Chicago: Fitzroy Dearborn, 1998. Covers five main topics in depth, including a serious and scholarly explanation of Watergate as well as the Iran-contra affair.

SPECIALIZED SOURCES

Ball, Howard. *"We Have a Duty": The Supreme Court and the Watergate Tapes Litigation.* Westport, CT: Greenwood, 1990. Concise narrative describing the trial with respect to the concept of executive privilege. The author had access to Justice Brennan's notes and observations.

Bernstein, Carl and Bob Woodward. *All the President's Men.* (1974). Reprint. Touchstone Books, 1994. The classic work on the Watergate break-in traces the event and the investigative procedures by the two newspapermen.

Emery, Fred. *Watergate: The Corruption of American Politics and the Fall of Richard Nixon.* New York: Times Books, 1994. Perhaps the definitive work on Watergate; up to date, detailed, and well written.

Feinberg, Barbara S. *Watergate: Scandal in the White House.* New York: Franklin Watts, 1990. Easy-to-read account of the break-in and the consequences.

Friedman, Leon, and William F. Levantrosser, eds. *Watergate and After-*

ward: The Legacy of Richard M. Nixon. Westport, CT: Greenwood, 1992. A collection of papers from a Hofstra University conference, with several targeting Watergate, the crisis, and the abuse of power.

Kutler, Stanley I. *The Wars of Watergate: The Last Crisis of Richard Nixon.* New York: Norton, 1992. Lengthy and thorough account detailing activities of the Nixon administration during the Watergate period.

Sussman, Barry. *The Great Coverup: Nixon and the Scandal of Watergate.* New York: New American Library, 1974. Popular paperback providing insight into the Watergate scandal and the role of the *Washington Post.*

Tretick, Stanley, and William V. Shannon. *They Could Not Trust the King: Nixon, Watergate, and the American People.* New York: Collier Books, 1974. An older work but still useful and accurate. Foreword by Barbara W. Tuchman.

BIOGRAPHICAL SOURCES

Aitken, Jonathan. *Nixon, a Life.* Washington, DC: Regnery Publishing/ National Book Network, 1993. Recent and detailed biographical study providing insight into Nixon's life and career.

Larsen, Rebecca. *Richard Nixon: Rise and Fall of a President.* New York: Franklin Watts, 1991. Easy-to-read biography of the former president; covers his younger days, political career including Watergate, and retirement.

Nadel, Laurie. *The Great Stream of History: A Biography of Richard M. Nixon.* New York: Atheneum, 1991. Concise account of Nixon's life and political career.

AUDIOVISUAL SOURCES

Watergate. Bethesda, MD: Discovery Home Entertainment, 1994. 3 videocassettes. Thorough treatment, with contributions by participants, prosecutors, and reporters. 135 minutes.

WORLD WIDE WEB

Farnsworth, Malcolm. *Watergate.* 1997; updated July 1998 http:// www.vcepolitics.com./wgate.htm Overview of Watergate developments with many leads and links to relevant information. Treats background, political context, the burglary, casualties and convictions, and aftermath.

86. Strategic Arms Limitation Agreements (SALT I and SALT II) (1972, 1979)

In 1972 President Richard Nixon visited Moscow and signed the Strategic Arms Limitation Agreement with Soviet leader Leonid Brezhnev. The agreement imposed only minor limitations on the arms race, but it did produce a détente between the two superpowers. The agreement lapsed in 1977; in July 1979 the United States and the USSR signed a second SALT accord, which further reduced the stockpile of weapons and weapons delivery systems. American critics, however, blamed President Jimmy Carter for having proposed either too many or too few cuts. When the Soviet Union attacked Afghanistan later that year, Carter withdrew the treaty from consideration by the Senate.

Suggestions for Term Papers

1. Analyze the conditions that made SALT I possible.
2. Compare the military strength of the United States with that of the USSR at the time of the SALT I.
3. Should President Carter have withdrawn the SALT II agreement from Senate consideration?
4. Analyze how and why President Ronald Reagan and Soviet leader Mikhail Gorbachev were able to achieve sweeping weapons reductions.
5. Discuss public reaction to SALT I and II.

Suggested Sources: See entry 97 for related items.

REFERENCE SOURCES

Encyclopedia of Arms Control and Disarmament. Richard D. Burns, ed. New York: Scribner, 1993. 3 vols. More than seventy-five essays on arms control both historically and as a contemporary policy; comprehensive coverage of the issue on an international basis.

GENERAL SOURCES

Carnesale, Albert, and Richard Haass, eds. *Superpower Arms Control: Setting the Record Straight.* Cambridge, MA: Ballinger, 1987. Collection of essays on results of arms control negotiations; SALT I and II are included.

Croft, Stuart. *Strategies of Arms Control: A History and Typology.* New York: Manchester University Press, /St. Martin's, 1996. Brief, comprehensive history of the strategies employed to control arms and weaponry.

Krepon, Michael, and Dan Caldwell, eds. *The Politics of Arms Control Treaty Ratification.* New York: St. Martin's, 1991. Detailed and thorough treatment of the history of arms control in the United States; consideration of foreign relations, politics, and treaties.

————. *Strategic Stalemate: Nuclear Weapons and Arms Control in American Politics.* New York: St. Martin's, 1984. The authors' earlier work on arms control, with a section on SALT talks.

Russett, Bruce M. *The Prisoners of Insecurity: Nuclear Deterrence, the Arms Race, and Arms Control.* San Francisco: W. H. Freeman, 1983. Examination of world politics and the policies of the United States and the Soviet Union.

Smoke, Richard. *National Security and the Nuclear Dilemma: An Introduction to the American Experience.* Reading, MA: Addison-Wesley, 1984. An examination of U.S. military policy and foreign relations in the latter half of the twentieth century.

————. *Think about Nuclear Arms Control: Understanding the Arms Race.* New York: Walker, 1988. Easy-to-read, informative description of the arms race providing historical background and impact.

Szilard, Leo. *Toward a Livable World: Leo Szilard and the Crusade for Nuclear Arms Control.* Helen S. Hawkins et al., eds. Cambridge: MIT Press, 1987. Volume 3 of the collected works of Leo Szilard. Provides insight into the history of nuclear disarmament and nuclear nonproliferation.

Talbott, Strobe. *Deadly Gambits: The Reagan Administration and the Stalemate in Nuclear Arms Control.* New York: Knopf/Random House, 1984. Informative account of the Reagan period and attempts at arms reduction.

Williamson, Jr., Samuel R., and Steven L. Rearden. *The Origins of U.S. Nuclear Strategy.* New York: St. Martin's, 1993. Good description of the development of nuclear policy in the United States.

Wirls, Daniel. *Buildup.* Ithaca, NY: Cornell University Press, 1993. Interesting and useful attempt to examine the large peacetime military buildup in the 1980s; includes the six-year debate on SALT II.

SPECIALIZED SOURCES

Bell, Robert G. *Implications of Extending the SALT I Interim Agreement.* Washington, DC: Library of Congress/Congressional Research Service, 1977. A brief examination of the SALT agreement from the U.S. government. Available in microfilm from University Publications of America, Arlington, VA.

Carter, Jimmy. *SALT II Agreement: Message from the President of the United States Urging the Ratification of the SALT II Agreement.* Washington, DC: GPO, 1979. The president's message to Congress. Available in microfiche from the U.S. Government Printing Office, Washington, DC. (six pages).

U.S. Congress. House Committee on Foreign Affairs. *Calling for a Mutual and Verifiable Freeze on and Reduction in Nuclear Weapons and for the Approval of the SALT II Agreement.* 97th Congress, 2d session, House of Representatives; No. 97–640. Washington, DC: GPO, 1982. Twenty-one-page report together with minority and supplemental views.

U.S. Department of State. Bureau of Public Affairs. *SALT II Agreement, Vienna, June 18, 1979.* Washington, DC: GPO, 1979. Complete documentary evidence of the agreement and the preceding events in fifty-four pages.

BIOGRAPHICAL SOURCES

Carter, Jimmy. *Keeping Faith: Memoirs of a President.* (1982). Reprint. Fayetteville, AR: University of Arkansas Press, 1995. Detailed recollections of the former president; SALT agreements are included.

AUDIOVISUAL SOURCES

United States Presidents Series. Memphis: City Productions Home Video, 1995. 5 videocassettes. Accomplishments and controversies for each president from Washington to Clinton; Jimmy Carter is treated in volume 5. 60 minutes each.

WORLD WIDE WEB

U.S. Arms Control and Disarmament Agency—ACDA. July 1997. http://www.acda.gov/initial.html The home page of this agency, with speeches, treaties, reports, historical documents, and fact sheets. Click on "Treaties" for excellent background information.

87. President Nixon Visits China (1972)

By 1971 badly deteriorating relations between the Soviet Union and the People's Republic of China (PRC) allowed President Nixon to achieve a dramatic shift in Sino-American relations. After sending national security adviser Henry Kissinger on a secret trip to Beijing that year, Nixon publicly announced that he would visit China the following year. A longtime bitter foe of the PRC, once in that country he courted and in turn was courted by party leaders. His trip in 1972 led to cultural exchanges, the possibility of trade resumption, and, most significant, the acceptance in principle that Taiwan was part of China. Diplomatic recognition came in 1979.

Suggestions for Term Papers

1. Analyze why the United States did not recognize the People's Republic for three decades after the communists had seized power.
2. Discuss why President Nixon reversed American diplomacy toward China.
3. Discuss public reaction to the change in U.S. policy toward the People's Republic.
4. Discuss the events in Tiananmen Square (Beijing) in the spring of 1989 and their effect on Sino-American relations.
5. Discuss the relations between the United States and Taiwan since the U.S. recognition of the People's Republic of China.

REFERENCE SOURCES

Dictionary of the Politics of the People's Republic of China. Colin Mackerras et al., eds. New York: Routledge, 1998. Comprehensive dictionary treating events, issues, personalities, and institutions of the PRC.

GENERAL SOURCES

Baum, Richard, ed. *Reform and Reaction in Post-Mao China: The Road to Tiananmen.* New York: Routledge, 1991. Concise examination of

Chinese politics, governance, and economic policy from the mid-1970s.

Feignon, Lee. *China Rising: The Meaning of Tiananmen.* Chicago: Ivan R. Dee, 1990. Good overview of politics and government in the PRC, with emphasis on student activity leading to Tiananmen.

Garson, Robert. *The United States and China since 1949: A Troubled Affair.* Madison, NJ: Fairleigh Dickinson University Press, 1994. Concise account of the difficult relationship between the two countries in the latter half of the twentieth century.

Goldman, Martin S. *Richard M. Nixon: The Complex President.* New York: Facts on File, 1998. Even-handed assessment of Nixon's impact and achievements, including his historical visit to China.

Harding, Harry. *A Fragile Relationship: The United States and China since 1972.* Washington, DC: Brookings Institution, 1992. Examination of the conflicts in the relations between the two countries since Nixon's historic trip.

Litwak, Robert. *Détente and the Nixon Doctrine: American Foreign Policy and the Pursuit of Stability, 1969–1976.* New York: Cambridge University Press, 1985. Good overview of the Nixon presidency and foreign relations, including China.

Salisbury, Harrison E. *Tiananmen Diary: Thirteen Days in June.* Boston: Little, Brown, 1989. Brief, insightful history of the incident by one of the leading authorities on China.

Shambaugh, David. *Beautiful Imperialist China Perceives America, 1972–1990.* Princeton, NJ: Princeton University Press, 1991. Examination of Chinese perceptions and misperceptions of the United States over the twenty-five years since Nixon's visit.

Terrill, Ross. *China in Our Time: The Epic Saga of the People's Republic from the Communist Victory to Tiananmen Square and Beyond.* New York: Simon & Schuster, 1992. Comprehensive history of China from 1949 to the present.

Wu, Fu-mei Chiu. *Richard M. Nixon, Communism and China.* Washington, DC: University Press of America, 1978. Brief examination of foreign relations with China under Nixon.

SPECIALIZED SOURCES

Buss, Claude A. *China: The People's Republic of China and Richard Nixon.* (1972). Reprint. San Francisco: W. H. Freeman, 1974. Concise, informative examination of foreign relations with China under Nixon.

Walker, Ann C., et al. *China Calls: Paving the Way for Nixon's Historic Journey to China.* Lanham, MD: Madison Books/National Book

Network, 1992. Detailed account of the preparations undertaken to make the visit possible.

Wilson, Richard, ed. *The President's Trip to China*. New York: Bantam Books, 1972. Account of Nixon's visit to China.

BIOGRAPHICAL SOURCES

Li, Lu. *Moving the Mountain: My Life in China from the Cultural Revolution to Tiananmen Square*. London: Macmillan, 1990. Interesting and informative personal account of life in modern China up to the Tiananmen Square incident.

AUDIOVISUAL SOURCES

Nixon: A Tribute. Seattle: Paragon Home Video, 1995. Videocassette. 52-minute presentation of the Nixon years from his own perspective.

Tragedy at Tiananmen Square: The Untold Story. Columbus, OH: Coronet Film & Video, 1989. Videocassette. 1-hour presentation on the incident at Tiananmen Square.

WORLD WIDE WEB

Luo, Ning. "*Some Thoughts on the US-China Relation (II)*." *Chinese Community Forum*. March 1996. http://www.china-net.org/ccf9613–4.html An interesting summary of current conditions between the two nations as a result of the Nixon initiative in 1972. The *Forum* is a weekly electronic journal of news, poetry, arts, etc. The opinions expressed are those of the editors and contributors.

88. Equal Rights Amendment (1972)

In 1923 the National Woman's party proposed a constitutional equal rights amendment that would end legal inequalities between the sexes. Long dormant, the amendment resurfaced during the 1960s, particularly through the efforts of the National Organization for Women (NOW). Congress passed an equal rights amendment in 1972 and sent it to the states for ratification. The amendment initially seemed destined for adoption, but opponents, ranging from traditionalist Phyllis Schlafly to conservative religious televangelist Pat Robertson, stopped the amendment's momentum. With the approval of only two more states needed, Congress extended the deadline for passage from 1978 to 1982, but no more states concurred.

Suggestions for Term Papers

1. Compare the arguments for and against an equal rights amendment.
2. Discuss why and how Phyllis Schlafly opposed the amendment.
3. Why did popular support for the amendment decline?
4. Is an equal rights amendment still needed?
5. Compare how different religious groups regarded the equal rights amendment.

Suggested Sources: See entries 12, 45, 93 and especially 77 for related items.

REFERENCE SOURCES

The ABC-CLIO Companion to Women's Progress in America. Elizabeth Frost-Knappman. Santa Barbara, CA: ABC-CLIO, 1994. Alphabetically arranged collection treating themes, personalities, issues, and events; detailed chronology.

The Equal Rights Amendment: A Bibliographic Study. Hazel Greenberg, ed. and comp. Westport, CT: Greenwood, 1976. Comprehensive bibliography published during the height of the struggle for passage under the auspices of the Equal Rights Amendment Project.

The Equal Rights Amendment: An Annotated Bibliography of the Issues, 1976–1985. Renee Feinberg, comp. Westport, CT: Greenwood, 1986. A more recent bibliography than the previous entry.

Women's Rights. Christine A. Lunardini. Phoenix: Oryx, 1996. Comprehensive treatment of topics, issues, personalities, events; well illustrated, with a detailed bibliography.

Women's Rights in the U.S.A.: Policy Debates and Gender Roles. Dorothy M. Stetson. 2d ed. Hamden, CT: Garland, 1997. Fine general resource for the study of women's rights; examines roles, expectations, societal issues, and ongoing controversies.

GENERAL SOURCES

Fetzer, Philip L., ed. *The Ethnic Movement: The Search for Equality in the American Experience.* Armonk, NY: M. E. Sharpe, 1996. Excellent essays by twelve individuals, including Betty Friedan, that explore politics, law, education, and other areas.

Ide, Arthur F. *Idol Worshippers in 20th Century America—Phyllis Schlafly, Ronald Reagan, Jerry Falwell, and the Moral Majority on Women, Work, and Homosexuality: With a Parallel Translation and Critical Commentary on Genesis.* Dallas: Monument Press, 1984. Critical examination of conservatism in modern U.S. politics.

Langley, Winston E., and Vivian C. Fox, eds. *Women's Rights in the United States: A Documentary History.* Westport, CT: Greenwood, 1994. Award-winning source book providing primary source documents relevant to the study of the legal and political development of women's rights in the United States.

McWhirter, Darien A., ed. *Equal Protection.* Phoenix: Oryx, 1995. Provides an overview of court decisions and fascinating cases regarding affirmative action, race, and sex discrimination. Part of the publisher's Exploring the Constitution series.

Schlafly, Phyllis. *The Power of the Positive Woman.* New Rochelle, NY: Arlington House, 1977. Popular tract examining the role of women in the United States and the burden of increasing feminism.

SPECIALIZED SOURCES

Becker, Susan D. *The Origins of the Equal Rights Amendment: American Feminism Between the Wars.* Westport, CT: Greenwood, 1981. Informative history of the background of the ERA with examination of early efforts by the National Woman's party.

Boles, Janet K. *The Politics of the Equal Rights Amendment: Conflict and the Decision Process.* New York: Longman, 1979. Informative, concise overview of the political considerations driving the passage of the amendment by the states.

Hatch, Orrin. *The Equal Rights Amendment: Myths and Realities.* Virginia Beach: Savant, 1983. Brief overview of the equal rights amendment and its attendant considerations by a U.S. senator.

Slavin, Sarah, ed. *The Equal Rights Amendment: The Politics and Process of Ratification of the 27th Amendment to the U.S. Constitution.* New York: Haworth, 1982. Concise, comprehensive examination of the amendment and the approval process; published during the final year of the effort.

Steiner, Gilbert Y. *Constitutional Inequality: The Political Fortunes of the Equal Rights Amendment.* Washington, DC: Brookings Institution, 1985. Brief account of the decline of the political impetus to pass the amendment.

BIOGRAPHICAL SOURCES

Carroll, Peter N. *Famous in America—The Passion to Succeed: Jane Fonda, George Wallace, Phyllis Schlafly, John Glenn.* New York: Dutton, 1985. Collective biography of four famous but politically diverse Americans; Fonda and Schlafly were on opposite sides of the ERA issue.

Felsenthal, Carol. *The Sweetheart of the Silent Majority: The Biography of Phyllis Schlafly.* Garden City, NY: Doubleday, 1981. Interesting biography of the arch-conservative political reformer.

AUDIOVISUAL SOURCES

Equality: A History of the Women's Movement in America. Bala Cynwyd, PA: Library Video/Schlessinger, 1996. Videocassette. 30-minute documentary on the women's movement from the eighteenth century to the present.

WORLD WIDE WEB

Freeman, Jo. *From Protection to Equal Opportunity: The Revolution in Women's Legal Status.* July 1994. http://www.inform.umd.edu/EdRes/Topic/WomensStudies/ReadingRoom/AcademicPapers/womens-legal-status Originally published in *Women, Politics and Change*, edited by Louise Tilly and Patricia Gurin (Russell Sage, 1990), this 25-page paper provides a detailed history and analysis of the impact of the struggle to pass the ERA.

89. *Roe* v. *Wade* (1973)

On January 23, 1973, the Supreme Court handed down what, with the exception of the 1953 desegregation case, was its most controversial decision in the twentieth century. Although forty-six states had enacted some form of antiabortion legislation, the High Court in *Roe* v. *Wade* ruled that the right of privacy permitted a woman to undergo an abortion during the first trimester of her pregnancy. Women's rights advocates and civil libertarians generally hailed the decision, while some religious groups and most conservatives denounced it. "Right-to-life" forces formed in opposition to the *Roe* decision, but thus far legal attempts to reverse the decision have failed.

Suggestions for Term Papers

1. Discuss the origins of *Roe* v. *Wade.*
2. Compare the arguments of pro-choice and right-to-life advocates.
3. Discuss how other countries treat abortion.
4. Discuss the use of violence and threats of violence against abortion clinics and physicians who perform abortions.
5. Discuss the abortion controversy in your own community.

Suggested sources: See entries 77 and 88 for additional relevant items.

REFERENCE SOURCES

Abortion. 2d ed. Marie Costa. Santa Barbara, CA: ABC-CLIO, 1996. Revised and updated version of Costa's award-winning work; contains a chronology, statistics, a listing of major court cases, information on harassment of abortion providers, and biographies.

Abortion Decisions of the United States Supreme Court. Maureen Harrison and Steve Gilbert, eds. Beverly Hills, CA: Excellent Books, 1992. Exposition of cases and decisions rendered by the Supreme Court in relation to abortion. Part of the publisher's Abortion Decision series.

Encyclopedia of Social History. Peter N. Stearns, ed. Hamden, CT: Garland, 1993. Broad, comprehensive treatment of periods and regions; abortion is an issue treated.

The 1995 Information Please Women's Sourcebook. Lisa DiMona and Constance Herndon, eds. Boston: Houghton Mifflin, 1994. The first issue of an annual publication presenting an overview of the major issues of concern to women (education, child care, politics, etc.). Includes graphs, tables, charts, judicial and legal decisions, and other material.

The Supreme Court A to Z: A Ready Reference Encyclopedia. Rev. ed. Elder Witt. Washington, DC: Congressional Quarterly, 1994. Alphabetically arranged topics with cross-references to other pertinent cases. Abortion is the first topic treated; historical overview with full description of *Roe* v. *Wade.*

Women's Issues. Margaret McFadden, ed. Englewood Cliffs, NJ: Salem, 1997. 3 vols. Treats all relevant issues and topics in encyclopedia-like fashion. Balanced treatment on volatile themes such as abortion, with fine historical coverage. Part of the publisher's Ready Reference series.

Women's Studies Encyclopedia, Vol. 3: *History, Philosophy, Religion.* Helen

Tierney, ed. Westport, CT: Greenwood, 1991. The history, definitions, and basic information about the women's movement as an international issue, as well as an American focus that includes NOW.

GENERAL SOURCES

Byrnes, Timothy A., and Mary C. Segers. *The Catholic Church and the Politics of Abortion: A View from the States.* Boulder, CO: Westview, 1992. Examines state politics in relation to the Catholic church and abortion.

Cozic, Charles P., and Jonathan Petrikin, eds. *The Abortion Controversy.* San Diego: Greenhaven, 1995. A collection of essays providing varying opinions on this volatile issue. Easy to read and understand, with an extensive bibliography. Well indexed.

Joffe, Carole E. *Doctors of Conscience: The Struggle to Provide Abortion before and after Roe v. Wade.* Boston: Beacon, 1995. Examines the ethical and social aspects of providing abortion and the pressures that physicians face.

Mersky, Roy M., and Gary R. Hartman, comps. *A Documentary History of the Legal Aspects of Abortion in the United States.* Littleton, CO: F. B. Rothman, 1993. 3 vols. Thorough compilation of documents and reports relevant to the abortion question.

Pojman, Louis P., and Francis J. Beckwith, comps. *The Abortion Controversy: 25 Years after Roe v. Wade.* Rev. ed. Belmont, CA: Wadsworth, 1998. A new examination of the abortion issue in the light of current thinking regarding moral and ethical aspects of it.

Segers, Mary C., and Timothy A. Byrnes, eds. *Abortion Politics in American States.* Armonk, NY: Sharpe, 1995. Good examination of the political aspects of abortion and state politics in the United States.

SPECIALIZED SOURCES

Faux, Marian. *Roe v. Wade: Marking the 20th Anniversary of the Landmark Supreme Court Decision That Made Abortion Legal.* New York: Mentor, 1993. A detailed examination of the trial and the principal participants, as well as the nature of legislation on abortion.

Herda, D. J. *Roe v. Wade: The Abortion Question.* Hillside, NJ: Enslow Publishers, 1994. Easy-to-read, brief description of the participants, the issue, and the trial. Part of the publisher's Landmark Supreme Court Cases series.

Romaine, Deborah S. *Roe v. Wade: Abortion and the Supreme Court.* San Diego, CA: Lucent Books, 1998. An easy-to-read work describing the controversy over the ruling. Part of the publisher's Famous Trials series.

Rubin, Eva R., ed. *The Abortion Controversy: A Documentary History*. Westport, CT: Greenwood, 1994. Useful collection of documents on the issue; balanced treatment.

———. *Abortion, Politics, and the Courts: Roe v. Wade and Its Aftermath*. Rev. ed. Westport, CT: Greenwood, 1987. Good examination of the legal issues surrounding the outcome of *Roe* v. *Wade*.

Tompkins, Nancy. *Roe v. Wade and the Fight over Life and Liberty*. Franklin Watts, 1996. Concise and lucid description of the struggle and its complexities.

BIOGRAPHICAL SOURCES

McCorvey, Norma, and Andy Meisler. *I Am Roe*. New York: HarperCollins, 1994. Well-written description of the life of McCorvey, the defendant (Roe) in the case.

AUDIOVISUAL SOURCES

Abortion in America. New York: Routledge. CD-ROM. Multimedia interactive CD-ROM addressing the abortion question in the context of other societal considerations.

Butler, J. Douglas, ed. *Abortion and Reproductive Rights: A Comprehensive Guide to Medicine, Ethics and the Law*. Phoenix: Oryx, 1997. CD-ROM. Comprehensive collection of articles, audio and video clips, images, and other material relating to abortion.

Supreme Court Decisions That Changed the Nation. Mount Kisco, NY: Guidance Associates, 1986. Videocassettes. 17-minute presentation in volume 2 analyzing *Roe* v. *Wade*.

WORLD WIDE WEB

National Organization for Women. *Roe v. Wade 25th Anniversary*. http://www.now.org/issues/abortion/roe25/ Issue-oriented link that provides awareness of developments since the decision. Calendar for celebration of the twenty-fifth year (1998), challenges, and some historical insight.

The Ultimate Abortion Law Homepage. December 1997 http://members.aol.com/abtrbng/ Excellent links and leads. Click on "Roe in a Nutshell" for syllabus of the case with numerous links to relevant text. The filed opinions of the six justices are edited for brevity.

90. Panama Canal Treaties (1978)

Negotiations to give Panama control over the Panama Canal had taken place fitfully until the administration of Jimmy Carter. Aware of strong anti-U.S. sentiment in Panama and throughout the rest of Latin America, the president urged Congress to accept two treaties that would permit Panama both ownership and control of the canal by century's end. After acrimoniously debating them in 1977, Congress the following year barely ratified these controversial treaties—opinion polls showed strong opposition—and then only after inserting a clause giving the United States the right to intervene to protect the canal. The treaties provided a source for debate during the 1980 presidential election between Carter and his Republican opponent, Ronald Reagan.

Suggestions for Term Papers

1. Compare the arguments both for and against giving Panama control over the canal.
2. Analyze the Senate debate over the treaties.
3. Discuss public reaction to the treaties.
4. How important were the Panama Canal treaties as a factor in the 1980 presidential election?
5. Discuss why President Carter decided to give Panama control over the canal.

Suggested Sources: See entry 4 for related items.

GENERAL SOURCES

Falcoff, Mark. *Panama Canal: What Happens When the United States Gives a Small Country What It Wants.* Washington, DC: AEI, 1998. Recent survey of politics and government in Panama; includes examination of the Panama Canal treaties.

Germond, Jack W., and Jules Witcover. *Blue Smoke and Mirrors: How Reagan Won and Why Carter Lost the Election.* New York: Viking, 1981. Detailed contemporary examination of the election and such issues as the Panama Canal.

Lindop, Edmund. *Panama and the United States: Divided by the Canal.* New York: Twenty-First Century, 1997. Easy-to-read description of foreign relations between the United States and Panama, especially regarding the canal.

Major, John. *Prize Possession: The United States and the Panama Canal, 1903–1979.* New York: Cambridge University Press, 1993. Informative account of the administration and the importance of the canal; based on government documents from Teddy Roosevelt to Jimmy Carter.

Ropp, Steve C. *Panamanian Politics: From Guarded Nation to National Guard.* New York: Praeger, 1982. Concise overview of Panamanian politics, with an emphasis on treaties and foreign relations.

SPECIALIZED SOURCES

Augelli, John P. *The Panama Canal Area in Transition.* Hanover, NH: American Universities Field Staff, 1981. 2 vols. Compilation of reports on the economic and social conditions as well as the treaties. Detailed examination of the issues.

Crane, Philip M. *Surrender in Panama: The Case against the Treaty.* New York: Dale Books, 1978. Tract providing the opposition voices to the canal treaties; examines issues of human rights and civil liberties. With an introduction by Ronald Reagan.

Furlong, William L. *The Dynamics of Foreign Policymaking: The President, the Congress, and the Panama Canal Treaties.* Boulder, CO: Westview Press, 1984. Informative examination of policymaking developments with respect to Panama and the canal treaties.

Jorden, William J. *Panama Odyssey.* Austin: University of Texas Press, 1984. Detailed examination of all aspects and issues regarding the ratification of the Panama Canal treaties in 1978. Well-written insider's account of negotiations, maneuvering, and personalities in both countries.

LaFeber, Walter. *The Panama Canal: The Crisis in Historical Perspective.* Exp. ed. New York: Oxford University Press, 1979. Useful overview of the historical developments with respect to the canal treaties from 1903 to 1977.

Moffett, George D. *The Limits of Victory: The Ratification of the Panama Canal Treaties.* Ithaca, NY: Cornell University Press, 1985. Describes the lengthy struggle to ratify the treaties; well-written and informative examination of public opinion and diplomacy.

Stoll, Samuel J. *Canalgate: A Panama Canal Brief for the People.* Exp. ed. Livingston, NJ: S. J. Stoll, 1988. Detailed history of the Canal Zone, with a critique of all the treaties from 1903 to 1977.

Summ, Harvey, and Tom Kelly, eds. *The Good Neighbors: America, Panama, and the 1977 Canal Treaties.* Athens, OH: Ohio University Center for International Studies, 1988. Brief history of foreign relations between Panama and the United States, with an emphasis on the 1977 treaties.

PERIODICAL ARTICLES

Kitfield, James. "Yankee, Don't Go!" *National Journal* 28 (8):420 (1996). Some Panamanian concerns over the 1977 treaties that provided for withdrawal of U.S. military forces and transfer of the canal.

"War of Words over Panama Canal" *Congressional Quarterly Weekly Report* 53 (36):2775 (September 16, 1995). Examines the debate over the treaties in 1977 and the intense dispute between the parties.

AUDIOVISUAL SOURCES

The Panama Canal. Columbus, OH: Coronet/MTI, 1978. Videocassette. Very brief (11 minutes) but useful look at the construction and operation of the canal, including the 1977 treaties.

Presidential Debate—President Jimmy Carter vs. Ronald Reagan. Washington DC: NBC-TV/National Archives Collection, 1980. 2 videocassettes. 2-hour coverage of and commentary on the debate in Cleveland. Anchored by John Chancellor.

WORLD WIDE WEB

Panama Canal Commission. "The Panama Canal." 1988. http:www.pancanal.com Provides general background data, canal history, transition information as well as relevant sites. (Use of the material requires consent of the commission.)

91. Camp David Accords (1978)

Hostile relations had ensued between Israel and its Arab neighbors ever since Israel's statehood in 1948. After Egyptian president Anwar Sadat paid a dramatic visit to Israel in 1978, President Jimmy Carter, hoping to further the peace process, invited Sadat and Israeli prime minister Menachem Begin to the presidential retreat in Camp David, Maryland. There the latter two signed accords by which Egypt agreed to recognize Israel, in return for which Israel would return occupied land in the Sinai and negotiate the Palestinian refugee problem. The accords nearly unraveled but then became part of a treaty in 1979. Arab hostility to the treaty, however, led to Sadat's assassination in 1981, and Begin thwarted hopes for a Palestinian solution.

Suggestions for Term Papers

1. Analyze the relations between Egypt and Israel between 1948 and 1978.
2. Analyze U.S. foreign policy in the Middle East between 1948 and 1978.
3. Analyze the role of President Carter in the negotiations between Egypt and Israel.
4. What have been the long-term consequences of the Camp David Accords?
5. Has U.S. foreign policy with regard to Israel and its Arab neighbors changed since the Camp David Accords?

GENERAL SOURCES

Bar-Simian-Tov, Yaacov. *Israel and the Peace Process, 1977–1982.* Albany: State University of New York, 1994. Analysis of the change in Israel's stance from war to peace with Egypt during the Begin period.

Carter, Jimmy. *Talking Peace: A Vision for the Next Generation.* New York: Dutton Children's Books, 1993. Brief, easy-to-read, informative narrative of Carter's basic philosophy, which governed his actions as a peacemaker.

Mansour, Camille, and James A. Cohen. *Beyond Alliance: Israel in U.S. Foreign Policy.* New York: Columbia University Press, 1994. Interesting analysis of Israel's privileged position in American politics from its beginning in 1948 to the Camp David Accords. From the Palestinian perspective.

Peleg, Ilan. *Begin's Foreign Policy: Israel's Move to the Right.* Westport, CT: Greenwood, 1987. Examines Begin's life and political career and his desire to annex the West Bank; treats ramifications for foreign relations.

Spanier, John W., et al. *American Foreign Policy since World War II.* Washington DC: Congressional Quarterly, 1997. Recent examination of foreign policy over the past half-century, placing events like the accords in historical perspective.

SPECIALIZED SOURCES

Friedlander, Melvin A. *Sadat and Begin: The Domestic Politics of Peacemaking*. Boulder, CO: Westview, 1983. Interesting account of foreign relations between Israel and Egypt, the two principal leaders, and internal politics.

Kamil, Mohamed I. *The Camp David Accords: A Testimony*. Boston: Routledge & Kegan Paul, 1986. Thorough and detailed account of the agreement exploring the thought processes and rationale of the Egyptian ministry. The author is opposed to the pact.

Telhami, Shibley. *Power and Leadership in International Bargaining: The Path to the Camp David Accords*. New York: Columbia University Press, 1990. Examination of the steps and events leading to the accords; treats the factors that led to the outcomes.

BIOGRAPHICAL SOURCES

Finklestone, Joseph. *Anwar Sadat: Visionary Who Dared*. Portland, OR: Frank Cass, 1996. Recent biography of Sadat by a journalist who knew him; examines his political career and his astuteness from the time he took over from President Gamal Abdel Nasser.

Israeli, Raphael, and Carol Bardenstein. *Man of Defiance: Political Career of Anwar Sadat*. Totowa, NJ: Barnes and Noble, 1985. Interesting account of Sadat and his capacity to govern; Sadat's first wife is one source employed by the author.

Sofer, Sasson. *Begin: An Anatomy of Leadership*. New York: Oxford University Press, 1988. Critical examination of Begin and what the author views as his lack of judgment in governance during a critical period.

Troester, Rod. *Jimmy Carter as Peacemaker: A Post-presidential Biography*. Westport, CT: Greenwood, 1996. Recent study of Carter's life and career as a diplomat.

AUDIOVISUAL SOURCES

Israel: A Nation Is Born. Momence, IL: Baker & Taylor, 1993. Videocassette. A good retrospective, hosted by Abba Eban, with archival footage examining important events in the history of Israel, including the Camp David Accords. 60 minutes each.

WORLD WIDE WEB

"The Middle East Peace Process: The Agreements." *Washingtonpost.com.*
    January 1997. http://sunsite.unc.edu/sullivan/CampDavid-Accords-
    homepage.html Excellent graphic tour of all aspects relating to the
    accords; divided into four stages or parts, concluding with a descrip-
    tion of the impact on modern history.

92. Iran Seizes American Hostages (1979)

Revolution struck Iran in 1978, and in January 1979 President Jimmy
Carter convinced the beleaguered pro-U.S. shah, Mohammed Reza
Pahlavi, to abdicate. In late October he allowed the mortally ill shah
to enter the United States for medical treatment. With the blessings
of the Ayatollah Ruhollah Khomeini, the country's new strongman,
a mob stormed the U.S. embassy in Teheran. Iran released thirteen
hostages, but neither UN entreaties nor Carter's trade embargo and
freezing of Iranian assets could obtain the release of the remaining
fifty-three captives. A daring rescue attempt by helicopter in April
1980 proved a dismal failure. Finally, Carter issued the release of
Iranian assets, and on January 20, 1981, Iran freed the remaining
hostages after 444 days in captivity.

Suggestions for Term Papers

1. Discuss U.S.-Iranian relations during the shah's rule.
2. How aware was the United States of conditions in Iran at the time
   of the revolution?
3. Should the United States have allowed the shah to enter the country for medical treatment despite threats from Iran?
4. Could the military's attempted rescue of hostages have succeeded?
5. Analyze President Carter's handling of the hostage crisis.

Suggested Sources: See entry 95 for related items.

GENERAL SOURCES

Buhite, Russell D. *Lives at Risk: Hostages and Victims in American Foreign
    Policy.* Wilmington, DE: Scholarly Resources, 1995. Interesting gen-

eral history of foreign policy crises and taking of hostages; examines government policy.

——, ed. *Major Crises in Contemporary American Foreign Policy.* Westport, CT: Greenwood, 1997. Comprehensive survey of crises in modern times from the cold war to the Persian Gulf War; good exposition of the Iranian hostage crisis.

Dreyfuss, Robert, and Thierry LeMarc. *Hostage to Khomeini.* New York: New Benjamin Franklin House, 1980. Good examination of Iranian politics and government before and after the crisis.

Haykal, Muohammad H. *The Return of the Ayatollah: The Iranian Revolution from Mossadeq to Khomeini.* London: Deutsch, 1981. Concise account of Iranian affairs from World War II to 1979; good background information.

Kaufman, Burton I. *The Presidency of James Earl Carter, Jr.* Lawrence: University of Kansas Press, 1993. Concise, informative examination of Carter's presidency and the difficulties it faced during critical periods.

Stich, Rodney. *Defrauding America: Encyclopedia of Secret Operations by the CIA, DEA, and Other Covert Agencies.* 3d ed. Alamo, CA: Diablo Western, 1998. A lengthy account of government corruption and abuse; examines the "October Surprise," among other things.

Wright, Martin, ed. *Iran: The Khomeini Revolution.* Chicago: St. James, 1989. Brief account of the Khomeini years. Part of the Countries in Crisis series.

Wright, Robin B. *In the Name of God: The Khomeini Decade.* New York; Simon & Schuster, 1989. Broad treatment of the Khomeini years from the beginning to his death in 1989.

SPECIALIZED SOURCES

Christopher, Warren, et al. *American Hostages in Iran: The Conduct of a Crisis.* New Haven, CT: Yale University Press, 1985. Thorough examination of the hostage crisis and government activities in their behalf.

Moses, Russell L. *Freeing the Hostages: Reexamining U.S.-Iranian Negotiations and Soviet Policy, 1979–1981.* Pittsburgh: University of Pittsburgh Press, 1996. Recent detailed account of the crisis and its effect on Soviet foreign policy.

Sick, Gary. *October Surprise: America's Hostages in Iran and the Election of Ronald Reagan.* New York: Times Books, 1991. Interesting and informative examination of the hostage crisis and the presidential election that followed.

BIOGRAPHICAL SOURCES

The Major Players

Cockroft, James D. *Mohammed Reza Pahlavi, Shah of Iran.* New York: Chelsea House Publishers, 1989. Brief and easy-to-read biography of the shah. From the publisher's World Leaders Past and Present series.

Gordon, Matthew. *Ayatollah Khomeini.* Rev. ed. New York: Chelsea House Publishers, 1988. Concise, readable, illustrated biography. From the publisher's World Leaders Past and Present series.

Haas, Garland A. *Jimmy Carter and the Politics of Frustration.* Jefferson, NC: McFarland, 1992. Interesting and informative sketch of Carter and his difficult presidency.

Mohammed Reza Pahlavi. *Answer to History.* New York: Stein and Day, 1980. The shah's own story; interesting for that reason. Translated from Farsi, the Iranian language.

Personal Narratives

Kennedy, Moorhead. *The Ayatollah in the Cathedral.* New York: Hill and Wang, 1986. An insider's view of the crisis by a U.S. diplomat.

Paen, Alex. *Love from America: A Newsman's Account of Efforts to Aid Hostages in Teheran.* Santa Monica, CA: Roundtable Publications, 1989. Useful perspective supplied by a journalist.

Sickmann, Rocky. *Iranian Hostage: A Personal Diary of 444 Days in Captivity.* Topeka, KS: Crawford, 1982. From Sickmann's personal account.

Wells, Tim. *444 Days: The Hostages Remember.* San Diego: Harcourt Brace Jovanovich, 1985. Detailed and thorough account of personal recollections of the incarceration.

AUDIOVISUAL SOURCES

Iran: Days of Crisis. Atlanta: Turner Home Entertainment, 1993. Videocassette. 3-hour television miniseries dramatizing the important period; excellent perspective from Hamilton Jordan and others.

WORLD WIDE WEB

"Robin Wright." *Booknotes Transcript.* June 1997. http//38.217.109.100/mmedia/booknote/lambbook/transcripts/10173.htm Transcript of interview with Robin Wright, author of *In the Name of God: The Khomeini Decade*, which aired November 5, 1989. Wright describes the background and conditions that enabled Khomeini to achieve power.

93. First Woman Appointed to the Supreme Court (1981)

In the summer of 1981 President Ronald Reagan appointed and Congress confirmed Sandra Day O'Connor as the first woman to serve on the Supreme Court. The choice of the appointee drew a mixed response. Conservatives generally applauded her belief in judicial restraint rather than judicial activism, but opposed her known beliefs in abortion rights and her support for the equal rights amendment. Liberals, in contrast, were pleased that the president had named a woman to the High Court but were unhappy with her overall conservative views. In her years on the Court, Justice O'Connor has usually sided with conservatives, led by Chief Justice William Rehnquist.

Suggestions for Term Papers

1. Analyze why Sandra Day O'Connor was considered a suitable appointee to the Supreme Court.
2. Discuss why Justice O'Connor is considered a conservative.
3. Compare the overall judicial achievements of the Court presided over by William Rehnquist with those presided over by Earl Warren.
4. Discuss the most important decisions rendered by the Rehnquist Court.
5. Analyze the judicial philosophy of a current Supreme Court justice.

Suggested Sources: See entry 99 for related items.

REFERENCE SOURCES

American Women's History: An A-to-Z of People, Organizations, Issues and Events. Doris Weatherford. New York: Macmillan, 1994. Useful handbook providing coverage of personalities, events, issues, and other topics. Sandra Day O'Connor is one entry.

The Columbia Encyclopedia. Barbara A. Chernow and George A. Vallasi, eds. 5th ed. Boston: Columbia University Press, Houghton Mifflin, 1993. An excellent one-volume encyclopedia with good coverage of Justice O'Connor, as well as other personalities and current topics.

The Oxford Companion to the Supreme Court of the United States. Kermit Hall et al., eds. New York: Oxford University Press, 1992. Covers all aspects and topics relevant to the Court: procedures, policies, cases, and personalities, including O'Connor.

Women in Law: A Bio-bibliographical Sourcebook. Rebecca M. Salokar and Mary L. Volcansek, eds. Westport, CT: Greenwood, 1996. Detailed profiles for forty-three women including O'Connor; thorough biographical sketches along with bibliographical references and publications listings.

GENERAL SOURCES

Sullivan, George. *The Day the Women Got the Vote: A Photo History of the Women's Rights Movement.* New York: Scholastic, 1994. Interesting photographic history of the women's movement from the time of the suffragists to the present. Justice O'Connor is included among the more recent photos.

SPECIALIZED SOURCES

Maveety, Nancy. *Justice Sandra Day O'Connor: Strategist on the Supreme Court.* Lanham, MD: Rowman & Littlefield Publishers, 1996. Study of O'Connor's judicial manner and procedural activity. Part of the publisher's Studies in American Constitutionalism series.

Van Sickel, Robert W. *Not a Particularly Different Voice: The Jurisprudence of Sandra Day O'Connor.* New York: P. Lang, 1998. Recent examination of O'Connor's rather conventional and predictable conservative stance on the Court.

BIOGRAPHICAL SOURCES

Bentley, Judith. *Justice Sandra Day O'Connor.* Rochester, NY: Messner, 1983. Brief and easy-to-read biography that examines the justice's background, views, and opinions on a variety of issues.

Berry, Dawn B. *The Fifty Most Influential Women in American Law.* Los Angeles: Lowell House, 1996. Interesting collective biography of historically important women ranging from the seventeenth century to Marcia Clark.

Cushman, Clare, ed. *The Supreme Court Justices: Illustrated Biographies, 1789–1993.* Washington DC: Congressional Quarterly, 1993. Contains biographical sketches of all 106 current and past justices; provides observations of contemporaries and anecdotes as well.

Felder, Deborah. *The 100 Most Influential Women of All Time: A Ranking Past and Present.* Secaucus, NJ: Carol Publishing Group, 1996. A collective biography, more interesting than serious, providing ranking and honorable mentions for women in all areas of endeavor.

Gabor, Andrea. *Einstein's Wife: Work and Marriage in the Lives of Five Great Women.* New York: Viking, 1995. Interesting and informative examination of the lives and careers of five talented married women, including Justice O'Connor.

Marshall-White, Eleanor. *Women, Catalysts for Change: Interpretive Biographies of Shirley St. Hill Chisholm, Sandra Day O'Connor, and Nancy Landon Kassebaum.* New York: Vantage, 1991. Interesting biographical treatment of three women from different points on the political spectrum.

AUDIOVISUAL SOURCES

"Sandra Day O'Connor." *American Women of Achievement.* Bala Cynwd; PA: Library Video Company, 1995. Videocassette. One of ten women covered in this series, based on the books by Chelsea House. 30 minutes.

WORLD WIDE WEB

Associate Justice Sandra Day O'Connor. September 1997. http://www2. cybernex.net/~vanalst/sandra.html Brief sketch with links to the justice's written opinions, 1990–1996, and to further biographical treatment.

94. Invasion of Grenada (1983)

A Marxist regime had been ruling tiny Grenada in the Caribbean since 1979, but an even more radical group staged a coup in October 1983 and killed the country's prime minister, Maurice Bishop. Noting that an extended airplane runway that the Grenadians, with Cuban help, had been building might be used for military purposes by Cubans or Russians, and that some 500 Americans attending the island's medical college might be in danger, President Reagan ordered a military invasion on October 25. A relatively easy U.S. victory followed, with the loss of few lives on either side. A non-Marxist government took power. Some protested U.S. intervention; others hailed it as necessary.

Suggestions for Term Papers

1. Analyze the reasons for the U.S. invasion of Grenada.
2. Discuss the reaction of Grenadians to the U.S. invasion.
3. Discuss the reaction of Latin America to the U.S. invasion.
4. Discuss the effect of the invasion on President Reagan's popularity at home.
5. Analyze U.S.-Grenada relations since the invasion.

Suggested Sources: See entries 96 and 98 for related items.

REFERENCE SOURCES

Schoenhals, Kai P., comp. *Grenada.* Santa Barbara, CA: Clio, 1990. Useful bibliography. Includes a map.

GENERAL SOURCES

Bishop, Maurice. *Maurice Bishop Speaks: The Grenada Revolution and Its Overthrow 1979–83.* Bruce Marcus and Michael Taber, eds. (1983). Reprint. New York: Pathfinder, 1991. Informative history of Grenada politics and government relevant to the communist takeover, written by the prime minister who was later killed by the radicals.
Cotman, John Walton. *The Gorrion Tree: Cuba and the Grenada Revolution.* New York: P. Lang, 1993. Revealing account of foreign relations between Cuba and Grenada prior to the U.S. invasion.
Emmanuel, Patrick. *Political Change and Public Opinion in Grenada, 1979–1984.* Cave Hill, Barbados: University of West Indies Press, 1986. Interesting and informative examination of public opinion in Grenada from the time of the Bishop government through the invasion and its aftermath.
Ferguson, James. *Grenada: Revolution in Reverse.* New York: Latin Amer-

ican Bureau/Monthly Review, 1990. Brief examination of social conditions, economics, and politics in Grenada since the invasion.

Heine, Jorge, ed. *A Revolution Aborted: The Lessons of Grenada.* Pittsburgh: University of Pittsburgh Press, 1990. Conference papers on politics and government, with an emphasis on the New Jewel Movement that overthrew the Bishop government.

Lewis, Gordon K. *Grenada: The Jewel Despoiled.* Baltimore: Johns Hopkins University Press, 1987. Brief, informative account and assessment of the achievements of the communist revolution; examines the murder of Bishop and the nature of the conspiracy.

Meeks, Brian. *Caribbean Revolutions and Revolutionary Theory: An Assessment of Cuba, Nicaragua and Grenada.* London: Macmillan Caribbean, 1993. Comparative treatment of revolutionary movements in the latter half of the twentieth century.

Noguera, Pedro. *The Imperatives of Power: Political Change and the Social Basis of Regime Support in Grenada from 1951–1991.* New York: P. Lang, 1997. Informative general history of Grenadian politics, leadership, and change during the past fifty years.

SPECIALIZED SOURCES

Adkin, Mark. *Urgent Fury: The Battle for Grenada.* Lexington, MA: Lexington Books, 1989. Detailed account of the battle itself; informative examination of the strategy and procedure.

Beck, Robert J. *The Grenada Invasion: Politics, Law and Foreign Policy Decisionmaking.* Boulder, CO: Westview, 1993. Informative examination of the invasion and sociopolitical and legal implications.

Burrowes, Reynold A. *Revolution and Rescue in Grenada: An Account of the U.S.-Caribbean Invasion.* Westport, CT: Greenwood, 1988. Concise account of the U.S. invasion in 1983 with its intention of overthrowing the radical regime.

Dunn, Peter M., and Bruce W. Watson, eds. *American Intervention in Grenada: The Implications of Operation "Urgent Fury."* Boulder, CO: Westview Press, 1985. Brief account of the politics of Grenada, with the emphasis on the invasion and its aftermath.

Lewis, Sybil Farrell, and Dale T. Mathews, comps. *Documents on the Invasion of Grenada, October, 1983.* Rio Piedras, PR: University of Puerto Rico Press, 1984. Compilation of documents relevant to the invasion, including text of the treaty.

O'Shaughnessy, Hugh. *Grenada: An Eyewitness Account of the U.S. Invasion and the Caribbean History That Provoked It.* New York: Dodd, Mead, 1984. Concise history of politics and government in Grenada from the time of the communist revolution to the U.S. invasion.

Payne, Anthony, et al. *Grenada: Revolution and Invasion.* New York: St. Martin's, 1986. Brief overview of Grenadian politics and foreign relations with treatment of the coup and the U.S. invasion.

AUDIOVISUAL SOURCES

Grenada Revisited. Ben Lomand, CA: Video Project Media for a Safe & Sustainable World, 1991. Videocassette. 30-minute examination of the possible causes and consequences of the invasion.

WORLD WIDE WEB

"Grenada—American Invasion." *War, Peace and Security Guide.* 1997. http://www.cfcsc.dnd.ca/links/milhist/grenad.html Links to the revolution, area studies, and personal narratives. From the Information Resource Center of the Canadian Forces College.

95. Iran-Contra Affair (1985–1987)

Despite the official trade embargo with Iran, the Reagan administration secretly arranged an arms deal in exchange for Iran's help in securing freedom for a few American hostages held in Lebanon. Meanwhile, funds from the arms payment were siphoned off to support the Nicaraguan contras in their fight against the Sandinista government, despite limits on such aid that Congress had imposed. Word of the arms deal broke in late 1984, and over the next few years various investigations brought forth fuller disclosures. The events of Irangate, as the scandal was dubbed, led to the convictions or guilty pleas of several individuals, notably National Security Council (NSC) director John Poindexter and marine colonel Oliver North.

Suggestions for Term Papers

1. Analyze the Reagan administration's negotiations with Iran.
2. Discuss the administration's policy toward the contras and the Sandinistas.
3. Discuss how and why Oliver North became and remained a controversial figure.

4. What were the immediate and long-range consequences of the Iran-contra affair?

5. Compare Watergate with Irangate.

Suggested Sources: See entry 92 for related items.

GENERAL SOURCES

Human Rights in Nicaragua under the Sandinistas: From Revolution to Repression. Washington, DC: U.S. Department of State, 1987. Examination of civil rights and political persecution in Nicaragua under the Sandinistas.

Miranda, Roger, and William Ratliff. *The Civil War in Nicaragua: Inside the Sandinistas.* New Brunswick, NJ: Transaction Publishers, 1993. Recent history of the Sandinista period and the war waged against the contras.

Morley, Morris H. *Washington, Somoza, and the Sandinistas: State and Regime in U.S. Policy toward Nicaragua, 1969–1981.* New York: Cambridge University Press, 1994. Comprehensive account of foreign relations between the United States and Nicaragua over the Sandinista period.

Ridenour, Ron. *Yankee Sandinistas: Interviews with North Americans Living and Working in the New Nicaragua.* Willimantic, CT: Curbstone/Talman, 1986. Interviews with Americans employed in Nicaragua exploring the social and political conditions of the time.

SPECIALIZED SOURCES

Kornbluh, Peter, et al. *The Iran-Contra Scandal: The Declassified History.* New York: New Press, 1993. Informative collection of documents relevant to the Iran-contra affair along with a chronology and editorial matter. Made possible by the Freedom of Information Act.

Marks, Stanley J. *A Year in the Lives of the Damned! Reagan-Reaganism—1986.* San Marino, CA: Bureau of International Affairs, 1988. Outspoken critic of Reagan and his policies; examines the agreement to sell arms to Iran.

Marshall, Jonathan, et al. *The Iran-Contra Connection: Secret Teams and Covert Operations in the Reagan Era.* Boston: South End Press, 1987. Examination of the political corruption and its link to the Iran-contra agreement. From a radical perspective.

Secord, Richard V., and Jay Wurts. *Honored and Betrayed: Irangate, Covert Affairs, and the Secret War in Laos.* New York: Wiley, 1992. Sweeping survey of government involvement in covert dealings from Ir- angate to war in Laos; interesting history of U.S. intelligence.

Terrell, Jack, and Ron Martz. *Disposable Patriot: Revelations of a Soldier in America's Secret Wars.* Washington, DC: National Press Books, 1992. Background on U.S. intelligence and the link to the contras.

Tobin, Jeffrey. *Opening Arguments: A Young Lawyer's First Case, United States v. Oliver North.* New York: Viking, 1991. Interesting insider perspective on the North trial.

U.S. Congress. House. Select Committee to Investigate Covert Arms Trans- actions with Iran. *Taking the Stand: The Testimony of Lieutenant Colonel Oliver L. North.* New York: Pocket Books, 1987. Detailed transcripts of the testimony of Colonel North before the committee; examines the Iran-contra affair and military assistance provided by the United States.

Walker, Thomas W., ed. *Reagan Versus the Sandinistas: The Undeclared War on Nicaragua.* Boulder, CO: Westview, 1987. Perspective on the struggle between Reagan and the communist government of Nic- aragua.

Walsh, Lawrence E. *The Iran-Contra Conspiracy and Cover-Up.* New York: Norton, 1997. Thorough and detailed coverage of the Iran-contra affair and its investigation authored by the independent counsel; re- veals the intrigue, lies, and duplicity surrounding it.

Wroe, Ann. *Lives, Lies and the Iran-Contra Affair.* New York: Tauris, 1991. Good detailed account of the entire affair; useful bibliography and index.

BIOGRAPHICAL SOURCES

Bradlee, Ben, Jr. *Guts and Glory: The Rise and Fall of Oliver North.* New York: D. I. Fine, 1988. Detailed examination of the Oliver North story by the former editor of the *Washington Post.*

D'Souza, Dinesh. *Ronald Reagan: How an Ordinary Man Became an Ex- traordinary President.* New York: Free Press, 1997. Interesting ac- count of the fortieth president by a political conservative who credits Reagan's will and foresight for the breakup of the Soviet Union.

North, Oliver, and William Novak. *Under Fire: An American Story.* New York: HarperCollins, 1991. Popular biography of the colonel's life, military career, and the Iran-contra affair.

Parmet, Herbert S. *George Bush: The Life of a Lone Star Yankee.* New York: Scribner's Sons, 1997. Recent and informative biography by a re- spected historian; provides insight into Bush's life and career. Sees Bush as a major player in the Iran-contra affair.

Timberg, Robert. *The Nightingale's Song.* New York: Simon & Schuster, 1996. Collective biography detailing the lives and careers of five graduates of Annapolis, including North, Poindexter, and McFarlane, and their passionate anticommunist stance.

AUDIOVISUAL SOURCES

MacLaverty, Bernard. *Hostages.* Studio City, CA: Imperial Entertainment, 1993. Videocassette. 90-minute docudrama with news footage of prisoners and their families.

WORLD WIDE WEB

"Iran-Contra Affair—The American Presidency." *Grolier Online.* 1996. http://intl.grolier.com/presidents/aae/side/irancont.html Brief description from *Academic American Encyclopedia* with useful links to Reagan and Bush, as well as suggestions for further reading.

96. Invasion of Panama (1989)

General Manuel Noriega, the strongman who had functioned as the de facto leader of Panama since 1983, abetted the CIA but also was heavily involved in the drug trade and had also aided Fidel Castro on occasion. Although both Presidents Reagan and Bush had publicly praised Noriega, Bush decided to oust him after he had refused to accept the outcome of a recent Panamanian election and had denounced the United States. U.S. forces attacked on December 20, 1989, and quickly toppled the Panamanian leader. Brought to the United States, Noriega was convicted on drug and racketeering charges in 1992 and sentenced to prison.

Suggestions for Term Papers

1. Discuss the relationship between Noriega and the United States prior to the invasion.
2. Analyze why President Bush called for the invasion of Panama.
3. Aside from the ouster of General Noriega, what changes did the invasion bring about in Panama?

4. Discuss the reaction of Latin America to the invasion of Panama.

5. Analyze the relationship between the United States and Panama since the invasion.

Suggested Sources: See entries 94 and 98 for related items.

GENERAL SOURCES

Albert, Steve. *The Case against the General: Manuel Noriega and the Politics of American Justice.* New York: Maxwell Macmillan International, 1993. Examination of Noriega's role in drug trafficking and money laundering for which he stood trial in Miami.

Barry, Tom, et al. *Inside Panama.* Albuquerque, NM: Resource Center, 1995. A useful brief overview of Panama since 1981 in a book that describes itself as "the essential guide to [Panama's] politics, economy, society, and environment."

Musicant, Ivan. *The Banana Wars: A History of United States Military Intervention in Latin America from the Spanish-American War to the Invasion of Panama.* New York: Macmillan, 1990. Good survey of the U.S. incursion.

Scranton, Margaret. *The Noriega Years: U.S.-Panamanian Relations, 1981–1990.* Boulder, CO: L. Rienner Publishers, 1991. Relatively concise survey of the U.S. relationship with Noriega from the beginning to the end of his rule.

St. Malo Arias, Guillermo de. *The Panamanian Problem: How the Reagan and Bush Administrations Dealt with the Noriega Regime.* Los Angeles: Americas Group, 1993. A critical view of U.S. relations with Panama during the Noriega years.

SPECIALIZED SOURCES

Behar, David S., et al. *Invasion: The American Destruction of the Noriega Regime in Panama.* Los Angeles: Americas Group, 1990. Concise, illustrated presentation of the U.S. invasion; good photographs.

Johns, Christina J., and P. Ward Johnson. *State Crime, the Media, and the Invasion of Panama.* Westport, CT: Praeger, 1994. Brief examination of the invasion, along with the political and media considerations.

Maendez, Juan E., and Kenneth Anderson. *The Laws of War and the Conduct of the Panama Invasion.* New York: Human Rights Watch, 1990. Very brief examination of the human rights issues involved in the invasion.

McConnell, Malcolm. *Just Cause: The Real Story of America's High-Tech Invasion of Panama.* New York: St. Martin's, 1991. Interesting account of the invasion and the need to overthrow Noriega.

The U.S. Invasion of Panama: The Truth behind Operation "Just Cause." Boston: South End Press, 1991. Concise report on the invasion prepared by an independent commission.

Wheaton, Phyllis E., ed. *Panama Invaded: Imperial Occupation vs Struggle for Sovereignty.* Trenton, NJ: Red Sea, 1992. Anti-invasion sentiment expressed clearly; brief and readable.

BIOGRAPHICAL SOURCES

Dinges, John. *Our Man in Panama: The Shrewd Rise and Brutal Fall of Manuel Noriega.* New York: Times Books/Random House, 1991. Detailed account of Noriega's life and career with all its political corruption and ethical violations.

Marvin, David. *George Bush and the Guardianship Presidency.* New York: St. Martin's, 1996. Recent examination of the Bush presidency, including the Panama invasion.

AUDIOVISUAL SOURCES

Kasper, David. *The Panama Deception.* Los Angeles: Rhino Home Video, 1992. Videocassette. 90-minute British television presentation examining the Panama invasion and the human rights violations that occurred. Narrated by Elizabeth Montgomery.

Stuart, Charles C. *Frontline: The Noriega Connection.* Santa Monica, CA: PBS Home Video, 1990. Videocassette. 58-minute exposition of the use of Noriega as an intelligence intermediary by the U.S. government long before it became necessary to remove him. Part of the popular PBS series.

WORLD WIDE WEB

Chomsky, Noam. *Deterring Democracy.* November 1996. http://world-media.com/archive/dd/dd.html Chomsky's complete work published in 1991; chapter 5 deals with the post–cold war era and treats "Operation Just Cause." Sees the United States as an aggressive bully.

97. The Breakup of the Soviet Union

Becoming head of the Soviet Union in 1985, Mikhail Gorbachev initiated a new era for his nation by announcing and introducing the policies of *glasnost* (openness) and *perestroika* (restructuring). In 1987 he visited the United States and signed the Intermediate Nuclear Force Treaty, which stipulated reductions in U.S. and Soviet nuclear weapons. Two years later, he acquiesced in the razing of the Berlin Wall and the overthrow of communist regimes in Eastern European satellite states, thus ending the Soviet empire and the cold war. Intending reform, Gorbachev had unwillingly brought about a revolution.

Suggestions for Term Papers

1. Analyze Gorbachev's reasons for initiating reforms in the Soviet Union.
2. Did the cold war end primarily because of Soviet weaknesses or pressures exerted by the United States?
3. Was the Strategic Defense Initiative ("Star Wars") instrumental in ending the cold war?
4. Why did Mikhail Gorbachev fall from power in the early 1990s?
5. Discuss the overall consequences of the cold war for the United States.

Suggested Sources: See entry 52 for related items.

REFERENCE SOURCES

Cambridge Encyclopedia of Russia and the Former Soviet Union. Archie Brown, et al., eds. Cambridge: Cambridge University Press, 1994. Examines all aspects of life in the former Soviet Union from the earliest times through the era of *glasnost* and the 1991 coup attempt. Written by more than 100 specialists.

Gorbachev Bibliography 1985–1991: A Listing of Books and Articles in English on Perestroika in the USSR (1985–1991). New York: Norman Ross, 1996. Good bibliography of books and articles both scholarly and popular.

Reinterpreting Russia: An Annotated Bibliography of Books on Russia, the Soviet Union, and the Russian Federation, 1991–1996. Steve D. Boilard. Lanham, MD: Scarecrow/Salem, 1997. Good listing of items for study and research.

GENERAL SOURCES

DeKovner, Barbara. *Shattered Silence: Feelings from Former Soviets Struggling with Freedom at Home.* Los Angeles: Americas Group, 1993. Interesting and informative examination of the feelings of former Soviets; treats hopes, aspirations, and frustrations.

Drobizheva, Leokadia, et al., eds. *Ethnic Conflict in the Post-Soviet World: Case Studies and Analysis.* Armonk, NY: M. E. Sharpe, 1996. Contains sixteen case studies of ethnic conflict following the breakup of the USSR. Good insight into factors that have caused the unrest since then.

Findling, John E., and Frank W. Thackeray, eds. *Events That Changed the World in the Twentieth Century.* Westport, CT: Greenwood, 1995. Description, explanation, and photographs of the collapse of the Soviet Union, as well as nine other major world events.

Kort, Michael. *The Soviet Colossus: History and Aftermath.* 4th ed. Armonk, NY: Sharpe, 1996. Popular and informative general history of twentieth-century Soviet Union and its transition back to Russia.

Moskoff, William. *Hard Times: Impoverishment and Protest in the Perestroika Years: The Soviet Union, 1985–1991.* Armonk, NY: Sharpe, 1993. Excellent description of the social and political history of *perestroika* in the years just prior to the breakup.

Nelson, Lynn D. *Property to the People: The Struggle for Radical Economic Reform in Russia.* Armonk, NY: Sharpe, 1994. Good history of economic conditions and privatization of resources since the breakup.

Pearson, Raymond. *The Rise and Fall of the Soviet Empire.* New York: St. Martin's, 1997. Brief, general history of the USSR, with a useful section on its disintegration.

Rywkin, Michael. *Moscow's Lost Empire.* Armonk, NY: Sharpe, 1994. Relatively concise but comprehensive examination of ethnic relations in the former Soviet republics.

SPECIALIZED SOURCES

Adelman, Deborah. *The Children of Perestroika.* New York: Sharpe, 1992. Based on interviews with Moscow teenagers prior to the revolution. The author updated the information with a second trip following the revolution in an article for *School Library Journal* (August 1994).

Bonnell, Victoria E., et al., eds. *Russia at the Barricades: Eyewitness Accounts of the August 1991 Coup*. Armonk, NY: Sharpe, 1993. Personal narratives of individuals who witnessed the August 1991 coup attempt.

Buckley, Mary, ed. *Perestroika and Soviet Women*. Cambridge, UK: Cambridge University Press, 1992. Examines the implications for women as workers and consumers in the new Russia following *perestroika* and *glasnost*.

Daniels, Robert V. *The End of the Communist Revolution*. New York: Routledge, 1993. Examination of the changes between Gorbachev's selection in 1985 and the breakup in 1991; treats current and future prospects.

Ellman, Michael, and Vladimir Kontorovich, eds. *The Destruction of the Soviet Economic System: An Insider's History*. Armonk, NY: Sharpe, 1998. Analysis of issues and events that led to the collapse of the economy. Examines the standard of living, ideology, arms race, and other topics through a survey of important officials.

Fisher, Marc. *After the Wall: Germany, the Germans, and the Burdens of History*. New York: Simon & Schuster, 1995. Interesting anecdotal account of the razing of the wall and German unification.

Hosking, Geoffrey A. *The Awakening of the Soviet Union*. London: Heinemann, 1990. Interesting treatment of the social and cultural developments underlying the revolution; gives attention to *perestroika* and Chernobyl.

Kaufman, Richard F., and John P. Hardt. *The Former Soviet Union in Transition*. Armonk, NY: Sharpe, 1993. Compilation of about sixty articles on a variety of topics, prepared for the Joint Economic Committee in the U.S. Congress.

Neimanis, George J. *The Collapse of the Soviet Empire: A View from Riga*. Westport, CT: Praeger, 1997. Authoritative study of the breakup of the Soviet Union and implications for an independent state; treats Latvia's nationalism and struggle.

Satter, David. *Age of Delirium: The Decline and Fall of the Soviet Union*. New York: Knopf, 1996. Detailed and thorough examination of the history of the Soviet Union.

Silverman, Bertram, and Murray Yanowitch. *New Rich, New Poor, New Russia: Winners and Losers on the Russian Road to Capitalism*. Armonk, NY: Sharpe, 1997. Good description of the costs and benefits associated with the new order; examines some inequities in the reform movement.

Strayer, Robert. *Why Did the Soviet Union Collapse? Understanding Historical Change*. Armonk, NY: M.E. Sharpe, 1998. Examines power conflict, revolution, colonialism, and other topics using a case study approach.

Tishkov, Valery. *Ethnicity, Nationalism and Conflict in and after the Soviet*

Union: The Mind Aflame. Thousand Oaks, CA: Sage, 1997. Up-to-date historical treatment of nationalism and ethnic minorities in the former Soviet Union republics.

BIOGRAPHICAL SOURCES

Gorbachev, Mikhail S. *The August Coup: The Truth and the Lessons.* New York: HarperCollins, 1991. Gorbachev's reflections on the attempted coup in 1991. Interesting personal narrative.

————. *Memoirs.* New York: Doubleday, 1996. Detailed and broad-based autobiography providing insight into the man's philosophical perspective and his current observations.

AUDIOVISUAL SOURCES

Russia for Sale: The Rough Road to Capitalism. New York: Cinema Guild, 1992. Videocassette. 56-minute presentation examining the lives of three Russians (a steelworker, a police officer, and an entrepreneur) in the transition from communism to capitalism.

WORLD WIDE WEB

Dixon, Ursula Grosser. "My Homeland Reunited—The Story of the Reunification of Germany." *Ursula's History Web.* January 1997. http://members.tripod.com/~Nevermore/homeland.html Part 2 of an autobiographical sketch of a German-born woman who rejoices at the demolition of the Berlin Wall. Her account in the form of a diary or log is useful in comprehending the moment.

98. Persian Gulf War (1991)

On August 2, 1990, Iraq invaded its tiny oil-rich neighbor, Kuwait. Fearful of the Iraqi threat to both Kuwait and Saudi Arabia, the United States sent a half-million troops to Saudi Arabia as part of a larger multinational force. After Iraq failed to comply with a UN resolution to vacate Kuwait and convinced that an economic embargo was futile, President George Bush ordered military air attacks and a ground offensive (Operation Desert Storm). By late February 1991 a cease-fire took effect. The Iraqis had sustained huge losses and were forced to withdraw from Kuwait. To the surprise and consternation of some, however, Saddam Hussein, Iraq's dictator, remained in power.

Suggestions for Term Papers

1. Could the United States have prevented Iraq from invading Kuwait?

2. Discuss President Bush's decision to use military force rather than other measures against Iraq.

3. Analyze the reasons for the military victory against Iraq.

4. Analyze why the multinational forces did not depose Saddam Hussein.

5. Discuss the consequences of the Persian Gulf War.

Suggested Sources: See entries 94 and 96 for related items.

REFERENCE SOURCES

Encyclopedia of The Persian Gulf War. Mark Grossman. Santa Barbara, CA: ABC-CLIO, 1995. Award-winning reference source providing comprehensive background of the war—its personalities, tactics, and weaponry. Well illustrated.

Gulf War Debriefing Book: An After Action Report. Andrew Levden. Grants Pass, OR: Hellgate, 1997. Comprehensive reference source providing facts, figures, chronology, and documentation; covers events with photographs.

The Harper Encyclopedia of Military History: From 3500 B.C. to the Present. Ernest R. Dupuy and Trevor N. Dupuy. 4th ed. New York: HarperCollins, 1993. Thorough, detailed, and comprehensive treatment of the Persian Gulf War.

The Macmillan Dictionary of Military Biography: The Warriors and Their Wars, 3500 B.C.-Present. Alan Axelrod and Charles Phillips. New York: Macmillan, 1998. Comprehensive biographical dictionary covering five hundred influential leaders from Julius Caesar to Colin Powell.

Persian Gulf War Almanac. Colonel Harry G. Summers, Jr. New York: Facts on File, 1995. Detailed chronology, lengthy topical essays, and valuable bibliographies; A to Z coverage of major military units, key battles, issues, and personalities.

GENERAL SOURCES

Duncan, Stephen M. *Citizen Warriors: America's National Guard and the Reserve Forces and Politics of National Security.* Novato, CA: Presido, 1997. Interesting study of the call-up for the Persian Gulf War, along with a comprehensive history of the National Guard from its beginning to the present.

Hyland, Terry, et al. *Letters from the Front: Boys Town Battlefield from Pearl Harbor to the Persian Gulf War.* Boys Town, NE: Boys Town, 1995. Interesting documentary history from servicemen in the field who once attended Boys Town; covers the period from World War II to the Persian Gulf War.

Tibi, Bassam. *Conflict and War in the Middle East: From Interstate War to New Security.* 2d ed. New York: St. Martin's, 1998. Updated version of an earlier work treating the history of the Middle East and conflicts from 1967 to the Gulf War in 1991.

SPECIALIZED SOURCES

Atkinson, Rick. *Crusade: The Untold Story of the Persian Gulf War.* Boston: Houghton Mifflin, 1994. Based on more than five hundred interviews of participants along with an observation of contemporary history; somewhat critical of General Norman Schwarzkopf. From the author of *The Long Gray Line.*

Eddington, Patrick. *Gassed in the Gulf: The Pentagon-CIA Cover-up of Gulf War Syndrome.* Washington, DC: Insignia Publishing, 1997. An insider's view of the dishonesty of the government in concealing the troops' exposure to chemical agents. Written by a former CIA analyst.

Friedman, Norman. *Desert Victory: The War in Kuwait.* Annapolis, MD: Naval Institute, 1991. Detailed background and examination of the war with numerous photographs, some in color.

Gay, Kathlyn, and Martin Gay. *Persian Gulf War.* New York: Twenty-first Century, 1995. Easy-to-read, concise history of the war. Part of the publisher's Voices from the Past series.

Gordon, Michael. *The General's War: The Inside Story of the Conflict in the Gulf.* Boston: Little, Brown, 1996. Unique insight by a Pentagon correspondent for the *New York Times* and retired marine general into the friction and conflict among the generals under the Allied command. Based on declassified documents and insider observations.

Kent, Zachary. *The Persian Gulf War.* New York: Facts on File, 1994. Concise account of the war that provides documentation and stories, as well as a chronology and maps.

Record, Jeffery. *Hollow Victory: A Contrary View of the Gulf War.* Washington, DC: Brassey's, 1993. Brief, critical commentary on the conduct and planning of the objectives achieved by the war.

Scales, Robert H., Jr. *Certain Victory: The U.S. Army in the Gulf War.* Washington, DC: Brassey's, 1994. Interesting, readable, and profusely illustrated official account by a brigadier general of the performance of the U.S. Army during the Gulf War.

Smith, Perry M. *How CNN Fought the War: A View from the Inside.* New York: Carol Publishing, 1991. An interesting examination of television coverage of the war and the effect on public opinion.

Yant, Martin. *Desert Mirage: The True Story of the Gulf War.* Buffalo, NY: Prometheus Books, 1991. Brief examination of the Gulf War. Highly critical of the manipulation of public opinion and the hypocrisy of American leadership who seemed to want the war.

Yetiv, Steve A. *The Persian Gulf Crisis.* Westport, CT: Greenwood, 1998. Brief examination of the war; contains primary documents and extensive interviews.

BIOGRAPHICAL SOURCES

Baker, James A., and Thomas M. DeFrank. *The Politics of Diplomacy: Revolution, War, and Peace.* New York: Putnam's Sons, 1995. Good political biography of the secretary of state under George Bush.

Coughlin, Sean T. *Storming the Desert: A Marine Lieutenant's Day-by-Day Chronicle of the Persian Gulf War.* Jefferson, NC: McFarland, 1996. Firsthand personal perspective. Contains photographs and maps.

Garcia, Rafael J., Jr. *Paladin Zero Six: A Desert Storm Memoir by a 101st Airborne Attack Helicopter Company Commander.* Jefferson, NC: McFarland, 1994. Personal perspective. Includes photographs.

Powell, Colin L., and Joseph E. Persico. *My American Journey.* New York: Random House, 1995. Best-selling autobiography by the most influential figure in the Gulf War.

Schwarzkopf, H. Norman, and Peter Petre. *It Doesn't Take a Hero: General H. Norman Schwarzkopf, the Autobiography.* New York: Bantam Books, 1992. Detailed and thorough autobiography of the general who led the forces that crushed the enemy.

AUDIOVISUAL SOURCES

Persian Gulf: Images of a Conflict. Orland Park, IL: MPI Home Video, 1991. 4 videocassettes. Thorough and detailed coverage by ABC news team of all facets of the war; treats strategy, weaponry, procedures, and other topics. 390 minutes.

WORLD WIDE WEB

1990: The Iraqi SCUD Threat. September 1996. http://www.cdiss.org/ scudnt3.htm A brief description from Lancaster University of the SCUD deployment with numerous relevant links. Click on "Special Forces in Desert Storm."

99. Clarence Thomas Appointed to the Supreme Court (1991)

In 1991 President George Bush nominated Clarence Thomas, a federal appeals court judge whose conservative views on various public issues were well known, to fill the vacancy created by Justice Thurgood Marshall's retirement. An African American, Thomas had headed the Equal Employment Opportunity Commission (EEOC) during much of the Reagan administration. During Thomas's confirmation hearings, Anita Hill, a law school professor, testified that Thomas had sexually harassed her when she worked for him at EEOC. Despite these charges, which he denied, Thomas won Senate confirmation by a narrow majority, thus becoming the second African American to sit on the High Court.

Suggestions for Term Papers

1. Discuss why President Bush nominated Clarence Thomas to the Supreme Court.

2. Why was Clarence Thomas considered to be a conservative?

3. Discuss public reaction to Thomas's confirmation hearings.

4. What effect did the confirmation hearings have on the women's movement?

5. Should the Senate have confirmed Clarence Thomas?

Suggested Sources: See entry 93 for related items.

REFERENCE SOURCES

Guide to the U.S. Supreme Court. Joan Biskupic and Elder Witt. 3d ed. Washington, DC: Congressional Quarterly, 1997. 2 vols. Provides detail on and insight into the workings of the Court; treats decisions, changes, and appointments.

GENERAL SOURCES

Danforth, John C. *Resurrection: The Confirmation of Clarence Thomas.* NY: Free Press, 1994. A partisan defense by the U.S. senator from Missouri who first promoted Thomas's candidacy and then stalwartly supported it during the bitter confirmation hearings.

Reed, Ishmael. *Airing Dirty Laundry.* Reading, MA: Addison-Wesley, 1993. General examination of the double standard by which black behavior is judged by the white media and white public mind; treats the Thomas-Hill hearing.

Simon, Paul. *Advice and Consent: Clarence Thomas, Robert Bork, and the Intriguing History of the Supreme Court's Nomination Battles.* Washington, DC: National Press Books, 1992. Interesting and informative history of the selection and appointment process in controversial cases.

SPECIALIZED SOURCES

Brock, David. *The Real Anita Hill: The Untold Story.* New York: Free Press, 1993. Interesting examination of Hill's character and her credibility; analyzes immediate events.

Chrisman, Robert, ed. *Court of Appeal: The Black Community Speaks Out on the Racial and Sexual Politics of Clarence Thomas vs. Anita Hill.* New York: Ballantine Books, 1992. Perspectives of black people on the impact of the hearings.

Mayer, Jane. *Strange Justice: Selling of Clarence Thomas.* Boston: Houghton Mifflin, 1994. Interesting, informative, and detailed account of the Thomas hearing and confirmation; evidence weighs favorably for Anita Hill.

Morrison, Toni, ed. *Race-ing Justice, En-gendering Power: Essays on Anita Hill, Clarence Thomas and the Construction of Social Reality.* New York: Pantheon, 1992. Collection of essays on the Hill-Thomas affair; examines the case, context, conditions, politics, and outcomes.

Phelps, Timothy M. *Capitol Games: The Inside Story of Clarence Thomas, Anita Hill and a Supreme Court Nomination.* New York: HarperPerennial, 1992. Detailed account of the backgrounds of the two principals, political manipulation, and the conduct of the hearings. It appears that Hill spoke the truth.

U.S. Congress. Senate. Committee on the Judiciary. *The Complete Transcripts of the Clarence Thomas-Anita Hill Hearings.* Chicago: Academy Chicago, 1994. The complete account; reveals rudeness and crudity on the part of Thomas.

BIOGRAPHICAL SOURCES

Cushman, Claire, ed. *The Supreme Court Justices: Illustrated Biographies, 1789–1995.* 2d ed. Washington, DC: Congressional Quarterly, 1996. In-depth biographies on all Supreme Court justices up to the present time; describes background, career, and major issues in cases they heard.

Halliburton, Warren. *Clarence Thomas, Supreme Court Justice.* Hillside, NJ: Enslow, 1993. Easy-to-read, concise biographical sketch of the Supreme Court justice from childhood to the present.

Smith, Jessie C., ed. *Notable Black American Men.* Detroit: Gale, 1998. Provides biographical sketches of 500 men in alphabetical order, including Clarence Thomas. Modeled after *Notable Black American Women.*

AUDIOVISUAL SOURCES

"Thomas as Supreme Court Nominee." *Nightline.* Orland Park, IL: MPI Home Video, 1991. Videocassette. 30-minute television presentation examining the wisdom of the Bush selection.

Thurgood Marshall: And Justice for All. New York: A&E Home Video, 1998. Videocassette. 60-minute presentation of quality and balanced perspective from the Biography series. Provides insight into the man whom Thomas replaced on the Court.

Thurgood Marshall: Portrait of an American Hero. Santa Monica, CA: PBS Home Video, 1985. Videocassette. 30-minute overview of Marshall's career as a Supreme Court justice, especially his involvement in the civil rights movement. His sociopolitical philosophy stands in sharp contrast to that of Thomas.

WORLD WIDE WEB

"Hill, Anita." *alt.culture*. September 1997. http://www.pathfinder.com/
altculture/aentries/a/anxhill.html Brief biographical sketch with link
to full testimony of seventeen pages.

100. North American Free Trade Agreement (NAFTA) (1993)

The Bush administration negotiated the North American Free Trade
Agreement that would remove tariffs and generally provide free trade
among the United States, Canada, and Mexico over a fifteen-year
period. Newly elected president Bill Clinton steered the agreement
through Congress, which passed in January 1993 after much controversy. Proponents argued that NAFTA would benefit both consumers
and the overall economy; opponents warned that American jobs
would be lost to the low-paying Mexican labor market and that environmental concerns would suffer.

Suggestions for Term Papers

1. Compare NAFTA with the European Community.
2. Analyze the arguments for and against NAFTA.
3. Has NAFTA proved more or less successful since its inception?
4. Discuss the reaction of people in your community to NAFTA.
5. Should the United States pursue a policy of general free trade
   elsewhere, or should it have tariffs to protect its domestic industries?

REFERENCE SOURCES

America's International Trade: A Reference Handbook. E. Willard Miller.
Santa Barbara, CA: ABC-CLIO, 1995. Comprehensive listing of in-
formation, with a section on NAFTA; good bibliography.
*Cross-Border Links: A Directory of Organizations in Canada, Mexico and the
United States*. Ricardo Hernandez and Edith Sanchez. Albuquerque,

NM: Inter-Hemispheric Education Resource Center, 1993. Directory of organizations divided by issue and country; lists their position on free trade, with a description of purpose.

Encyclopedia of U.S. Foreign Relations. Bruce W. Jentleson and Thomas G. Paterson. New York: Oxford University Press, 1997. 4 vols. Up-to-date, comprehensive treatment of foreign relations; good topical coverage.

The McGraw-Hill Dictionary of International Trade and Finance. Carolyn Gipson. New York: McGraw-Hill, 1994. Comprehensive coverage of organizations, issues, definitions, and other topics. Useful two-page account of NAFTA and the modification of U.S. policies.

GENERAL SOURCES

Eckes, Alfred E. *Opening America's Market: U.S. Foreign Policy since 1776.* Chapel Hill, NC: University of North Carolina Press, 1995. Comprehensive, general history of free trade; presents the debate over free trade.

Kreuger, Anne O. *American Trade Policy.* Washington, DC: AEI Press, 1995. Brief account of American trade policy; analyzes the effect of NAFTA on U.S. economy and foreign policy.

Preeg, Ernest H. *Traders in a Brave New World: The Uruguay Round: The Future of International Trading.* Chicago: University of Chicago Press, 1996. General treatment of regional free trade initiatives; discusses NAFTA and the General Agreement on Tariffs and Trade (GATT).

Randall, Laura, ed. *Changing Structure of Mexico: Political, Social and Economic Prospects.* Armonk, NY: Sharpe, 1996. Collection of thirty-five essays treating diverse topics, such as the current economic crisis and various policy issues.

Suchlicki, Jaime. *Mexico: From Montezuma to NAFTA, Chiapas and Beyond.* Washington, DC: Brassey's, 1996. Brief, comprehensive history of Mexico up to the time of NAFTA.

SPECIALIZED SOURCES

Bulmer-Thomas, Victor, et al., eds. *Mexico and the North American Free Trade Agreement: Who Will Benefit?* New York: St. Martin's, 1994. Useful analysis of the free trade situation and the economic conditions surrounding it.

Drummond, Ian. *North America without Borders: Integrating Canada, the United States and Mexico.* Calgary: University of Calgary Press, 1993.

Examination of economic relations between Canada, Mexico, and the United States under NAFTA; covers a variety of aspects and issues.

Garber, Peter M., ed. *The Mexico-U.S. Free Trade Agreement.* Cambridge, MA: MIT Press, 1993. Compilation of papers prepared for a professional conference in 1991 on various aspects of the agreement.

Hufbauer, Gary C., and Jeffrey J. Schott. *NAFTA: An Assessment.* Washington, DC: Institute for International Economics, 1993. Concise evaluation of the potential effects of NAFTA; a follow-up to the popular 1992 publication (see the next entry).

———. *North American Free Trade: Issues and Recommendations.* Washington, DC: Institute for International Economics, 1992. Thorough treatment of NAFTA in terms of commercial policy; examines the effects and possible future.

Krooth, Richard. *Mexico, NAFTA and the Hardships of Progress: Historical Patterns and Shifting Methods of Oppression.* Jefferson, NC: McFarland, 1995. Thorough examination of capital and labor relations in the United States and Mexico, with an emphasis on NAFTA.

Orme, William A., Jr. *Understanding NAFTA: Mexico, Free Trade, and the New North America.* Austin: University of Texas Press, 1996. Informative account of the commercial and economic policies of both the United States and Mexico, with a focus on NAFTA.

AUDIOVISUAL SOURCES

Ross Perot: Straight Talk. Charleston, WV: Cambridge Educational, 1992. Videocassette. 60-minute interview conducted by David Frost; Perot discusses issues of importance in his campaign for the presidency in 1992, among them his opposition to NAFTA.

WORLD WIDE WEB

"No More NAFTAS, No Fast Track!" *NAFTA Section.* September 1997. http://www.teamster.org/nafta_section.html From the Teamsters Union comes this anti-NAFTA tract. Contains links to news releases, congressional updates, and assorted information.

Index

About the Authors

ROBERT MUCCIGROSSO is Professor Emeritus of History at Brooklyn College in New York, where he taught for thirty-seven years. He has edited three volumes of the *Research Guide to American Historical Biography* (1988). He has written, among other works, *American Gothic: The Mind and Art of Ralph Adams Cram* (1980), *Celebrating the New World: Chicago's Columbian Exposition of 1893* (1993), and with David R. Contosta, *America in the Twentieth Century* (1988).

RON BLAZEK is Professor of Information Studies at Florida State University, where he teaches courses in reference/information services and bibliography. He is author of *The Humanities: A Selective Guide to Information Sources* (4th ed., 1994) and *United States History: A Selective Guide to Information Sources* (1994), both of which were named *Choice* Magazine Outstanding Academic Books. He has written numerous other works and articles.

TERI MAGGIO is Deputy Directory of Technical Services and Outreach Coordinator for the Southwest Georgia Regional Library in Bainbridge, Georgia.